P9-CKR-479

305.42   R 1

Rubin, Nancy.
    The new suburban woman.

PASADENA CITY COLLEGE
LIBRARY
PASADENA, CALIFORNIA

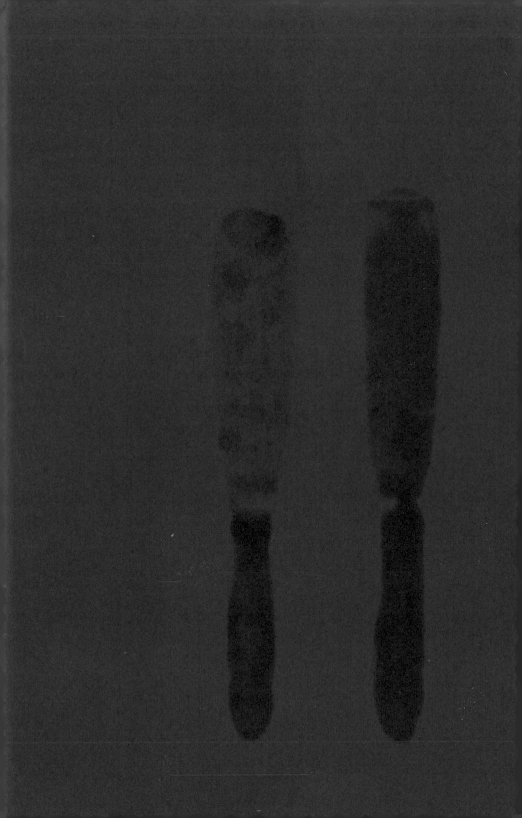

The New Suburban Woman

THE
NEW
SUBURBAN
WOMAN

Beyond Myth and Motherhood

NANCY RUBIN

Coward, McCann & Geoghegan/New York

Copyright © 1982 by Nancy Rubin. All rights reserved. This book, or parts thereof, may not be reproduced in any form without permission in writing from the publisher. Published on the same day in Canada by General Publishing Co. Limited, Toronto.

Library of Congress Cataloging in Publication Data
Rubin, Nancy.
The new suburban woman.

Bibliography: p.
1. Women—United States. 2. Suburbs—United States.
I. Title.
HQ1420.R8   1982   305.4'2'0973   81-19622
ISBN 0-698-11133-8   AACR2

Grateful acknowledgment is made to the following for permission to reprint the materials listed:
From *The Two-Paycheck Marriage*, by Caroline Bird. Copyright © 1979 by Caroline Bird. Reprinted by permission of Rawson, Wade Publishers, Inc.
From a TV Jingle for Enjoli Perfume. Reproduced by permission of Charles of the Ritz Group Ltd. © Charles of the Ritz Group Ltd. 1978.
The Feminine Mystique, by Betty Friedan. Copyright © 1963, 1974 by Betty Friedan. By permission of W. W. Norton & Company, Inc., and Curtis Brown, Ltd.
Between Myth and Morning: Women Awakening, by Elizabeth Janeway. Copyright © 1972, 1973, 1974 by Elizabeth Janeway. By permission of William Morrow & Company, Inc.
"The Squeeze on the Middle Class," by William Severini Kowinski. From a July 13, 1980, *New York Times Magazine* article. Copyright © 1980 by The New York

Times Company. By permission of *The New York Times.*

The Culture of Narcissism: American Life in an Age of Diminishing Expectations, by Christopher Lasch. Copyright © 1979 by W. W. Norton & Company, Inc. By permission of W. W. Norton & Company, Inc.

The Lonely Crowd: A Study of the Changing American Character, by David Riesman. Copyright © 1950. By permission of Yale University Press.

Women of a Certain Age: The Midlife Search for Self, by Lillian B. Rubin. Copyright © 1979 by Lillian B. Rubin. By permission of Harper & Row, Publishers, Inc., and the William Morris Agency.

The Power of the Positive Woman, by Phyllis Schlafly. Copyright © 1977 by Phyllis Schlafly. By permission of Arlington House Publishing, Westport, CT 06880.

The Third Wave, by Alvin Toffler. Copyright © 1980 by Alvin Toffler. By permission of William Morrow & Company, Inc.

Reprinted from *The Declining Significance of Race: Blacks and Changing American Institutions,* by Wilford Julius Wilson. By permission of the University of Chicago Press. Copyright © 1978 by the University of Chicago.

The Organization Man, by William H. Whyte, Jr. Copyright © 1956 by William H. Whyte, Jr. Reprinted by permission of Simon & Schuster.

The text of this book has been set in Primer.

PRINTED IN THE UNITED STATES OF AMERICA

FIRST EDITION

WITHDRAWN

Acknowledgments

THIS BOOK could not have been written without the remarkable warmth and generosity of hundreds of women throughout America who gave so openly of themselves and their lives, and whose stories remain etched in my memory as I have attempted to share them with readers in these pages.

Nor could this book have been created without the faith of two individuals who were excited about the idea from the beginning, and who provided me with heartening encouragement at each step of the research and writing process. The first was the talented editor Thomas Ward Miller, whose provocative suggestions inspired me as I sat daily at the typewriter to strive for a work that would honestly reflect the state of modern suburban womanhood, and whose astute literary sense is evidenced throughout the book. The second is my literary agent Dominick Abel, whose sensitivity, faith and unflappable objectivity in all matters relating to this book have made him an invaluable friend as well as a professional advocate.

Among the women who gave most generously of themselves and helped me reach others in their communities were Jennifer Elliott, Martha Moffet, Muriel "Nikki" Beare, Janet Cohen, Earline N. King, Amanda Smith, Helene Von Rosenstiel, Marion Behr, Wendy Lazar, Kathleen Donovan, Karen Freifeld, Doris Gonzalez Stratmann, Pauline Nelson, Cynthia Lowe, Virginia Goode, Rebecca Curto, Jane Goldstein, Sallie Ann Cardno, Susan Gentry, Millicent Susens, Susan Easton, Joan Mills, Barbara Robertson, Mary Lou Andrews, Catherine Gaugler, Opal Hoffman, Marilyn Preston, Carol Kleiman,

Mary Lou Gadin, Sandra Wolkoff, Mardi DeLardi, Ann Eisner, Carmen Chavez, Maura McNiel, Lucy Polter, Vicki Downing, Sue St. John, Betty Coughlin, Babette Feibel, Jerre Cotter, Les Wright, Mary Tedrow, Carolyn Duvall, Carol Goodman, Nancy Siegle and Elaine Leach.

I want to thank John Stinson, Diane Wescott, Elizabeth Waldman and Allison Grossman of the U.S. Department of Labor, Bureau of Labor Statistics, who offered me repeated assistance with government data on working women, some of which was still unpublished and untabulated at the time of my research, but all of which was invaluable to the chapter on working women. Frank Reilly at the U.S. Department of Transportation research library located studies of female commuting patterns to the workplace for me. Steve Rawlings and Ed Welniak of the U.S. Department of Commerce, Bureau of the Census, tirelessly provided me with census updates on population and income levels. Mary Tobin, regional administrator at the Women's Bureau of the U.S. Department of Labor in New York, furnished me with names, studies and documents relevant to the chapters on divorced, working, and single women. Michael F. Woods, first deputy commissioner of the New York State Department of Commerce, aided me in obtaining state labor statistics. Floyd Lapp, assistant planning director of the Tri-State Regional Planning Commission, helped me with information on regional housing patterns. Paul Davidoff of the Suburban Action Institute and Thomas Gale of the National Urban League provided me with studies, books, and personal contacts in my research for the chapter on minority women. Jane Newitt and Paul Bracken of the Hudson Institute spent several afternoons in 1980 and 1981 talking with me about the future of the suburbs. I owe much of the content of the last chapter to their ideological expertise and generosity.

I am also grateful to many academic experts, some of whom took special pains to acquaint me with the full scope of relevant data in their respective fields. Dr. Herbert Gans of Columbia University, Dr. Bertram Cohler of the University of Chicago, Dr. Richard Gelles of the University of Rhode Island,

ACKNOWLEDGEMENTS

Michelle Seltzer Seligson of the Wellesley College Center for Research on Women, Professor Hugh Wilson and Dr. Sally Ridgeway of the Institute for Suburban Studies of Adelphi University, Dr. Thomas Clarke and Dr. Robert Lake of Rutgers University, Dr. Francena Thomas of Florida International University, Dr. James Lynch of the University of Maryland Medical School, Dr. Harold Feldman of Cornell University, Dr. Graham Spanier and Dr. Gunhild Hagestad of the Pennsylvania State University, Dr. Michael Wachter and Dr. Janice Fanning Madden at the University of Pennsylvania and Dr. Stanley Nollen of Georgetown University.

Special thanks to Dr. Edward Zigler, Dr. Sharon L. Kagan and Susan Muenchow at Yale University who gave me the opportunity to read from parts of this book at the Bush Center in Child Development and Social Policy.

Mrs. Mary Kearn and Miss Mary Brooks at the Mt. Vernon, New York, Public Library were extremely helpful to me in researching the historical sections of the book.

Other experts who offered their insights on suburban women but whom I was not able to quote directly in the book include Dr. Ruth Neubauer, president of the American Association of Marriage and Family Therapists, Clara Allen, director of the New Jersey Division on Women, Phyllis Clay of the National Committee for Citizens in Education, Virna Canson, regional director for the San Francisco Bay Area of the NAACP, Dr. Gerald Foster and Paula Hunchar Black of the Westchester Service Council, Deborah Seidel, executive director of the Association of Junior Leagues, Dr. Quincalee Brown, executive director of the American Association of University Women, Dolores Brinkley, director of Volunteer Training for the Young Women's Christian Association, and Lee Porter, executive director of the Fair Housing Council for Bergen County, Inc.

Friends and writers who helped me with the original conception of this book include Sara Ann Friedman and Elizabeth Einstein, both of whom encouraged me in the summer of 1979 to write a proposal for my book idea; Edward Fiske, Joseph Michalak, James Feron and Geraldine

Shanahan of the *New York Times*, who continued to be supportive of my writing during my absence from the paper; Ron Powers, who offered advice and helpful suggestions in the early research and writing stages; Ronni Sandroff and Judith Wershil Hasan, who listened patiently and offered cogent advice during the writing period; Mary Dee Benjamin, Jeri and Richard Stone, Louise and Matthew Baudoin, Gisella and Herbert Klein, friends who always said they understood even when they didn't; Helen Rubin for her unequivocal support of my work, and Etheline Van Riel for her loving attention to my family.

I am especially indebted to Dr. Ira Silverstein, whose wisdom permeates these pages in more ways than even he could know.

I am grateful to two artists' institutions for the genesis and final evolution of the book—to the Bread Loaf Writers' Conference in Middlebury, Vermont, which, in the summer of 1979, provided me with a rich environment for growth and self-discovery as a writer, and to the MacDowell Colony where I spent three memorable weeks in 1981 in the solitude of a tree-shaded studio in the New Hampshire woods completing the final chapter.

Finally, it is to my family that I owe the greatest debt of all—to my children, Elisabeth and Jessica, who have tolerated the absences and inaccessibilities of their mother with good spirits for almost two years, and to whom the completion of this book itself must seem a myth—and to my husband Peter, who first brought me back to the suburbs, who has given courageously of himself as editor, friend and lover, and without whose tenderness and encouragement this book would surely never have been written.

To Peter, for his love and willingness to grow,
To Elisabeth and Jessica, tomorrow's women.

Contents

INTRODUCTION 15

CHAPTER 1/*An Overview of the Modern Suburbs* 21

CHAPTER 2/*From Rose-covered Cottage to Split-level Ranch: A History of the Suburban Woman* 39

CHAPTER 3/*Nine to Five: The Working Suburban Woman* 72

CHAPTER 4/*The Circuit Breaker: The Divorced Suburban Woman* 104

CHAPTER 5/*Liberation and Backlash: The Suburban Woman Who Stays at Home* 131

CHAPTER 6/*The New Pioneers: Single and Childless Suburban Women* 163

CHAPTER 7/*Charity Begins at Home: The New Volunteer* 200

CHAPTER 8/*Skin Deep: The Minority Suburban Woman* 225

CHAPTER 9/*Options: New Directions for the Suburban Woman* 255

NOTES 276

BIBLIOGRAPHY 305

INDEX 315

Introduction

THE CONCEPT OF A BOOK begins deep in the unconscious of its author and seldom becomes recognizable until weeks, even months, after it has first taken root. So it was for me when *The New Suburban Woman* was first conceived. Originally shadowy, the idea had a curiously compelling claim upon me, like a newborn infant demanding nurture, even as I tended to other, more pragmatic affairs of my life.

Despite my efforts to ignore those demands, the book persisted in my thoughts, the inevitable product, it seemed, of my personal experiences as a suburban wife and mother and as a free-lance reporter for the Westchester section of the *New York Times*. Without realizing it, I had been disquieted by what I had observed around me during those first years of suburban living, even though I could not at first synthesize my impressions into a cohesive whole. Gradually I came to realize that the events I witnessed in my own neighborhood— in the lives of my children and friends and in the social, political and economic trends I reported for the newspaper— were part of a new suburban reality, one far less perfect than the idyllic image I had always had of suburban living, or than the memories of my own suburban childhood.

Through my work as a reporter, I made several surprising discoveries: many families living in unmitigated poverty in otherwise affluent suburban counties, inflation and money crises in middle- and upper-middle-class families, unexpected divorce, racial strife, an aging population, communities looking for an enlarged tax base, corporate intrusion upon what was once pasture and woodland, traffic jams at 5:00 P.M. As I looked around I saw children wearily routed to school, sports activities and music lessons by mothers resentfully chained to their cars as chauffeurs. I saw women dazed by divorce, after leading lives of blind devotion to their homes and families. I saw young women, bored, angered, restless in their housewife roles yet paralyzed in their suburban environment, unable to find healthy outlets for their energies.

And I saw a new population of dynamic women who had succeeded in combining family and career, but who were seldom visible in their neighborhoods.

Somehow there had been slippage in the golden suburbs, in the American dream. More often than not, the women I knew expressed their discontent in terms of personal unhappiness about the schools, the hours their husbands worked, or the feeling that they had fallen into a rut. These women vaguely sensed that they were caught between two different time zones, that they had contradictory expectations for themselves and the suburban communities they lived in. Many of them readily acknowledged they could not fit into one or the other mode very well—that they were neither the suburban house-wives of memory nor the self-actualized feminists of the media, who have apparently learned to live happily in their suburban environments.

Gradually I came to realize that in spite of our present disavowal of the traditional values of the suburbs, the image of the archetypal suburban community persists in our minds—a landscape lush, affluent and tranquil, inhabited by women eternally serene in their roles as caretakers and consumers.

Opposed to this idealized image is the reality of a trans-formed suburban female population: over half the women work; many others attend school; many are divorced; others are married, but have no children. The image most of us grew up with and hoped to find when we moved back to the suburbs, after we had lived away from them, has all but disappeared.

Are there really rats in affluent Westchester County? Wife batterings? Grisly murders? Foreign business investments in community-based corporations? A decline in the female volunteer work force? Yes.

Even the editors in the downtown newsroom at the *Times* are occasionally intrigued by these events—despite the generally held urban conviction that the suburbs, particularly wealthy ones like Westchester, seldom experience such events.

In time, I understood that the utopian myth of the suburbs has powerful, even irrational, claims on our collective psyche, lingering seductively in our memories even as we are forced to confront the harsh new realities. The more liberated of us still blush when we realize how much we are still enamored of that myth, as we anxiously leave the dirty dishes behind to commute to our jobs, or as we explain to our children why we cannot head a scout troop or attend a PTA meeting. We are a different generation of women, we patiently say to our youngsters, trying to justify why we no longer fit contentedly into that old suburban pattern. At the same time, another, more private part of us wistfully wishes we could.

It was because of my personal involvement with that heretofore unexamined controversy that I set about writing this book. By doing so, I hoped to gain insights into the meaning of suburban life for young women today, to discover what it suggests about the evolution of women into more autonomous roles and the future of American family life. The suburbs, after all, are where most people live today, where new social trends must be integrated into behavioral norms to become contemporary American characteristics.

Despite the influence of the suburbs on our national personality, surprisingly little has been written about the life of these communities, either in popular or academic books. Even less attention has been focused on the suburban experience with regard to women, who are still its principal daytime inhabitants.

Yet anyone who has lived in the suburbs will tell you that suburban women are different. Like many of her urban contemporaries, the suburban woman is well educated and sophisticated, with cosmopolitan ideas, tastes and ambitions. In contrast to the life of her city sister, though, the suburban woman's life is tempered by the realities of geographical distances between home, school, shopping mall and the business community. In contrast to the country woman, the suburban woman has, until recently, lived a life of enforced leisure. In terms of her values, expectations and appetites, she is a hybrid, a distinctive blend of two different social realities. In my early research for this book I came to realize that the study I had undertaken was unique—the first major popular investigation of suburban women.

To conduct a comprehensive inquiry into the American women of the suburbs required work well beyond the confines of Westchester County. Because I was concerned that the suburbs of New York may be atypical in their trends, I determined to widen my private investigation into other parts of the country, into other suburban communities.

First, I had to define what I mean by "suburban." The U.S. Census Bureau and the U.S. Bureau of Labor Statistics were useful in helping me arrive at a definition. According to them, each suburb is a part of a Standard Metropolitan Statistical Area (SMSA), the densely populated group of communities of 50,000 people or more which surround and include a large central city. For statistical purposes, I defined suburbs as communities within an SMSA but outside the central city limits.

In conceptual terms, however, when I sought interviewees for this book, or thought about the suburbs in terms of their peculiar social characteristics, my definition became even more specific. According to my understanding, suburbs are primarily residential, originally created as "bedroom" or "dormitory" communities for the workers of the central cities but which have recently evolved beyond that earlier stage and now include rapidly growing business centers and economies of their own. With the influx of a free-standing economic life independent of the parent city, these communities have become what I often call the "middle landscape," a kind of intermediary environment retaining aspects of both city and country, a unique amalgam of both, without being either one or the other.

Next, I settled upon five metropolitan areas on which to concentrate my observations: Miami, San Francisco, Chicago, Dallas, Columbus, Ohio, and New York. From time to time I also drew upon information from suburban communities surrounding other American cities as my contacts grew or when individual women living in other places expressed an interest in talking to me about their lives.

My research methods were simple and direct. I spent about a week in the suburban communities surrounding each central city and set about interviewing women from as broad a spectrum of the population as I could gather. Most interviews were conducted with a tape recorder. Sometimes, however, the background noise in a restaurant, a park or an office was so distracting that it made tape recording impractical. As a result, I also carried a notebook, which, over the many months of interviews, proved to be the most dependable way to record all meetings.

I quickly discovered that the writing of a book depends heavily on the kind of people written about. Happily, I was blessed with a remarkable group of dynamic, vibrant interviewees. It was these suburban women—about 400 of them, culled from a variety of sources and walks of life—who have given this book its flavor. They gave generously of their time and resources and invited me into their homes, their back yards and, often, their hearts. Many of them could not be included in these chapters, but their stories and observations provided me with a rich backlog of human experiences to draw on. As I wrote they often filled me with a glowing faith in the potential of suburban womanhood.

Inevitably, in the course of my research for this book, I also met many men and children, some of whom were eager to share their perceptions and feelings with me about the suburban environment. While the lives of most suburban women are intricately intertwined with those of their men and children, it was not my purpose in this book to examine the suburbs from their perspective. Occasionally I have included an insight or anecdote from suburban men and children, but only when I felt it was illustrative of a larger female issue. First and foremost, this was meant to be a book about women, about what life in the suburbs means to them today, from their candid, highly specialized viewpoint.

Some of these women I met through national organizations such as the Girl Scouts of the U.S.A., the National Organization for Women, the Urban League, the Association of Junior Leagues, the National Association for the Advancement of Colored People, the American Association of University Women, the National Association of Commissions for Women, the League of Women Voters and the National Board of the YWCA. Others were reached through conventional news sources, the help of government officials and universities, and through local organizations such as day-care councils, churches, civic committees and social service organizations. Still others were reached through friends, and they, in turn, put me in touch with other friends. Many of the most articulate women of the suburbs, in fact, were "third-" or "fourth-generation" contacts—the acquaintances of acquaintances of an original source. Some women were encountered without any plan at all, but were met casually at social gatherings, conventions or parties.

It was through this eclectic approach that I built up a "network" of suburban women throughout the country who served as subjects for this book. My method was frankly personal, admittedly rather unscientific, although many of the observations I made were, much to my delight and relief, later verified by my review of relevant studies by social scientists and government agencies.

This book is one suburban woman's view of the new women now living in the nation's suburbs, women who are stepping beyond the myths to confront their full potential.

1

An Overview of the
Modern Suburbs

The garden of a house is but its outer expression
and it can be full of a woman's thoughts. It can have
the romance of an old-fashioned flower garden, the
modern trimness of shrubs, or the beauties of the
woodland; and in its very care a woman will not only
find a sweet peace but a charming bond with all the
growing world about her, the world of flowers,
shrubs and trees.

Antoinette Rehmann Perrett, "The House,"
Good Housekeeping, October 1909

IT WAS LATE. Almost too late to sit at the breakfast table
with Jim and the kids and gulp down a cup of coffee. But she
was determined not to give that up too—there were already
the rushed dinners, the kids' homework and the various
chores at night—so Anita Corgan sat another five minutes in
the sunny kitchen of her North Palm Beach home, knowing
she was out of time, swishing the coffee around in her mouth
and listening to her 8-year-old daughter Allie. The story was a
familiar one: about the child who sat behind her in school and
wrote on her shirt with a Magic Marker.

Anita heard the faint thud of an overripe grapefruit falling from the tree in her back yard, joining the others behind the porch with the hanging plants in a pile that was beginning to rot in the hot May sun. "We must get out in the back yard this weekend," she said to her husband absently as she glanced at her watch. "Time for me to go." The pretty 36-year-old woman kissed her husband and her four children and hurried to the front door. "Have a good day," she called to them cheerfully before slamming the front door.

Time, Anita thought, as she pulled the car out of the driveway, was becoming a bit like money in the Corgan household—there was always enough for the essentials if she was careful to spread it around, but rarely was there any left over. It hadn't always been that way.

A decade ago, when the twins were little and the other two not yet born, time hung heavily upon Anita, so heavily that it was stale and tasteless. But time was a luxury now, to be savored on rare days off. Buying the house in the suburbs had been worth it. And her job with a Palm Beach periodical had benefits—interesting work, friendly colleagues and a respectable paycheck. Besides, the money Anita made was important: it was the only way the Corgans could have pulled themselves out of the rent trap.

Jim knew that. He was glad Anita had found a good job and willingly assumed responsibility for the children every morning when she left. "Hurry up now, Chris," he said to his 4-year-old son who was dawdling over his Cheerios this particular morning. "Bob, you're on dish duty this week, right?"

"Right, Dad." The oldest boy rose from the table abruptly and began to rinse the breakfast dishes. Silently his 12-year-old twin sister Barbara placed the milk and butter in the refrigerator and then dashed off to her room to gather her books. There was an accelerating pace to the children's actions. Hair brushed. Homework collected. And, most important, a recital of the day's after-school activities, an announcement of where everybody would be and what they would be doing. For there were no baby-sitters to watch the Corgan children when school ended: they were thought too expensive and unreliable.

The children gathered in the living room in front of their father. Today Barbara would go to the library after school. Bob would return home with Allie and Chris. Yes, Allie could ride her bike provided she didn't wander out of the neighborhood. She wouldn't forget to set the table for dinner as she had last night. Chris should take a nap today. "Yes, Dad," the children said, nodding dutifully in response to their father's last-minute instructions.

There was nothing remarkable about the morning ritual. The Corgan children had been doing it for over a year. The big test had come the previous summer when the children had school vacation and took care of themselves for three full months. Only once was there serious trouble—when Chris got lost for an afternoon. Another time the twins had a fight and called Anita at work, screaming incomprehensibly through the receiver like angry, wounded cats.

Now it was too late for idle chatter or summer memories. Kisses for Jim. An extra hug for Chris.

"Bye, Dad."

"Bye, kids. See you tonight. Don't forget to call around four. Make it a good day."

The children gathered at the picture windows of their pretty suburban home and waved good-bye to their father as he backed the car out of the driveway. He honked the horn once as he turned the corner of the street. At 9:00 A.M. the Corgan children locked the front door of the white house and began their walk to school.

It is the same routine every morning. There are few variations. It is simply part of what the elder Corgans consider the good life for a young up-and-coming suburban family.

Rhythms. You can almost feel them on suburban streets, divine the hour of the day without consulting a clock from the sounds heard in the cool, loafy neighborhoods. In the early morning, the abrupt departures of the commuters, their cars filling the streets with roaring engine sounds; an hour later the yawning wheeze of air brakes from school buses; by nine, silence, except for the haphazard departure of women in quieter vehicles leaving for the clubs, shops or volunteer service organizations.

In midafternoon the pattern reverses: first the random return of women to their homes; then the rumble of school buses with gangs of chattering youngsters spilling unceremoniously onto the streets, the front lawns and back yards; much later, as the angle of light dims, a dark tide of returning commuters appears, swelling the streets once again with vehicles amidst the clatter of women preparing dinner, ending at last in the hypnotic twilight of cocktail hour.

So it has been in the suburbs for the better part of a century. And so it might have continued if not for a different rhythm discerned by many women decades ago, now openly played in a thousand communities throughout the land. That counterpoint rhythm is transforming suburbia today as profoundly as the energy shortage, high mortgage rates and the outflow of population from major cities. I shall write about woman's impulse to change her own rhythms in the face of an environment constructed to retain her as guardian of the suburban hearth, as well as about the social and economic forces that have acted upon her. We have lived through civil rights, the drug culture, new sexual mores, the energy shortage, the women's movement, economic recession and abortion and have been transformed.

But these changes are just beginning to make their full impact upon the American suburban experience: in the sprawling counties surrounding New York, Boston and Philadelphia, where population has dwindled in the last decade as the young have delayed marriage or moved to warmer climates; in the Sunbelt suburbs of Houston, Dallas and Miami, where an expanding economy and corporate relocation have spawned new suburban developments on the sites of reclaimed farmlands; in the western suburbs of Phoenix, Los Angeles and San Francisco, where heavy industry, traffic congestion and skyrocketing real estate values have all but forced the young middle class into rental units, distant suburbs and small towns.

There has already been considerable attention to these changes in our suburbs: in the news stories and television documentaries that trace the population shifts, rising crime rates, unemployment trends and the new economies of our metropolitan areas. But few authors have focused attention on the women of these evolving suburbs, the caretakers of those once-idealized communities nestled between city and country. It is the purpose of this book to do so. For the economic and social changes of the last twenty years have most profoundly affected its women.

No longer are the suburbs homogeneous enclaves of young middle-class couples, nurseries for white youth, playgrounds and prisons for housewives. No longer are they the static sanctuaries of conformity deplored by the social critics of the fifties. No longer are their women uniformly content to remain within the confines of a post-World War II technicolor picture, tending garden, home and children with unquestioning equanimity.

Women have begun to venture from the proverbial suburban nest, some because of their personal beliefs about women's liberation—their need to realize their own potential as individuals beyond the traditional roles of wife and mother. Others—indeed, we are told the majority of women—have returned to work simply because they need the money.

But whatever their reasons, the steady exodus of women from the home is wreaking profound changes in the suburban way of life: friendship patterns, education, neighborhood groups, volunteerism. To some, "housewife" has become a dirty word. Suburban housewifery, in particular, has been renounced, even in affluent residential communities where women were traditionally domestic and leisured—and proud of their life stations. Today, it is acceptable for all women to work, even if one's husband is a corporate executive or professional.

In the suburban heyday of the fifties, women rarely held

jobs. Those who did work were readily identifiable—widows, wives with husbands who provided inadequately, single women and the occasional professional female doctor, lawyer or scientist. A few were divorced, although divorce was rare in suburbia, and still considered scandalous. But very few of the working women were married or had children. Working women were, in the main, those who had no men to support them.

Today, there has been an abrupt change in attitude toward women and work. Work for women has become commonplace. In fact, in some suburban circles—not necessarily those identified with the feminist movement—it is considered downright commendable, a status symbol for good cocktail party conversation. In many areas it is seen as a sign of personal failure if one remains "just a housewife." Few women readily identify themselves with that role today.

As Elizabeth Janeway writes in *Between Myth and Morning:* "The modern world has made the Women's Movement, made it possible and now inevitable. What women are doing now is making the downfall or decline of the Movement clearly impossible. That awkward new presence in the world is here to stay."

The trickle-down effect of that "awkward presence" on the lives of suburban women has probably been irreversible. As a result, today's suburban communities are vibrant, fragmented municipalities—more divided now than they have been at any other time in their histories—populated with working women, singles, childless couples, female-headed households, minorities, families of second marriages and the aged. The blend has made the middle landscape between city and country less predictable, and for the women at home, often more lonely.

This is not to suggest that the old suburban symbols—the bridge games, the country club luncheons, the kaffee-klatsches and the station wagons—do not endure. Without question they do, and will continue to exist as permanent fixtures—but they are inevitably archaic traditions in view of the profound reshuffling of population and personal priorities that has foreshadowed a new national order.

Drive through the suburban communities of any large city during the week. What you will discover is deserted houses, empty back yards and silent streets, community agencies bereft of female volunteers, schools searching for room mothers and parent participants, hospitals and nursing homes anxious to attract volunteer workers: communities swept clean of women in an environment that has always demanded their presence.

The great suburban mansions and modest tract homes are often silent all day, mausoleums to a dream, the streets hushed until the schoolchildren return home. These are the new silent streets of suburbia, where tricycles and bikes ridden by a generation of baby-boom children once intimidated the suburban driver, and every house had a lawn chair mom and a kitchen filled with the smell of freshly baked chocolate-chip cookies.

Given these changes, it is little wonder that a powerful backlash has arisen—a vocal contingent of suburban women who have taken issue with what they perceive as the excessive narcissism and materialism of their female peers, and who lament the fact that others have forsaken old values. These dissenters are ardent, still committed to the duties of motherhood, trusting in the economic prowess of their mates and in the institution of marriage.

The battle lines between these opposing camps have been well drawn in our national press and in our political figures, groups and expressions during the last decade: pro choice, pro life, abortion, the Eagle Forum, Betty Friedan, the ERA, the Total Woman, Phyllis Schlafly, women's lib, stop ERA, profamily, radical feminists, bra burners, the Moral Majority, Right to Life. These name tags have become as familiar to every American woman as Tide, Maxwell House coffee and Lux soap, but are charged with far more emotional content. So explosive are the issues behind those names that they became major issues in the 1980 national elections. And they have quietly cut wide paths of dissension through our suburbs.

Everywhere there are signs of disruption in the traditional patterns of female suburban life. Last year, a 40-year-old

Scarsdale, New York, matron who had devoted a dozen years to volunteer work suddenly resigned her position in the Junior League and the PTA and embarked on a determined search for paid work. Her complaint: she was "the last of all the women at home."

A mother from Groveport (a suburb of Columbus, Ohio) demanded that the school bus stop be changed and placed outside her home because, as the one mother in the community remaining at home, she watched over the children of her working neighbors every morning.

A 33-year-old mother of two young children from Hollywood (a suburb of Miami, Florida) confided to a friend that she was "very depressed" when she heard that a contemporary had been accepted to law school.

A hairdresser from Arlington (a suburb of Ft. Worth, Texas) told of a next-door neighbor who committed suicide in her ninth month of pregnancy. "In a way, I blame myself for her death," the woman said. "I knew she was unhappy, but I was just too busy to listen. I had recently started my own business and wasn't home very much."

"Nobody came to welcome us when we moved into the neighborhood," mused a bright-eyed young woman living in Palo Alto, California, near San Francisco. "It took months to discover there were other children in this neighborhood for my son. This wasn't the way I remembered the suburbs of my childhood. Those communities seemed a lot more friendly."

She may be right. The suburbs *are* less friendly now than they used to be; fewer women remain home during the day. But how many of us really think of that when we first contemplate having our own homes in the suburbs? More often than not, we assume that our neighborhoods will contain a ready-made community of like-minded women, settled happily into the suburban life-style we remember from our childhoods. So it was for me when we first moved from Manhattan to Westchester County in 1975. But where are the children? I began to wonder a few days after we moved in. And where are the other women on the street? Many of them are older. Others are employed. Some are divorced. Still others, I discovered, remain home all day, but seem discontent in that situation.

Fifty-one percent of all American women work. And the rate for suburban women is even higher—over 53 percent of all suburban women were working in 1980. Many other women have returned to school.

Community volunteer organization numbers have dwindled. The League of Women Voters, one of the oldest and most respected volunteer organizations, composed largely of middle-class suburban women, has watched its membership decline by 23 percent within the last decade. Recent polls from the National Opinion Research Center indicate that only 8 percent of well-educated, affluent Americans now participate in political organizations compared to 17 percent in 1967. That decline is thought caused as much by a growing lack of interest in volunteerism as by public disillusionment with politics in the post-Watergate era. Other volunteer organizations such as the National PTA and the Girl Scouts of the U.S.A. have reported significant declines in their adult membership.

Yet the tranquil image of suburbias of the past remains, and continues to influence us, as do traditional concepts of femininity, which saw a renaissance in the suburbs in the early 1950s, in a fervent return to family life.

It was a unique period in American history, those years between 1945 and 1960 when neighborly and homogeneous suburbs were an important new national phenomenon. Some have called it the golden age of suburbia. They were also years of expanding educational opportunity, technological advances and unprecedented prosperity for the middle classes. Monied confidence produced a cornucopia of goods, services and material ease, bolstering the national conviction that middle-class values would perennially yield bountiful results. Consumerism was embraced as a national right, a patriotic imperative.

But in the long run, it may not have been a good era for the family. The rise of the suburbs was an anomaly in our

country's history because, for the first time, there was enough
for everybody. As University of Chicago sociologist Dr.
Bertram Cohler observed: "The expectation of the suburb was
that it would provide people with the ideal setting for a happy
life. But in reality, the fathers hated commuting, the mothers
were lonely and the kids grew up embittered and discontent."

Even before the peak of suburban expansion, social critics
cautioned about the dangers of the suburban life. A 1954
article in *Harper's* magazine dubbed the suburban experience
a "manless matriarchy" where the wife "busies herself
furiously in organizations of all sorts, as if to rid herself of the
frustrating feeling that the place where things are really going
on is somewhere else." In the same year, the *New York Times*
noted that the women of the suburbs "find no outlets for their
talents and energies and tend to focus all their efforts upon
their children. Everything that the mothers do, all the little
chores, tend to take on disproportionate significance, so that
the children feel the pressure while the mothers cannot help
feeling frustrated and discontented."

In 1963, Betty Friedan published *The Feminine Mystique*, a
shattering analysis of women's "problem without a name."
Those seemingly healthy and prosperous years of the 1950s
witnessed their own demise in the student protests, bloody
riots, futile wars and political shifts of the 1960s.

Many families have shunned the suburbs from the beginning, choosing the urban life, high-rise apartments and
demanding careers in lieu of lawn chairs, large families and
station wagons. When asked why she lived with her husband
and daughter in a congested part of Miami instead of a suburb,
a free-lance editor said: "I wouldn't live in the suburbs for
anything. I see it as a cop-out, a trap that my mother fell into. I
mean, given those distances, what else can you do out there
but carpool and shop? It seems to me that women either
develop the skills needed to make it in the business world, or
they have to retreat into the domesticity that is suburbia."

A similar sense of disdain was expressed to me by a Texas

financier as we drove through downtown Dallas and she proudly pointed out a residential reconstruction project to me in the summer of 1980 while I was researching this book. "We call this the 'Swiss Village' section of Dallas. These houses are filled with women who have fled suburbia, who frankly couldn't swallow the suburban life-style any longer. Instead they have opted for the excitement and convenience of the city. We're one of those families and proud of it."

Much publicity has been given to the "urban renaissance," the return of the middle-class professionals to the cities, where they have restored town houses and brownstones and provided new economic vitality to decaying sections of New York's West Side, Chicago's North Shore, Baltimore's Inner Harbor and Philadelphia's Queen Village among many other areas. Initially, an urban migration appeared to be under way: between 1976 and 1977 over 2.5 million people moved from the suburbs to the urban centers. In 1977 Eric Sevareid proclaimed to his television audience: "What is beginning to happen now in America is a flowback of people from suburbs to inner cities."

But it seems to me that the so-called "gentrification" of the cities has done little to reverse the outward movement of the middle class to less sparsely populated places. A 1980 article in *Chicago* magazine observed that "the suburbs have lost their glitter," but also cautioned that the cultural rebirth of downtown Chicago was a product of young childless professionals and was not therefore a promising sign of urban health. In 1980 a *New York Times* investigation of population patterns in the nation's largest cities confirmed that analysis, concluding that despite new "pockets of plenty" and the return of young middle-class individuals, the urban centers were still rapidly losing population and per capita wealth at the end of the 1970s.

Some young middle-class families continue to settle outside the city, beyond the older suburbs, in search of a better life than their parents had known. With the steady relocation of corporations in suburban areas, the industrial trend toward regionalization and our increased reliance on computers and telecommunications, the cities have indeed begun to lose their singular grasp on the national economy. The most recent census and population studies show that the national growth of suburban population has continued, albeit at a slower rate than before, since the early 1950s; the suburbs now include nearly 45 percent of the population. At the same time the central cities have become consistently less crowded: within the last decade, they have lost nearly 5 percent of their population.

The younger generation's fascination with a return to the land takes many forms, from camping, outdoor life, wilderness sports, natural foods, country music, environmentally designed homes, to what is thought of as the purity of rural values. In the late sixties that idealized vision manifested itself in a burst of communes, cults and throngs of "hippies" retreating to the farmlands of Vermont, Maine, Oregon and New Mexico.

Today, after a decade of energy shortages and economic recessions, the trek back to the land continues, but for more pragmatic reasons. Our young people may return to the farms, but usually when there is an economic incentive for them to do so. The recent publicity given to the 10 percent increase in the area of New England farmlands after 160 years of decline, for instance, can be attributed as much to rising energy costs (which have made locally grown products economically competitive) as to the return-to-the-land movement.

Corporations, faced with escalating city rents, have also moved to exurban areas with increasing frequency, but also only when there is a financial advantage in doing so. The search for better facilities and cheaper space is the primary motive for the move. As a result, we have made cities out of our suburbs, and now, with the corporate drift from urban centers, are beginning to make suburbs out of our cities.

Yet the illusion of a pastoral life—a suburb without its social trappings—tempts us to move still farther out, to build houses in the cornfields and pastures of our disappearing countryside. Sadly, there are few places left to go. The last frontier for increasing numbers of Americans has become the small town, with its ingrained, unworldly set of values.

A 43-year-old divorced woman about to leave an administrative job in a San Jose electronics firm for an uncertain future in a small northern California town explained her decision: "After living in 'Silicon Valley' for nearly two decades, I'm longing for a simpler, less competitive life-style. After years of trying to keep up with the cars, the boats and the hot tubs, I've become burned out on the Bay. We're moving to a rural area because I think people will judge us there for who we are, not for the clothes on our back. You can't hide the truth about yourself in a small town."

Similarly fervent feelings about the virtues of small-town living were expressed by a young mother of three boys who described her family's move from a suburb near Chicago to a small community in northern Illinois: "Buffalo Grove was just a developer's series of subdivisions with a commercial shopping strip. It had no reason to exist beyond that, and it showed up in the way people related to each other. Very superficially. To make matters worse, it was an organization-man type of community with everyone on their way somewhere else. Here it's different, because there's an authentic sense of history to the place, a population mix of different ages and old-time residents, people who care and don't want to see this town grow too quickly."

We have all experienced the effects of suburban communities that have grown too quickly, myself included. But the shock comes when you don't expect it. After moving from a tiny Manhattan apartment with my husband and first daughter to what we thought was going to be verdant tranquility, we became aware of the acrid fumes from the automobiles that sped by our door, heard the electric guitars, radios and stereos of our neighbors that first summer and realized that the suburbs were no verdant sanctuaries after all—at least not for the ordinary homeowner.

Two years later, while reporting a story on air pollution for the Sunday Westchester section of the *New York Times*, I discovered that our move to the suburbs for a "cleaner, more healthy life-style" was in some ways ironic. According to the scientists I interviewed at the Boyce-Thompson Institute for Plant Research, which was then still located in Yonkers, suburban air was in some ways less healthy than that breathed in the city! As my interviewees explained, the industry-polluted air of the New York-New Jersey metropolitan complex traveled slowly northward toward Westchester and Fairfield County, Connecticut, and during the course of its passage was acted on by the sun. By the time city air reaches the scenic hills of northern Westchester, the air contains higher levels of ozone and other photochemicals than there are in New York City—distressing facts for any newcomer to suburbia to contemplate.

It was then that the meaning of Scott Donaldson's words from *The Suburban Myth* took on a fuller meaning: "In any marriage between the city and the country today, the city is going to be the dominant partner." It is no wonder that people have fled. Or at least have wanted to.

Even with renewed interest in small-town living, however, it seems unlikely that our population will again become bucolic. Even if the stereotypical suburb is more artificial than the small town, its proximity to and interdependence with the still vital economic forces of the city cannot be denied. Suburbs are still growing, and with the continued impact of energy shortages on outlying towns and the distant countryside, they will continue to flourish.

As cities were melting pots in the nineteenth century, suburbs have become the twentieth-century equivalents. At least part of that new diversity reflects recent social trends: divorce, couples who remain childless and the increased presence of single people, minorities and the elderly. The Census Bureau tells us that the number of female-headed families in the nation increased sharply within the last two decades, nearly doubling from 4.5 million in 1960 to 8.5 million in 1979. Divorce has become commonplace in the suburbs; there are now about 1.5 million divorced women there. Many of these women (more than half of whom are mothers) are left to maintain litigated homes they can no longer support; others find themselves encumbered with suburban trappings they can no longer afford: the swimming pool, the club membership, the car wash, the casual social lunch, the well-manicured lawn. In order to maintain the bare essentials of daily life, about 70 percent of these divorced women have returned to work.

While earlier generations of young couples traditionally moved to the suburbs to raise families, growing numbers of childless couples have purchased homes purely as financial investments. Twenty-four percent of married women aged 20 to 24 remained childless in 1960; by 1979 that figure had grown to 41 percent and demographers expect that childlessness—despite the current baby boomlet—will become a permanent feature of American married life.

The emergence of childless couples in the suburbs has had a subtle but powerful effect upon school taxes, land values and suburban social life. School populations had already begun shrinking, partly because of improved methods of birth control and new abortion laws, by the beginning of the 1970s. They have been further eroded by the appearance of childless couples who now occupy homes once filled with children and parents. Rapidly rising real estate prices in some suburban communities have also been attributed in part to the formidable buying power of these childless two-paycheck marriages. These couples—the "new elite" of our inflation-ridden economy—are often more capable of buying homes than young couples with children. For many of these couples, the suburban home has become merely a place to hang their hats and invest their dollars, rather than a homestead for the setting down of family roots with commitment to a community.

Singles, once considered exceptional members of the traditional suburban population, have also emerged in the suburbs, paralleling their larger percentage of the national population. In 1979, one-quarter of all women over 14 years of age (the government's definition of womanhood) were single. In the same year, one-quarter of all households in the nation were maintained by singles—a 66 percent increase over their numbers a decade ago. Single women own nearly 5 million of the nation's homes, and have become potent forces in the suburbs.

Proof of their growing importance is visible everywhere— not only in the proliferation of suburban singles bars, night-clubs and social activities held at community centers, churches and clubs, but in the silent mushrooming of apart-ments and luxury condominiums atop California hills, on the prairies of Houston, Dallas and Fort Worth, on the sprawling flatlands of the Florida coast and on midwestern farmlands bordering Chicago and Cincinnati—self-selected communities for the free spirits of our time. Real estate builders and planners are constructing larger numbers of cluster and condominium homes each year. Fourteen percent of all new dwellings constructed in 1980 were condominiums—twice as many as were built in 1978—and projections indicate that the rate of building will continue to grow within the next decade.

Minorities, refugees and other population subgroups have also entered the suburbs. In the wake of the 1960s civil rights movement, the black population has grown dramatically in suburban areas. Between 1970 and 1977 the black population increased at an average rate of 4.1 percent each year, while the white population grew by only 1.2 percent. Even after a 45 percent increase in their numbers, blacks still accounted for only 6 percent of the total suburban population by the end of the decade, but their appearance in hitherto all-white areas has effected changes in neighborhood friendship patterns, school populations and real estate values.

Other minorities—Hispanics, Japanese, Chinese, Indo-Chi-nese and native American Indians—have also begun to appear in suburban communities, with varying degrees of comfort. Hispanics, although constituting the nation's fastest-growing minority group, still comprise only a small portion of the total suburban population—about 4 million compared to about 75 million Caucasians in 1979. But their influence as another new social entity is already being felt.

A final factor in the changing composition of suburbia is age. The suburbs were once the breeding ground for a generation of young men and women who came of age during the Depression, survived World War II, and moved into moderately priced, GI Bill-financed housing around the nation's cities. These mass-produced, ranch-style communities are now increasingly inhabited by older people who have remained long after their children have grown and left. A report entitled *The Graying of Suburbia* found that surprising numbers of older Americans live in today's suburbs. According to the study, over 4.5 million people over the age of 65 lived in the suburbs in 1976—only 8 percent less than in the central cities. In the 59 to 64-year-old category, the suburbs contain 20 percent more people than do the central cities. These figures suggest that within the next decade, the elderly will become an even more substantial suburban subgroup, a population that will, as the report predicts, produce "pressing needs for financial assistance and social services." In addition, social isolation will become a major problem "exacerbated in the suburbs by the lower population density and greater reliance on private automobiles."

I was amazed to discover that suburbs are communities in which over half the women work, where divorced mothers, childless couples, singles, minorities and the elderly are increasingly important components of the community, where a shrinking birth rate has resulted in fewer children, where child care is often left in the hands of day-care providers, nursery schools or the children themselves, where gasoline and oil shortages make the very distances between city and suburbs a threat, rather than an advantage.

Yet our old expectation that the suburbs are homey, tranquil and predictable places continues to gnaw at the feminine collective subconscious. The suburban home still begs for a presiding divinity—a keeper of keys and human cares, the archetypal mother of earlier ages. No matter what we say aloud, no matter how "liberated" we profess to be, the old suspicion lingers that women are particularly responsible for the children, the well-kept home and the suburban social life.

The result is an anxiety that turns our working women into "supermoms." Obviously, there is guilt among those who work, but there is guilt also, as well as apology and outrage, among those who remain at home.

As the decade of the seventies has evolved into the eighties, there has been a good deal of confusion among women about which role they should elect: subservience to the home and family or self-fulfillment. I believe that the ability to contemplate such a choice is a luxury, and it is in the heartland of affluence, the suburbs, as in no other place, that the polarities of the contemporary female dilemma have been most evident. Nowhere does it seem more selfish for women to opt for themselves with a career, since suburban communities demand special duties from women: those of consumers, chauffeurs and caretakers.

But the suburbs also serve a broader, more positive function: it is there that new attitudes and life-styles are ultimately accepted. The suburbs are the primary absorption point for new ideas, as advertisers long ago discovered, the cultural conduit for our national consciousness. Today's suburbs are now the crucibles of feminism, the critical centers of a changing female awareness. A new sense of energy pervades the air.

Adversity has already begun to mold some new suburban women; the economic tide will draw others; conscious feminism and social convention will sweep the rest along. It is only a matter of time. Undoubtedly, many women will continue to elect the suburban life-style in future years, deliberately choosing greenery over city glamor, but they will do so much more carefully.

2

From Rose-covered Cottage to Split-level Ranch: A History of the Suburban Woman

〰〰〰

> The greater number of American women have home and its affairs, wherewith to occupy themselves. Wifely and motherly occupation may be called the sole business of woman there. If she has not that, she has nothing.
>
> Harriet Martineau, *Society in America, 1837*

The housewife of the future will be neither a slave to servants nor herself a drudge. She will give less attention to the home, because the home will need less; she will be rather a domestic engineer than a domestic laborer, with the greatest of all hand-maidens, electricity, at her service. This and other mechanical forces will so revolutionize the woman's world that a large portion of the aggregate of

woman's energy will be conserved for use in broader,
more constructive fields.

Thomas A. Edison, *Good Housekeeping,*
October 1912

The Nineteenth Century

The suburban dream began innocently enough, one and a
half centuries ago, with a weariness of city life and a craving
for all things green, bright and pure. In 1833, the transcen-
dental philosopher Ralph Waldo Emerson proclaimed: "We
need nature, and cities give the human sense not room
enough." His generation of writers, thinkers and social reformers had a profound effect upon the national consciousness.

The belief that the city stifled man's innermost self, that
nature's primal beauty could redeem him, found expression
also in Henry David Thoreau's *Walden,* published in 1854,
nine years after the author had retreated to the woods near
Concord, Massachusetts. He wrote: ". . . what youth or
maiden conspires with the wild luxuriant beauty of Nature?
She flourishes most alone, far from the towns where they
reside."

By the mid-nineteenth century, while the United States was
rapidly transforming itself from an agricultural nation to an
industrialized power, the impulse to retain contact with the
agrarian heritage and ideals of the New World still burned
strong—a remnant of the Jeffersonian vision of a free nation of
yeoman farmers, the "chosen people of God." Manifestations
of that pastoral ideal and of the accompanying sympathy with
the common man were everywhere in the American cultural
expressions of the day: in the 1829 election of populist folk

hero Andrew Jackson to the presidency; in the writings and social experiments of reformers and intellectuals like Bronson Alcott, George Ripley, Margaret Fuller and Nathaniel Hawthorne; in the paintings of Thomas Cole, George Catline, and William Sidney; in the poems of William Cullen Bryant and Henry Wadsworth Longfellow; in a growing national pride in the native arts; and in the first burst of Romantic country homes for the wealthy. Many of those grand estates, such as Lyndhurst in Tarrytown, New York, and the Cottage in Fairfield, Connecticut, still stand today, mansions which spawned their own satellite communities in the middle landscape between city and country.

The railroads were an important part of that first industrialization. By the mid-nineteenth century, the "iron horse" had become an important social and economic force, transporting raw goods and finished manufactured products across the lonely stretches of wilderness to the major cities of the nation. Between 1830 and 1860 over 30,000 miles of railroad track were laid, and with the continued expansion of rail service from the urban centers to the countryside, a growing number of Americans found they could maintain homes in the country as well as jobs in the city.

As early as 1848, the suburban concept was recognized by influential writers and social commentators as a fortuitous means of reconciling city with country and reaping the benefits of both. In that year, the prominent landscape architect Andrew Jackson Downing wrote in *Horticulture:* "Hundreds and thousands, formerly obliged to live in the crowded streets of cities, now find themselves able to enjoy a country cottage, several miles distant—the old notions of time and space being half annihilated, and these suburban cottages enable the busy citizen to breathe freely and keep alive his love for nature . . ."

With characteristic pragmatism, Downing noted that the suburbs offered individuals living quarters that were not only more healthy and commodious than those that might be found in the city, but also could be constructed in a cheaper way than the country estates of the wealthy to accommodate the ordinary wage earner. Downing wrote in his 1850 guide, *The Architecture of Country Houses:* "An industrious man, who earns his bread by daily exertions and lives in a snug and economical little home in the suburbs of a town, has very different wants from the farmer. . . . We have been most anxious to give designs for the cheap cottages. There are tens of thousands of working men in this country, who now wish to be given something of beauty and interest to the simple forms of cottage life."

Downing was right, and his vision struck a responsive chord among his fellow countrymen, resulting in the first crop of nineteenth-century middle-class cottages. But what about the tens of thousands of women living in the mid-nineteenth century who were the wives, daughters and mothers of those working men? What were their living preferences? History unfortunately tells us little about women's domestic ideas of the day, even less about their architectural visions—if they dared to have any. The truth was that by the nineteenth century they had little choice but to follow their fathers or husbands wherever fortune might take them, through the city slums or town houses, and out into the sunlit air of the country cottages.

The tranquility and isolation that made the suburbs so appealing to the first generation of urban male workers dealt yet another blow to Victorian women, who had already experienced considerable loss of status, economic autonomy and self-esteem as a result of the Industrial Revolution. The declining position of women in the nineteenth century, particularly those of the middle class, who for the first time in America's history were prohibited from paid employment once they married and bore children, occurred simultaneously with the creation of the first suburbs and was one of the most profound effects of the Machine Age, reducing women to their homes as the physical and spiritual guardians of the family unit, while at the same time insuring their economic impotence.

It hadn't always been that way. We know that childbirth and a high infant mortality rate had always been problematic for women, yet they had enjoyed a considerably higher status in colonial North America than in the nineteenth century because value was placed on their economic contributions. Men and women worked side by side in the early days of America, both on the farm and in the home, where cottage-industry production of household goods and textiles was a cooperative effort. Even when colonial men were merchants, apothecaries, printers and wig-makers in the early cities, their wives often performed as their assistants, and if through their labor and enterprise their family prospered, it was to their mutual credit. A strong, capable and enterprising wife was an important asset to colonial man.

But with the invention of the spinning jenny by Richard Hargreave in England in the late eighteenth century and the subsequent introduction of the power loom in Waltham, Massachusetts, in 1805, the textile trade was never to be the same. Men and childless women journeyed from their country homes and farms to work in the first mills and factories of the cities, leaving married women with young children behind as new economic dependents. It was an important separation that might have produced a more angry response among nineteenth-century women except for the pervasive Victorian rationale of the "doctrine of two spheres"—the sanctioned division between labor and consumption, the flesh and the spirit, work and home life.

In the perversely contorted thinking of the day, nineteenth-century women were conventionally seen as the spiritual and moral, if not the intellectual and legal, superiors of men. Suddenly able to purchase many of the household goods they were once forced to manufacture themselves, women assumed new roles as consumers, and were encouraged to devote more of their time to the educational, social and spiritual well-being of their families. As a result, they began to assume more authority over the affairs of the home while men worked in the offices, factories and mills and sported in the clubs, bars and brothels of the rapidly growing nineteenth-century cities. When Victorian women did venture outside the sphere of home and family, it was as the spiritual watchdogs of the age, to identify with the causes of religion, charity, abolition and temperance, the Cult of True Womanhood, what is now called "the feminine mystique."

Many of us had grandmothers of that school, myself included. A strong, doughty woman who raised four sons to adulthood, she was the unquestioned intellectual, cultural and charitable leader of the family, while my grandfather spent his days engrossed in the cash-and-carry concerns of the dry-goods business.

One reaction to the relatively powerless position accorded women in the nineteenth century was the early feminist movement that began with Elizabeth Cady Stanton and Lucretia Mott's famous 1848 *Declaration of Sentiments* protesting man's mistreatment of woman and demanding the right to vote. Among the grievances was that man had, in fact ". . . compelled her to submit to laws in the formation of which she had no voice . . . has made her, if married, in the eyes of the law, civilly dead . . . has venerated a false public sentiment by giving to the world a different code of morals for men and women . . . has endeavored in every way that he could to destroy her confidence in her own powers, to lessen her self-respect, and to make her willing to lead a dependent and abject life."

The last accusation, which was an angry, if honest, assessment of the role accorded women during the Victorian Age, was dismissed, forgotten or denounced in the subsequent seventy-two-year fight that occupied feminist energies in their quest for suffrage. It came to have special meaning again only to a generation of women a hundred years later, who found themselves "trapped" in the suburban environment.

As Alice Rossi writes in her social history of the women's movement, *The Feminist Papers*, women's identity with the abolitionist cause was applauded, even seen as a "social and political reinforcement of family and church solidarity between the sexes," but when they engaged in a fight for their own civil rights, women were seen as a threat and ostracized. Faced with these alternatives, most nineteenth-century women naturally chose safe, socially sanctioned outlets for their energies.

The Female Society for the Promotion of Sabbath Schools, the Social Purity Movement, the New York Female Reform Society, Jane Addams's Hull House, the Women's Christian Temperance Union and the National Congress of Mothers were formed in the nineteenth century. Nor should it come as any great surprise to us that nineteenth-century middle-class women were portrayed as sexually unresponsive, physically frail, intellectually stunted and economically dependent creatures who were pushed further back into the confines of the home—shuttered from the world of commerce, politics and industry—when they moved to the early suburbs at the end of the century.

One of the most compelling arguments for women's new role as the primary social and spiritual guardians of the family was promoted by Catherine Beecher, a daughter of Reverend Lyman Beecher and the older sister of Harriet Beecher Stowe. A spinster, educator, founder of the Hartford Female Seminary in Connecticut and the author of many manuals on women's domestic obligations, Miss Beecher was a highly respected spokeswoman for Victorian womanhood even before her *Treatise on Domestic Economy for the Use of Young Ladies at Home and at School* appeared in 1841.

In contrast to other widely read books on domestic practices of the nineteenth century, such as Lydia Maria Child's *The American Frugal Housewife* of 1830 and earlier household guides such as H. L. Harwell's *The Domestic Manual* and Thomas Green Fassaden's *The Husbandman and Housewife*, all of which addressed the housekeeping obligations of both sexes, Miss Beecher's *Treatise* urged women to assume an authoritative position in the home as spiritual minister and secular guardian. Women, she argued, must systematize or professionalize their roles as household managers. The *Treatise* helped provide us with a moral rationale for our modern concept of the housewife.

Basing her arguments upon woman's undeniable biological

function as childbearer, Beecher reasoned that women had a particularly sacred role in the American democracy, which depended upon the intellectual and moral character of its citizenry. It is the mother, Beecher reminded her readers, who "writes the character of the future man" and the wife "who sways the heart, whose energies may turn for good or for evil the destinies of a nation."

But in order to accomplish those spiritual tasks, women first had to be strong and healthy in body, something few Victorian women apparently achieved, with sexual frigidity, childbearing ills and chronic invalidism so commonplace as to be stereotypical feminine characterizations. Beecher wrote: "The Writer has heard some of her friends declare that they would ride fifty miles to see a perfectly healthy and vigorous woman out of the laboring class. This . . . was not an entirely unfair picture of the true state of female health in the wealthier classes."

Taking her readers to task for their avoidance of fresh air, exercise and healthful foods in the hope of attaining a pale complexion and properly delicate silhouette, Beecher railed against those conventions. If young girls and women led healthier lives in their youths, she said, they would be fitter wives and mothers.

Finding another source of stress in the unreliability of the American servant, Beecher pleaded with her readers to assume the duties and obligations of the housewife themselves, urging them to teach that role to their daughters as well. Miss Beecher proposed that "study and intellectual excitement in a young girl" should be postponed until she had "passed the most critical period of her youth" and developed a "vigorous and healthful constitution." She added that "physical and domestic education should occupy the principal attention of mothers in childhood and the stimulation of the intellect should be very much reduced. As a general rule, daughters should not be sent to school before they are six years old; and when they do go, far more attention should be paid to their physical development. They should never be confined, at any employment, more than an hour at a time; and this confinement should be followed by sports in the open air . . ."

Women, in other words, should be healthy and vigorous animals, educated enough to have a cursory knowledge of the world, but not so much as to impair their primary biological function. That message, so well reasoned and practical over a century ago, was to have an intellectually chilling effect upon American womanhood, and especially upon married suburban women who, severed as they were from the cultural and intellectual mainstream of the city, had little choice but to embrace the duties and obligations found within the confines of the self-sufficient and newly systematized home.

The scatterbrained schoolgirl. The dilettante housewife. The widely traveled, widely read, untrained-for-anything suburban middle-aged woman. The displaced homemaker. The origins of these modern feminine stereotypes are not hard for us to trace.

The rewards for total commitment to domesticity were presented in the most positive moralistic terms to women. The house was considered an outer manifestation of the inner female mind. A well-run house in a semirural setting was thought wonderful, for by the mid-nineteenth century, the rural environment was firmly equated in the popular mind with the values of warmth, sincerity and honesty. Even the early feminists inadvertently upheld the virtues of rural life and found it preferable to urban society. Harriet Martineau, the ardent English feminist who visited America, expressed an unabashed admiration for the country. In 1850, in *Harper's New Monthly Magazine,* she chided young women for their fashionable paleness and wrote: "I know a Phyllis, fresh from the country, who gets up at six and goes to bed at ten; who knows no perfume but a flower garden and has worn no bandage to her waist except a sash . . ."

It was inevitable that the American pastoral dream and the enshrinement of women in the home converged in a powerful union that has persisted to the present day, and has reached its apotheosis in the twentieth-century version of the American dream—the single-dwelling suburban home.

While the intellectual langour and economic dependency that such domesticity fostered upon American womanhood became a *cause célèbre* of American feminists for the next

century, a few intellectual and social critics of the time noticed
that the growth of the early suburban communities like Mt.
Vernon, New York, Riverside, Illinois, and Brookline, Massachusetts, was accelerating the cloistering of women. By the
last years of the nineteenth century, the early suburbs of New
York, Boston and Chicago were being ridiculed in urban
journals and magazines as "lonesomehursts" and "lone-
lyvilles." And with what was to become a characteristically
ambivalent attitude toward the suburbs in the next century,
these critics depicted the communities ringing the central
cities with a curious mixture of envy and ridicule—both as
the elite and tranquil havens for urban workers and their
families, and as unsophisticated cultural backwashes beyond
city limits.

In 1894, in *Harper's New Monthly Magazine,* a city dweller
endures an insufferably long train journey to visit a former
sweetheart and her husband in a New York suburb. The
author describes the ride as a "wondering as to how much
further from civilization they are going to take you . . ." After
spending two days with his suburban friends and taking
solemn notice of their growing detachment from the city, he
concludes that if they truly preferred the country life to that of
the city, then they were certainly wise to live in the suburbs.
But suburban living begets isolation, the author warns his
readers, for "he who ventures beyond the North and East
Rivers for fresh air and golf clubs, leaves his friends behind."

Turn of the Century

Although the personal identity of the suburban homeowner
was split between his intellectual allegiance to the city and
emotional preference for the country, the homeowner's wife
had little choice but to try to form a new life for herself in these
fledgling communities. In 1909, *Good Housekeeping* ran a

story called "The Commuter's Wife" that addressed the problems faced by women in those communities: "The days are long in these suburban towns. The busy men . . . leave on early trains and are at once plunged in the rush of their accustomed life among their usual associates. The little wife, left standing behind the struggling young vines of her brand new piazza, turns back into the house to face a day devoid of interest and companionship. She may read a little—she who has been brought up on lectures; she may practice a little—she who has been educated on concerts; she may sew or cook, neither of which interests her in the least, and both of which she does badly as yet . . . The most hopeful thing is the frequent perambulator with its tiny occupant."

While encouraging the young suburban matron to become involved in church activities as a way of improving social contacts and exercising talents, the author maintains that the commuter's wife is "still a woman apart." Her problems are unique. Like the women of later periods, the suburban mother has the "double problem" of deciding all alone "all minor matters of conduct and life." The author asks: "How much influence does the man have who leaves before his children are awake in the morning and sees at night only the sweet, rosy faces and curly heads of his sleeping boys and girls?"

The solution to the peculiar set of circumstances faced by suburban wives, the author of that article wrote, lay within the women themselves. They must learn to shoulder the additional burdens of suburbia and motherhood rather than to object to those conditions or expect more from their husbands. "It calls for independence, courage, cheerfulness, resources and it produces by its demands those eminently attractive and capable young women, each one of whom at heart is proud of her home and her children, proud of the little town she lives in, proud of one especial man on the 8:17—proud, in fact, of being a commuter's wife."

It was a solution that became a permanent way of life for women living in the suburbs for the next fifty years. But it was a solution that began to wear thin when economic uncertainties, rising divorce rates, reliable methods of birth control and widespread higher education finally allowed women to search beyond the parameters of their monolithic domestic obligation.

Domestic Science, or The New Housekeeping

The belief that women could find ultimate fulfillment in the maintenance of the suburban home persisted in the early twentieth century, dressed in the guise of "domestic science," the scientific management of the home. Bolstered by the addition of "household arts" programs at such prominent institutions as Teacher's College at Columbia University, Simmons College, Pratt Institute and the University of Illinois and by the 1909 appearance of the *Journal of Home Economics,* the cult of the "new housekeeping" aimed to legitimize housewifery for a generation of women still struggling with the concept of suffrage. The new domesticity, with its attention to an orderly household and a sanitary, efficient kitchen, created so much attention and anxiety among average women that it became a safe diversion for many, in the same way that the Victorian Cult of True Womanhood had been for their nineteenth-century mothers.

The leading figure for this movement was Mrs. Christine Frederick, a pioneer teacher of the application of industrial efficiency to household management and the household editor of the *Ladies' Home Journal,* "the Bible of the American Home," where her columns appeared regularly between 1910 and 1920.

In a series of articles reminiscent of Catherine Beecher half a century before, Mrs. Frederick advised her readers to schedule their household duties systematically. Adhering to a strict timetable of home care and supervision of the children was one answer, better home and kitchen design was another. Mrs. Frederick's columns were accompanied by plans and drawings for efficient homes and kitchens reminiscent of

Beecher's one-story servantless homes, engendering—in spirit, if not precisely in physical detail—the commonplace bungalows of the 1920s that still mark the outskirts of Chicago, San Francisco, Boston and New York.

"Pure food laws are now in effect: more intelligence is shown in weighing food values. Domestic science has come to stay. In an age of advancement, it is only natural that the cause of cookery should progress . . ." proclaimed a 1913 magazine advertisement for Crisco.

If the principles of domestic science were to relieve women of the time-consuming aspects of their chores, the promise of the countryside was an added bonus to a generation of women reared on the nature writings of John Burroughs, Dallas Sharp and John Muir. Country life, in the form of summer homes, camps, wilderness, park conservation and nature organizations, flourished and became a national passion. And with it, the suburbs were embraced as a sensible living arrangement.

The belief that life in the country was the superior life persevered, enticing a war-weary generation of young men and women to hasten to the suburbs with a freneticism characteristic of the Jazz Age. The post-World War I years witnessed the first major flowering of the suburbs, pictured as elegant, fashionable communities for the wealthy or as friendly bungalow neighborhoods where middle-class ex-flappers ran their homes and lives with a high degree of efficiency, as portrayed in the novels of F. Scott Fitzgerald and Sinclair Lewis.

By the mid-1920s, the suburbs had become, as a writer of the period observed, "a footnote to urban civilization affecting the near-by countryside." They were not only an important feature of American life, they were fast becoming an economic threat to the cities that spawned them. Between 1899 and 1909 the wage earning population increased by 98 percent in the suburbs but only 41 percent in the nation's largest cities.

Henry Ford's decision to mass-produce automobiles affordable to the middle class hastened that suburbanization, and his early Model T's flooded the narrow roads with their human cargoes, routinely scaring chickens, cows and other livestock as they shuttled between city and suburb. The flood of new cars to the suburbs created the first rush hours and prompted the construction, in 1924, of the nation's first suburban highway, the Bronx River Parkway in Westchester County, New York.

The prosperity of the 1920s provided additional impetus to the growth of the suburbs with easy money, massive land speculation and the wide-scale construction of new homes. Many of those homes were reminiscent of the English manor houses, the Cottswold cottages and the French châteaus the "doughboys" who fought on the European front the decade before had seen. It was, as historians Samuel Eliot Morison and Henry Steele Commager have said, "an age of materialism and reaction."

Even after winning the vote in 1920, the undisputed place for most women was believed to be the home. The burden as most women saw it was not so much that they were confined to the home after their children were born, but that their homemaking duties were so onerous. "What good does it do to open to women the door to political occupation, of civil achievement, when the machinery of the average home is so irrational, wasteful, medieval that the majority of women cannot fully meet even the basic demands for a complete home life?" the *Woman's Home Companion* asked readers in 1922.

Commonly proposed solutions to women's work were cooperative laundries, nurseries and kitchens, whereby women could gain some free time for themselves and "get a start toward developing their individual talents and gaining more financial freedom"—precursors of today's public day-care facilities. Seldom was the idea of soliciting male help, or even cooperation, mentioned, for by that time the words "home" and "women" had become practically synonymous.

As I have discovered in my research, from the nineteenth century until the end of the baby boom there was in the public eye an increasingly close identity between women and their homes. For suburban women especially, whose homes were often handsome, the house became a proud symbol of their inner worth, a personal extension of the self. In 1925, a feature in *Better Homes and Gardens* asked: "Did you ever stop to think that your kitchen is the most truly self-expressive room in your home? A woman's attitude toward the whole job of homemaking shines out right there. The kitchen is a great betrayer of one's chronic state of mind, and by the same token it has much influence upon one's daily state of mind."

Fashion was exceptionally important to women of the day, and if a product was associated with people of fame, style or fortune, the housewife was assured it was also appropriate for her use. "Coined in Paris to express originality plus taste, the word 'chic' has come to mean many things to many people. In London, swagger, in America, pertness, in Japan, genuineness. The original and last meanings are the ones contained in the undoubted chic of Crane bathrooms . . ." Glamor could be attained by housewives even through plumbing fixtures.

Women commonly appeared on the covers of popular magazines as golfers and tennis players, and in frankly sexual roles as well. That women could be popularly regarded as athletic, adventurous and even sexual in the 1920s was a new concept, a direct product of the suffrage movement and the flapper era.

That women might have been discontent in their glamorous new role was seldom considered. The glitter of fashion and a frank acknowledgment of women as sexual beings was a far more pleasurable diversion for feminine energies during the Jazz Age than the painful issues raised by old-line feminists. Once again, women were cloistered in the suburban home— this time by the glamorization of their sexuality and the romanticization of their household duties.

But at least one social scientist, Harlan Paul Douglass, had begun to notice distressing signs of stress, "defects in suburban character," as he called them. In his 1925 book *The Suburban Trend,* one of the first serious studies of the suburbs, Douglass noted that while suburbs were indeed a promising aspect of urban civilization, separating the home from the bustle of the commercial, political and industrial world, they divided men's loyalties between the city and his residence. He also noticed that the suburbs treated men and women in different ways: "One systematically goes and comes to and from work; the other stays at home and goes occasionally . . . in brief, the suburb decentralizes women unless they are gainfully employed more completely than it does men." Male workers, he noted with distress, are "not in key with actual suburban domesticity as typified in the wife and children, are housemates, rather than members of the family, and yield little social allegiance to their place of technical residence."

Someone must keep the home fires burning, and seldom, in suburbia, is it the man. The problem persists, plaguing suburban women, keeping them tied to the home even if they are employed.

To be sure, the challenge of combining careers with traditional roles as wives and mothers is an awesome one for all women, whether they be city or country bred. The plethora of women's studies in our colleges and universities, the women's centers, the women's libraries, bookshops, businesses and publications devoted to exploring the nuances of that dilemma provide ample testimony to the arduousness of that dual role. While women's rights have been advanced in recent years by the passage of the Civil Rights Act of 1964, as well as by equal-opportunity laws and the "new feminism," women nevertheless remain so firmly welded to traditional expectations that there are still many practical and psychological obstacles to autonomy. For suburban women—informed by ideas of economic independence and social equality, but far from the city centers and bound by over a century of carefully prescribed social values—the obstacles loom even larger.

How, suburban women have often wondered, can they hold jobs if they are compelled by school systems to prepare lunch for elementary schoolchildren sent home daily at noon? How can they justify the expenditure of time to further their own educations if no one is at home to pick the children up from school and drive them to sports activities or the homes of friends? And how, after years of remaining in the suburban neighborhoods, can they justify their first job offer—often at an entry level wage—if it would cost them nearly as much, or more, to obtain a baby-sitter, a driver or a housekeeper? How can they break away from long-term friendships, with their subtle social pacts of conformity and interdependence, without being ostracized? How can they accept top-paying jobs in the cities, requiring still more travel, expense and absence from the home, instead of nearby positions where salaries and growth opportunities may be fewer? How can they retain any connection with community life if their time is already jealously divided between employment, housekeeping chores and the demands of their children?

Doubts such as these frequently darken the suburban female mind. It is the double demand implicit in our role—the middle-class mandate that we must be well-organized, thoughtful, resourceful and sophisticated human beings but at the same time must perform the many servile functions demanded by the suburban experience—that has continued to confound so many women. It is the same mixed message which had led so many into inactivity, unhappiness and the symptoms of discontent so commonly attached to them—alcoholism, sexual promiscuity, drug dependency and neuroticism.

It is no wonder. The contradictory expectations of woman's role are buried deep in our national consciousness, historically entwined with the genesis of the suburbs themselves. These expectations are still to be confronted by millions of new suburban women.

The Baby Boom

"We married in 1953 and lived in a small apartment in Jackson Heights. After the birth of our first son we moved to Westchester County. I guess we were probably the last generation to live the lives that were expected of us and to have no questions about what we wanted to do. And what we wanted was to be wives and mothers."

The woman sitting across from me on the living room couch of her comfortable New Rochelle home smiled as she reflected upon the 1950s, a time when her female neighbors were home, the back yards were noisy with children and the kaffeeklatsch was a relief from the monotony of housework. Even today, when Elly Doctorow has traded her housewife role for dual responsibilities as the first New Rochelle city councilwoman and as the director of a local nursery school, she still describes herself as a nurturer, rather than as a politician or a careerist. Her primary identity, she insists, is as a proud wife and the mother of three sons. "That's the way women of my generation were brought up. We never thought to challenge that way of looking at ourselves," she says simply.

The 1950s were a remarkable period in our history, resonating with the aftershocks of World War II as returning veterans married, bore children and moved to the moderate-priced houses of the raw, treeless developments mushrooming in concentric circles around America's large cities. Rosie the Riveter, that fabled working woman of the war years who had come to include a record 37 percent of the nation's female population, disappeared into family scrapbooks and museum memorabilia after 1945, giving up her job for men, matrimony and motherhood. "Finally we can return to a normal way of life" was the prevailing mood among the 6.5 million women who had spent years working in the wartime factories, shipyards and ammunition mills. If anyone should have jobs, the women thought or were told by their employers, it was the returning veterans and young men with families.

A 1945 *Fortune* poll mirrored the attitude that was to structure the social expectations of the fifties: 63 percent of all Americans questioned believed that married women should remain at home if their husbands could earn a living.

By 1950 the female work force had begun to decline. Most of those who worked were older women, widows and young single girls. Married working mothers with young children, who had worked during the war, were now a rarity. In 1950 less than 12 percent of all women with children under 6 held jobs. Woman's place was clearly in the home.

For middle-class women the social mandate was especially well defined: be feminine, sexy and bright, but not *too* brainy. While middle-class girls were often encouraged to attain a college education, the anticipated reward was a "Mrs." degree rather than entry to graduate or professional school. And as the postwar economy made higher education possible for more daughters of the middle class, the college campus was seen as an increasingly important place for women to meet the bright young men of their generation. Once they were married, these college-educated women would become suitable life companions for their upwardly striving men. Going to college, getting married and having children became the prescribed formula for middle-class happiness for an entire generation of women just coming of age, like Elly Doctorow.

The suburbs were an essential part of that romantic promise. The 1950s were a time when women still thought they would fall in love, marry, move to the suburbs and live happily ever after. There was plenty of fuel to feed the fires of that suburban dream by the early 1950s. There had been the economic hardships of the Depression of the 1930s that compelled millions of young Americans to postpone marriage and childbearing in the prime years of their youth. Just as the economy was beginning to recover, World War II happened. With the bombing of Pearl Harbor on December 7, 1941, and the subsequent declaration of war, millions of ablebodied young men were drafted and their courtship patterns disrupted.

When the war ended in 1945, a national fever of matrimony swept the nation. Returning GIs married former sweethearts or new girl friends in a delirium of postwar nuptials, which reached its peak in 1946 with 2.2 million marriages. A serious housing shortage followed. Couples lived in cramped quarters or boarded with their parents. Jokes about mothers-in-law and Murphy beds were common. But the GI Bill and Federal Housing Administration loans offered young people a chance for a better way of life. Near New York, Philadelphia, Chicago and Los Angeles, wherever there was ample room for expansion, shrewd real estate developers snatched up vacant land parcels and turned them into mass-produced homogeneous communities for the nation's suddenly overcrowded and underhoused population. Young couples flocked to the hinterlands in waves of migration that were to continue for the next two decades. The years between 1945 and 1960 were an era of unprecedented growth and prosperity for the new suburbs, a time when the residential building industry boomed in the urban fringes, creating over 11 million new homes, when nearly half of the nation's 28 million new Americans (babies and immigrants) lived in those fledgling communities, when 4,000 families a day were leaving the cities for the new ranch and split-level subdivisions.

It was a boom time for the middle class; the young adults of that period were, as sociologists George Masnick and Mary Jo Bane observed years later, "members of that 'lucky generation' who came closer than any other to the ideal of American domesticity: a nice suburban home; a breadwinner husband and homemaker wife; dedication to childrearing; and status gained from a high level of consumption."

It was also a time when suburban sprawl was first taken seriously, when it became, as historian Constance Green has written, "suddenly a source of anxiety to both city and suburban administrators." The prediction of a 500-mile megalopolis stretching from north of Boston to south of Washington by 1975 began to look "perilously accurate." Between 1950 and 1960, the suburban population in the United States increased by 45 percent; 83 percent of the nation's population growth had occurred there. Nearly 60 million Americans now called the suburbs home. By 1957, the *New York Times* reported that the northeastern cities and suburbs had "grown into each other" to form eighteen district urban regions.

Suddenly, suburban zoning was an important public issue. Newspapers and magazines were filled with stories of small-town zoning battles and of the tug-of-war between land developers and the old-guard establishment of those once-stable suburban communities. In 1957, the *Reader's Digest* proclaimed that a "new age of pioneering" had begun—in suburbia, based largely on increased use of the automobile and the expanding highway system.

But while the automobile brought families to the suburbs, it was the appearance of babies in the nation's maternity wards at a rate of twelve a minute that was the compelling factor behind the middle-class population shift. For the postwar baby boom had continued long after demographers had predicted it would, reaching its apogee in 1957, when more than 4.3 million children were born. The parents of those new children thought of the suburbs as a "new frontier," a welcome relief from the crowded apartments, polluted air and high-crime zones of the central cities. The new suburbs became, as Landon Jones writes, "child-oriented societies, 'babyvilles,' teeming with new appetites, new institutions and new values."

The United States was a nation of nesters and, for most women, "Kinder, Küche, Kirche" was the order of the day. Once more, being a housewife was regarded as acceptable. Dr. Benjamin Spock, whose *The Common Sense Book of Baby and Child Care* first appeared in 1946, told women that "the reasonably good mother has the natural leadership qualities of an Eisenhower without any West Point training, the ability to keep order of an English policeman who is never armed." Being a good housewife and mother, Dr. Spock assured his readers in a 1952 article, was an occupation that is "as influential as any other regular job in the world." The women believed him and embraced his philosophy as religiously as they followed his feeding regimens, teething instructions and permissive approach to parental discipline. In 1955, in a commencement address to Smith College graduates, Adlai Stevenson said that motherhood "places upon you an infinitely deeper and more intimate responsibility than that borne by the majority of those who hit the headlines and make the news."

What started as a typical postwar baby boom became a reproductive mandate for the subsequent generation of women, who produced more than 42 million babies between

1955 and 1965. The average family size was 3.6 members in 1957, just slightly above what it had been in 1940, but unlike earlier eras, more and more women were marrying and giving birth. Everybody, it seemed, was getting married, and doing so at earlier ages. Women who had married at a median age of 21.5 years in 1940 were marrying at 20.1 years of age by 1957 and having babies earlier. College women were dropping out to get married and have children; only 37 percent of all women admitted to colleges during the 1950s graduated. Older women nearing the end of their reproductive years, who had delayed babies during the war, were having children for the first time. Women in their late twenties and early thirties were having their third, fourth and even fifth child.

Nowhere was the baby boom more visible than the suburbs. Gangs of children prowled the streets, crowded the schools and swelled the baby-food and baby-supply counters, the supermarkets and drugstores. Mounting school taxes, rapidly rising suburban land values and the incessant construction of three-bedroom suburban homes made the decade truly the midpoint of the "diaper century."

In the meantime, the popular periodicals were applauding the new homing instinct among women and praised their readers for their sensible approach to life. In 1956, *Look* magazine hailed the American woman as a "wondrous creature who also marries younger, bears more babies and looks and acts far more femininely than the 'emancipated' women of the 1920s or even 30s. . . . Today, if she makes an old-fashioned choice and lovingly tends a garden and a bumper crop of children, she rates louder housannas than ever before." "No sky-high tycoon or strong laborer works harder than a size 10 blonde with 2 children" read a caption above an article in the *Ladies' Home Journal* which proudly observed that the services performed by the average suburban housekeeper-mother were worth $10,000 in yearly wages.

Only a few writers, sociologists and social critics expressed concern about the new domesticity of American women. In 1949, sociologist David Riesman observed that middle-class women seemed to have shunned or avoided careers after the war in the belief that work skills would detract from their sexuality. Riesman wrote in *The Lonely Crowd* about the increased tendencies toward group conformity he observed among the young: middle-class women seemed to have "turned back in a futile effort to recapture the older and seemingly more secure patterns" of marriage and childbearing. "They have bowed not to authority or internalized inhibitions, but to a diffuse image of male expectations, female-peer group jealousies and reactionary counseling dressed up as the inside psychoanalytic story."

Riesman wrote that the deliberate sacrifice of individual talent to a blind compliance with group-sanctioned domesticity would result in a kind of death of the self, a "privatization" doomed to unhappiness and unproductivity. Middle-class suburban women, he suggested, may have an increased susceptibility to that kind of psychic strangulation because of the monolithic character of the suburban community: "The husband drives to work in the only car and leaves his wife a prisoner at home with the small children, the telephone, and the radio or television. Such women can easily become so uninteresting that they will remain psychological prisoners even when the physical and economic handicaps to their mobility are removed."

In 1956, Margaret Mead also wrote about what she perceived as wasted female talent resulting from the new domesticity. Although contemporary American women were educated like men and expected to fulfill many similar societal duties, at mid-century women exhibited a "striking paradox" in their continued choice of marriage over every other way of life. Comparing the American style with those of other nations, Dr. Mead said that 81 percent of all American women had married at one time or another in their lives, and that marriage seemed to have had a particularly deleterious effect upon their career aspirations and ability to remain financially autonomous. Women had "made home and marriage more important than they should be. American woman is still on a pedestal long after the conditions which placed her there have vanished."

Despite such disquieting interpretations of the new housewife cult, most women continued to defend the reproductive riot as a humanistic response to years of deprivation. What else, the new women of the fifties reasoned, could they do but have babies? And what else should they do?

"Why not? We had been in the work force long enough. We knew plenty about working. It had been tough and the jobs just weren't that good for women. I'd worked at a medical instrument company for years and never made as much money as a man. Babies were the natural way of life for women and when they finally came, we were just thrilled," says a 70-year-old woman living in a Boston suburb.

Total devotion to maternity was most common in the new suburbs, built as they were along strictly income-graded lines. The suburban women of those new communities were almost exclusively young and their motives for moving similar—to find good lives for themselves and their children. The suburbs developed strict social codes: the station wagon, coffee pot and carpool were common denominators of suburban sociability. Not to use them would be to fly in the face of one's suburban sisters. Most jobs were still located in the city center, and few women considered work a viable option, unless there was a compelling financial reason for them to do so.

In certain middle-class communities, the working woman was considered so aberrant that few people mentioned her in polite company or even in casual social conversation. "It was like somebody who was married a long time and had no children. You'd never mention it. You were just too embarrassed to say anything about it," recalled Ruth Sosne, a mother of two children, living in Brighton (a suburb of Rochester, New York) in the 1950s.

With the migration of families to the suburbs and the implicit understanding that young mothers remained at home, suburbia became a land of golden opportunity for big business, for a consumer market that would swell the gross national product and the nation's output of automobiles, home freezers, televisions, power tools and lawn mowers to record-breaking figures. In 1953, *Fortune* wrote: "Anybody who wants to sell anything to Americans should take a long look at the New Suburbia. It is big, lush, uniform . . ." A year later *Time* reported that suburban families had incomes 70 percent higher than those of the average American family and that since "business must follow the dollar," today's merchants "will have to follow the flight to the suburbs." By mid-decade, merchants and developers had staked out their territory, transforming strategically located pasture land and tangled thickets into hard-topped parking lots and shopping centers, as familiar fixtures of Americana as apple pie and motherhood.

New national attention to domestic pursuits such as home sewing, do-it-yourself home repair and gardening created whole new markets for big business. Power mower sales swelled from 42,000 in 1940 to 1,275,000 in 1953. Between 1946 and 1953 home freezer sales went from 210,000 to 1,200,000. Suddenly the kitchen gained new importance and a consumer craze for all kinds of cooking, canning and baking gadgets resulted. Electric can openers, blenders, toaster ovens, waffle irons and high-speed eggbeaters became new status symbols for women.

The kitchen grew larger, open walled in many of the new suburban homes, emerging as an important new living area for the family. As a Seattle housewife told a *Time* magazine reporter in 1954: "We spend at least 50 percent of our waking hours in the kitchen, it would be silly not to make it one of the nicest rooms in the house."

Half of one's waking hours in the kitchen? I found that concept amazing, but then I recalled that women of that era had also said the same things about their station wagons. Several mothers I knew, in fact, claimed they thought of their cars as substitute homes because they spent so much of their time in them. One mother from my past regularly used the time between dropping her daughter off and picking her up from ballet lessons to set her hair in pin curls. Another imaginative woman outfitted her car with blank stationery, stamps, yarn, knitting needles and unread magazines which kept her amused while waiting between carpools and family errands.

There is no doubt that by the mid-1950s housekeeping had become a national obsession: in 1954 over 3 billion dollars of housewares were sold and 500 million dollars' worth of kitchen furniture! Suburban women became the focal point for $11 million worth of advertising every year. With women's formidable economic power, the hand that rocked the cradle ruled the world in the 1950s, but few women were aware of it; most continued to see themselves as pretty but passive creatures in a world of men and machines, or in especially gray moments, as household drudges in a society that offered them few other options except for spinsterhood and poverty.

Unlike the small towns that had naturally evolved throughout history to accommodate the needs of all age groups, the new suburbs were designed as narrowly age-graded communities: two-generation towns—sunlit sanctuaries for the young and their parents, or, more accurately, for the young and their mothers.

In 1955, *House and Garden* wrote that "a good suburb is one that puts the needs of its children first." Good suburbs were places that provided well-run schools, safe streets, abundant recreational facilities for children and teenagers, baby-sitters and nursery schools. Women of the new suburbs found it discouraging that there was only a "half-finished community" outside their doors, but personal participation and volunteer service in their towns, it was felt, would make the suburbs a better place. Besides, as the magazine brightly reminded its female readers, such volunteer civic activities would immediately serve to "widen your circle of friends and your understanding of democracy."

The lure of getting out of the house for a few hours, exercising talents and improving their new communities through volunteer service proved irresistible to women. The message, coupled with a postwar patriotism, was straightforward: women could make this a better America, make their prefabricated communities character-forming civic models, if only they would volunteer. Many women were truly inspired by the message, others followed their friends and a few participated in volunteer activities because it was one of the few socially acceptable things they could do. The net effect of the participatory impulse was that suburban women became involved in volunteer work as at no other time in their history. In record numbers they flocked to the PTA, the Girl Scouts, the Boy Scouts, the League of Women Voters, the Campfire Girls, the Federated Women's Clubs, the Junior League, Great Books and the American Association of University Women.

"Suburbia" and "community service" became practically synonymous. Between 1945 and 1960, the League of Women Voters, a largely white middle-class organization with a strong constituency in suburban areas, watched its membership more than double, from about 53,000 members at the end of the war to 126,000 by 1960. The PTA watched its adult ranks swell from 3.4 million to 12 million in the same years; the number of adult volunteers for the Girl Scouts more than tripled between 1945 and 1960, reaching a peak in 1959 with more than three-quarters of a million women. Seventy percent of the Levittown, Pennsylvania, suburban adults were members of volunteer groups by the mid-1950s; 52 percent of the woman volunteers in that community when queried said they had joined organizations because of a newly perceived community need, rather than because they had any long-term interest in such groups. Women, in other words, were becoming increasingly enveloped in their communities and families. And what could be wrong with that?

Nothing, said the women's magazines, the big businesses, the advertisers, the volunteer agencies and most of the women themselves. It was the right thing to do. Here was the best life the American woman had ever experienced. She had washing machines, clothes dryers and dishwashers to help her with daily chores. She had the telephone, radio and television to keep her amused. She had nearby supermarkets in the newly built shopping centers and new department stores. She had back-fence and next-door neighbors like herself. She had her own car, increasingly important as she began to shuttle her children to sports activities, scout meetings, lessons and social engagements. Suburban life was "merely motherhood on wheels."

Donna Reed in "The Donna Reed Show," Lureen Tuttle in "Life with Father," Lucille Ball in "I Love Lucy" and Barbara Billingsley in "Leave It to Beaver" were sterling examples of that lucky new suburban woman. She was pretty, busy and happy. She was also a little zany, but her problems were simple ones that could be solved in thirty minutes, with time out for commercials. Like the suburban woman she was imitating and instructing, the television mother's life had innumerable interruptions. What she needed to set her straight was that Ipana Smile, Ivory Soap, Buster Brown shoes for her children and Tide for a Better, Brighter Wash. If only, I used to think when I was a kid, life could be that simple for me and my mother.

Problems in Paradise

But a curious change came over the American consciousness. The bubble of conformity and complacency burst in 1957 when the Russians launched the Sputnik satellite into space. Suddenly something was terribly wrong in America: wrong with our military, our scientific community, our educational system, our life. What was it? We had become apathetic. Smug. We had characteristically thought of ourselves as the biggest, brightest and best nation on earth. We had become a nation of complacent, well-fed sheep. Where were our inventors, our scientists, the leaders of the next generation?

What was at the root of our national malaise? Maybe it was the suburbs. Even before Sputnik, criticism of suburbia had been mounting.

Suddenly it was no longer regarded as the promised land. Something was inherently unhealthy about the suburban experience, the social critics said, something that engendered group banality and the compulsion to conform, produced juvenile delinquency among our youth, rendered the adult population neurotic, prone to alcoholism and spiritual sterility. Something was unnatural about it. Maybe it was the homogeneous character of the houses themselves. Maybe it was the narrow two-generation population mix. Maybe it was the transience of the upwardly mobile middle-class population, moving from suburb to suburb. Maybe it was because the men left home so early in the morning for city jobs and returned so late at night. Maybe it was because the suburbs were segregrated by race, ethnic groups, class and income levels.

In 1957, William Whyte observed in *The Organization Man* that Americans were becoming increasingly "intimidated by normalcy" and that the suburbs, with their homogeneous social milieu, exacerbated that tendency. Group pressure affected the women of those look-alike communities, who were "easily misled by the façade of those about them in suburbia." One result of keeping up appearances was that women often shouldered inordinately large civic and social obligations in addition to their duties as wives and mothers, and were thus compelled to maintain frantic social lives. The unfortunate end of this syndrome was that suburban women often developed serious emotional problems because their husbands no longer had sympathy for them. It was a frightening observation—an accurate one, touching the crux of the feminine suburban problem.

Vance Packard in *The Status Seekers* pointed to the recent American obsession with material symbols. Cars, suburban homes, televisions, hi-fi's and clothes were the trappings of newly acquired social stature, the only way modern man could prove who he was. The current danger in contemporary society was that materialism had become an end in itself. Like Whyte, Packard briefly scrutinized the women of the era, observing that "wives . . . tend to be more status conscious than their husbands" and that "emotionally insecure people are most vulnerable" to status symbol intimidation. But Packard spent little time in exploring the connection between women's search for status and emotional insecurity. Like *The*

Organization Man, Packard's *The Status Seekers* has been remembered for its criticism of faulty American values.

Suburban women and the problems they faced were still not focused upon, though a few sociologists, family doctors, psychiatrists, researchers and journalists noticed that there was increased depression among suburban women. They also noticed increased smoking, drinking, sexual promiscuity. And the gradual beginnings of a skyrocketing divorce rate.

Writer Eve Merriam boldly stated that full-time housewifery may not be necessary, that "staying at home full-time is not fit occupation for a full-time grown woman." "Is the housewife necessary?" she asked *Nation* readers in 1959 in an article with the same title. She is not, Merriam proclaimed, but she is made to believe that her place is in the home, because frankly our society has no other place for her. Besides, she was a necessary repository for consumer products. "She's an absolute must for Arthur Godfrey and his tea-bags."

In the same year, psychiatrist Dr. Richard Gordon and his social psychologist wife Katherine called attention to the real problems they had observed in suburban women. The Gordons maintained that suburbia seemed to contain certain psychological stresses which made its residents prone to higher incidences of heart attack, duodenal ulcers and hypertension than people living in small towns. One of the most startling findings of their five-year study was that it was suburban women who suffered the most. The reasons behind their angst were that suburban women experienced distinctive social and psychological separation from their husbands, that they were frustrated by the "dull, grubby diapers and dishes of a housewife's daily routine" and that they suffered from compulsive drives to "keep the homes meticulously clean, meeting trains on deadline and getting the children to school on time."

In *The Split-Level Trap,* published the following year, the Gordons observed that the suburban citizen with his mass-produced home and automobile thought he had achieved the epitome of the American dream, but in reality he "represents the great sad joke of our time." Something essential to the human psyche was missing, because the suburban homeowner "gropes for tranquillity and finds it only fleetingly in pill bottles and a cocktail glass." Suburban women, particularly young married mothers, were the most tragic casualties of the new Disturbia, as the Gordons called it. "Of all the people in the sample, thirty-six percent—more than a third—are young married women. The number of disturbed suburban young wives is more than half again as big as the number of young husbands, and more than three times as big as any other group. . . . There is a strong indication that things are troubling the young wives more often, or more severely, than anybody else."

This was shocking news to a generation of women weaned on the concept of female domesticity and the good life of suburbia. A flurry of newspaper and magazine articles followed. The *New York Times* and the *Daily News* reported that alcoholism was rampant among suburban women in the New York metropolitan area because of the loneliness of their existence. *U.S. News & World Report* wondered in 1962 if exodus from the suburbs was beginning. Other periodicals, like *Cosmopolitan, Good Housekeeping* and *Redbook,* began to examine the causes and consequences of feminine suburban angst and offered helpful suggestions. Today, the stereotype of the alcoholic or pill-popping suburban housewife persists and has become a national cliché despite the fact that studies on alcoholism and drug abuse during that time and today do not clearly implicate suburban women. Even if the "gin in the steam iron" or "two-Valium kaffeeklatsch" did exist in greater numbers among suburban women of the 1950s than in other geographical settings, popular magazines still recommended increased community activity and more involvement with friends. Seldom was the enforced domesticity of the suburban situation and its resultant effect upon the female psyche examined; instead, magazines implied that the fault lay within the women themselves for not exercising their own inner resources.

It was left to Betty Friedan, in 1963, to explore the housewife question on a more comprehensive basis in *The Feminine Mystique.* Women were trapped, said Friedan, stymied by the "feminine mystique" that dictated that the greatest accomplishment for women was the realization of their femininity through sexual passivity, childbearing and housekeeping, as extensions of their nurturing force. The woman with the worst case of "the problem without a name" was the suburban housewife. Her spacious living quarters and the wide distances between store, school and train station to which she must shuttle in her station wagon made her household obligations more demanding than those of her city sister. "Her day is fragmented as she rushes from dishwasher to washing machine to telephone to dryer to station wagon to supermarkets and delivers Johnny to the Little League field, takes Janey to dancing class, gets the lawn mower fixed and meets the 6:45."

Friedan observed that while the suburbs may have initially represented a tempting challenge to bright ambitious women, once the women became involved with home, children, consumerism and the demanding social rites of suburban life, they had little time left for meaningful work, even in the volunteer sector. As a result, young suburban housewives were "perfectly willing to fill their days with the trivia of housewifery," restricting their volunteer work to door-to-door collection, den mother jobs and lesser PTA responsibilities. "The housewife who doesn't 'have time' to take serious responsibility in the community, like the woman who doesn't 'have time' to pursue a professional career, evades a serious commitment through which she might finally find herself; she evades it by stepping up her domestic routine until she is truly trapped."

The end result of that syndrome, Friedan predicted, would be a generation of unhappy, unfulfilled older women whose skills, sense of self-esteem and personal growth had been so hampered as to render them psychologically noxious to their husbands and children, and useless to society.

Despite that controversial best-seller, the suburban pattern still held firm. By the mid-1960s, most suburban women still hadn't heard of or given serious thought to Friedan's book, or if they had, regarded it as heresy. Instead, suburban women continued to raise children, chauffeur, clean house and prepare dinner in a fashion similar to that of their sisters of the fifties. A diamond was forever. And so was marriage. The economy was holding strong and their men would support them. Besides, as the *Ladies' Home Journal* once reminded its readers, the housewife, unlike the career girl, had special benefits. She was "loved out loud." She had job security. And unlike the single working woman, she had a job from which she would never be fired.

Few mothers dreamed that the children they lavished so much love, attention and money on would reject those values in the decade to come, as those youngsters began to experiment with drugs, sex and civil disobedience on the college campuses and city streets of America. Even fewer women suspected that the three essentials of our modern suburban society—a stable economy, cheap energy and the sanctity of marriage—were about to undergo radical changes, changes that would, by the early 1970s, erode the foundation of the suburban home.

3

Nine to Five:
The Working
Suburban Woman

What happens to the dream of home when a wife goes to work? Other dreams jostle it for time, but it doesn't go away. Most working wives honor the service clause of the marriage contract. They keep it going by mirrors. The majority of their tasks are performed, hired done, or done without. But what they discover in the attempt is that the priceless center of the dream is the unfailing, 24-hour presence of a woman to respond to immediate needs and make everyone comfortable. When she earns the right to make plans of her own, the dream fades—but it continues to haunt both husband and wife.

Caroline Bird, *The Two-Paycheck Marriage*

IT IS 7:30 A.M. on a rainy Monday morning as an army of commuters' automobiles swarm like ants over the Grand Central Parkway toward Manhattan. "Jackknifed trailer truck, just east of the Throgs Neck Bridge," drones the CBS News

Traffic Watch helicopter over the radio. It is here, just south of the bridge, that the long, agonized crawl to the city begins in earnest every morning. It is here, too, that the red Chevy Malibu from Hempstead, Long Island, brakes quickly before coming to an abrupt stop. "Damn," mutters Barbara, the middle-aged driver, as she sees the stalled traffic. With undisguised irritation she unfolds the morning newspaper and impatiently proceeds to read the front page.

Her 30-year-old companion breathes a sigh of relief, removes a cosmetic case from her pocketbook and applies makeup to her face. Unlike her friend, Carol is glad for the traffic jam. It is a moment of respite from the driving pace of her day—the rasp of the 5:30 alarm, the hurried breakfasts for her husband and kids, the lunches to be packed, the dishes to be washed, the long hours of work ahead. If only she could be a housewife again. Life was so much simpler when she had three preschool youngsters running under foot and a husband who arrived home at 6:15 every night for dinner. Now she finds herself hoping for the most perverse events, like snarled commuter traffic on the Throgs Neck. Those few moments of enforced idleness provide restorative calm to the storm that has become her life since she returned to work.

An hour later, and it is sunrise over Columbus, Ohio. A 35-year-old woman kisses her two children and husband, closes the door to her car and pulls away from the curb of a fashionable street in Bexley, Ohio. Life seems easy for Gail. She has an easygoing husband who makes a good living. She has two bright young children. She is a tall, willowy woman whose serene manner and easy laughter have made her one of the most popular administrators at the University of Ohio. Her job is an exciting one. Yet as she drives west on Route 70 toward the university, a rising sense of anxiety overtakes her. Maybe I shouldn't leave the kids, she thinks, maybe they are too young. Maybe I should still be home with them. Maybe I shouldn't have taken this job. The freeway guilts, Gail calls these voices, the self-doubts that have become her constant companions as she commutes between home and the university.

In the evening as she leaves the school and heads south on Route 71, the inner monologue begins again, but this time with a different message. I really should be staying here longer. There's so much more I could do on this job, so much more I could contribute to the department. I was lucky after all to get this job in the first place. But it's so late already, and I haven't seen the kids all day . . .

6:00 P.M., the San Francisco Bay area. The doors to the Bay Area Rapid Transit train open at the Walnut Creek station and a distraught young woman named Natalie pushes her way out of the first car of the train. She runs down the station steps. She is late, woefully late. She missed the earlier train because she was delayed at work. Now she is overdue at the day-care center where her 3-year-old daughter is waiting. Now she will have to pay the center overtime. Frantically she unlocks the car, jumps in, careens out of the station parking lot and heads toward the day-care center. When she arrives, her daughter is in tears. "I thought you weren't coming, Mommy," says the little girl as Natalie runs to her, picks her up and kisses her gently. The teacher, waiting with the child, regards Natalie coldly.

"I'm sorry. I was late at work and missed the train," Natalie apologizes to the woman. "How much extra do I owe you for waiting?"

"Twenty dollars. A dollar for every two minutes overtime."

Natalie raises her eyebrows in surprise, but says nothing.

"We have to charge that much or the mothers begin to take advantage of us," snaps the teacher brusquely. "Please try to get here on time from now on."

They work for different reasons. Some take jobs to help pay the family bills, others for personal fulfillment, a few to keep themselves busy. But there is little doubt that they work in ever-increasing numbers. Rush hour gives new shape to their days. Fast foods, wash-and-wear fabrics, food processors and microwave ovens are its mass-market expressions.

"I can put the wash on the line, feed the kids, get dressed, pass out the kisses and get to work by five of nine, cause I'm a woman," goes a TV jingle for Enjoli perfume. And in the recent song "9 to 5" Dolly Parton laments the fact that today's working women spend their days pounding typewriters, answering phones and assisting male bosses with little hope of being promoted to positions of professional responsibility themselves.

By 1980, 57 percent of all mothers with minor children were working. They have become a permanent fixture in our society. New magazines have appeared in their honor: *Savvy, Venture, Working Woman, Working Mother*—bright testimonials to the working woman's new public image as increasingly urbane, glamorous and resourceful. And somewhere in the suburbs, the working woman scrambles to keep pace with that image.

Despite the publicized glamor of her new position, the suburban woman often finds herself caught between the demands of suburban home life and her job. Like the Hempstead woman, she may become chronically exhausted trying to fulfill both roles. Like the Columbus college administrator, she may be wracked with guilt as she tries to juggle home life and a challenging career. Like the California mother, she might discover that her rising career obligations as a young executive have come into conflict with suburban day-care services.

Torn between old expectations of suburban womanhood and new anxieties about an inflationary economy, she often returns to work only to find herself at the center of contemporary feminine dilemmas: equal opportunity, child care, equal division of household labor between husband and wife. Often she is shaken by the inequities of her position. How can she carpool and collect a paycheck at the same time? Should she take that high-paying job in the city even though it means an additional hour of commuting every day? Should she settle for a less challenging job closer to home so she can fulfill household duties without placing additional demands upon her family?

It is a dilemma that seems more difficult for her to resolve than for the woman living in either the city or the country. The opposing pulls of those demands may be enough to radicalize this most traditional of all American women and to turn her into one of three types: an ardent housewife, an anxious career "superwoman," or a bitter individualist.

"It was only when I returned to work that I realized what a disadvantage I was laboring under," a Bergen County, New Jersey, broker who works in Manhattan explained to me. "It was only when my child walked to school in snowstorms because I simply couldn't participate in carpools, that I began to appreciate the full onus of the suburban condition."

And it was only when neighborhood children began to congregate at her home every day after school because their mothers were working and their homes empty, a suburban Dallas Right to Lifer told me, that she became convinced not to seek employment until after her children were grown. "If you bring children into this world, your first responsibility is to them," she said fervently. "If money gets tight around here, we'll just do with less. We'll get by without me returning to work."

The resultant social fragmentation among women faced with these issues is the essence of the unique revolution taking place in today's suburbs. And at the bottom of it all is often the question of money.

Suburban women. The sneering sonority with which we tag a woman of our acquaintance a "suburban matron" by way of quick identification underlines the tenacity of that monied image, even as it acknowledges our evolving awareness of the underside of the fifties' feminine ideal. Sadly, for the contemporary woman of the suburbs, the ideological fallout from that earlier prosperous era of the golden age of suburbia has stuck. The glazed female sexuality of that older suburban image imbues our national psyche, often stifling a tremendous reservoir of energy and talent.

Suburban women. The discrepancy between the image and the real women is crucial, even as the old dreams about hard work and the rewards of thrift are shattered. Financial stability for many families has become a struggle. More often than not, it takes two paychecks to support a family in the suburbs today. And yet mothers are still expected to chauffeur their children to and from school in many suburban communities. Elementary schoolchildren in many suburbs are still sent home for lunch. Public transportation is notoriously poor, leaving children dependent upon the automobile—and their mothers—for after-school transportation. Baby-sitters, cleaning help, even well-paid housekeepers are increasingly difficult to find; after-school programs are uneven; suburban day-care centers inconvenient, overcrowded and expensive.

Given these circumstances, I find it amazing that suburban women work at all, but work they must. For a new factor has been added to the old suburban formula: the need for ever-increasing amounts of cash. It began with the inflationary spiral of the early 1970s that saw prices for food, clothes and shelter increase at an alarmingly rapid rate. In 1973, the first oil embargo and the resultant recession of 1973 and 1974 sent another twinge of fear through the nation's families; by the end of the decade, double-digit inflation, OPEC, runaway energy costs and an unstable economy had dealt a death blow to the middle-class standard of the breadwinner father, an at-home mother and several children. By 1978, only 7 percent of all families conformed to such a traditional pattern.

In 1980, the *New York Times Magazine* wrote that because of the unstable economy, the middle-class dream of hard work and thrift rewarded by economic security and the good life had been endangered, that the American dream was becoming increasingly inaccessible: "Squeezed in the middle of this madness is the middle class, for whom money in itself had become the medium that translated education and hard work into well-paid careers, suburban homes and the latest possessions that prosperity and technology provided, fashion suggested and revolving credit financed. . . . Now there is doubt and anxiety and even fear. Gross economic problems are complicated by subtler psychological ones, and together they are prodding the middle class to become more vocal on its own behalf, more insistent that its needs be met and less sympathetic to the needs of others."

National fertility rates went down as the cost of bearing children and maintaining single-dwelling homes leaped upward. Participation in the labor force among all women increased rapidly, growing from 38 percent in 1960 to 43 percent in 1970—and reaching an all-time high of 51 percent in 1980. Among young women aged 25 to 34, the rate was even more striking—rising from 36 percent in 1960 to 64 percent in 1979. Women with school-age children returned to work in dramatic numbers: 39 percent of all mothers with children aged 6 to 17 worked in 1960, but there were 64 percent by 1980.

By 1980, *Newsweek* reported, modern mothers had become transformed from just plain old apple-pie moms to "supermoms" who held paying jobs and kept house with varying degrees of success. "The American Woman is trapped in the superwoman squeeze."

Nowhere was that more true than in the suburbs, where rising mortgage rates, heating and air-conditioning bills and the high price of gasoline had taken an alarmingly large bite out of the family budget. Suburban women returned to work with unprecedented vigor. In fact, they are working in greater numbers than women from both the central cities and the rural communities. Historically, as the old stereotypes would have suggested, suburban women tagged behind the rest of the nation's female workers. But by 1975, the year after the recession had lifted, the number of working suburban women surpassed that of the rest of the nation for the first time. By 1980, 53.4 percent of all suburban women over the age of 16 worked (that is, 18 million women)—the rate for all women in the nation over the age of 16 was 51.6 percent. In the suburbs the working woman had become the rule, rather than the exception. But with a difference: nobody was ready to believe them yet.

Why Does She Work?

One of their problems was the issue of why they sought work. For many employers, the idea that they were looking for work because they needed the money still sounded odd— especially if they came from affluent communities. A Scarsdale, New York, matron who had looked for work for almost a year before finding a job, described a distinct skepticism among her interviewers when they learned where she lived. Although the woman had a Ph.D. in psychology, and equal opportunity laws prohibited interviewers from asking questions about her economic status, the air was heavy with doubts about her seriousness. "They wondered if I was for real, whether I'd be able to carry through on a long-term commitment. You could just see the look on many of their faces. They'd never say anything directly, of course, but sometimes they'd make oblique references, like repeatedly asking what kind of transportation I'd use, whether I intended to take the train or not, constant reminders that the vacation time was limited during the first year and the fact that the job might require overtime during peak periods."

Another woman, living in Alexandria, Virginia, who encountered the same type of attitude in her job search, finally decided to take matters into her own hands. "Since they couldn't very well ask me certain questions about my marriage or financial situation, I decided that I'd volunteer that information. I wanted to be taken seriously. I wanted them to know that I needed the money. I told them that my husband had just lost his job," the woman said with a wry smile. "He hadn't of course, but it worked. It changed their entire attitude toward me. Suddenly I wasn't just another bored suburban matron. I was somebody who really needed to work. The next day they called me back for another interview."

While public opinion surveys like the Roper Organization's American Women's Opinion Poll showed, in 1980, that 86 percent of all women work because they need the money, perceptions about what is true financial need and what is discretionary, or personal, income vary widely with social class and geographical area. What may be considered a standard accouterment in Birmingham, Michigan, such as a food processor or a video tape recorder, may be considered a luxury in Cicero, Illinois. This issue tells us much about the suburban dilemma surrounding work for women: where does true need begin and the need for the acquisition of status and comfort through material goods end? The gray area of subjective "need" seems to confound many middle-class women and complicate their decision to enter the labor force or remain at home.

Labor force statistics seem clearly to demonstrate that most women work because of financial need. Of all employed women in 1980, 44 percent were single, divorced, separated or widowed, and another 25 percent were married to men with incomes of less than $15,000 a year. But what of the other 31 percent of married women who work, those with higher family incomes, many of whom live in the suburbs? How can we account for the rising female suburban work force in areas where family incomes are known to be higher than anywhere else in the nation?

Economic need is only part of the reason. Today's suburban women are working as much for a sense of self-fulfillment and autonomy as for financial gain. Often, for married middle-class women—especially for suburban women, whose median family income is about 20 to 25 percent higher than for those living in the central cities and the rural communities ($22,801 in the suburbs, $17,549 in the cities and $16,301 in the nonmetropolitan areas in 1979)—the decision to return to paid employment is a highly personal one. It touches on a woman's views on feminism, on her sense of self-fulfillment, on her self-image. If a woman sees her primary purpose in life as a

wife, mother and housekeeper, her decision to remain home
will be a simple one. If, however, she is at all ambivalent about
that role—if she is bored, restless or just plain unhappy at
home—she may attempt to experiment with paid employment.
Nearly every woman can always use more money in her
pocket; financial need is a good excuse for a woman to return
to work. But even today, in an era of official recognition of the
notion that women should have the right to pursue activities
beyond those of the immediate family circle, many women I
have interviewed have been hesitant to give reasons such as
unhappiness or boredom at home to their friends and neighbors when they return to work.

As sociologist Helena Lopata observed in her landmark
study of suburban and urban Chicago area women, *Occupation: Housewife,* women in traditionally female jobs—
which include about 80 percent of all working women—are
more likely to tell others that they are working out of economic
necessity because it is a less threatening statement. On the
other hand, women in upper-level managerial and professional
jobs or in jobs they have created themselves, are much more
likely to cite "personal fulfillment" or "intellectual stimulation"
as an important factor in their decision to work. Feminism is at
least partially responsible for the suburban woman's return to
work, even though its true impact may be disguised.

What may have begun for many women as a "fun job" for
extra money or a legitimate way to get out of the house often
becomes financial necessity as women begin to make more
money and as inflation gnaws an increasingly large hole in the
family budget. A suburban Columbus, Ohio, woman who
returned to work eight years ago described such an evolution:
"Originally, I went to work just to keep from getting bored.
The money that came in from my first few years of work was
extra money we always used for luxuries—vacations, clothes,
a new TV. But with inflation and high energy costs, there's
been a real turnaround in our family budget. We *need* the
money I'm making now. Without it, in fact, we couldn't pay
the monthly bills."

Rapidly accelerating college costs have also taken many

families by surprise, causing many women to return to work or to continue their employment long after they had anticipated stopping. A 42-year-old mother of four children in Des Plains, Illinois, who now holds a responsible position with the Veterans Administration, looks back on her at-home days with a sense of wonder at her earlier naivete about long-term family finances. Recalling that she was "just starting to think about returning to work" when a local politician offered her a staff position five years ago, she said she had reluctantly agreed to try the job on an experimental basis. "The first job worked out really well, because my husband was very helpful, and we knew we could use the money. We knew we would have two children in college in a few years, but we didn't anticipate what that would really mean. If I hadn't gone back to work then, I honestly don't know how we would have gotten them through school. When I look back on it now, I wonder what I could have been thinking all those years by staying home."

Other suburban women freely admit that while they have seriously considered family finances, they sought work largely because they were bored at home. This seems to be particularly true among younger women, who, I discovered, have already demonstrated an unprecedented commitment to the work ethic. Many of the young women I have interviewed around the country have talked about their desire to return to work in reaction to what they were feeling at home—the sensation that they were withering away as housewives, as though their mental faculties were diminishing. For many of these young women, who left the work force for the first time to bear children, the suburban environment seemed terribly bleak and monotonous. Just how abrupt the break between the world of work and the suburban environment can be was vividly portrayed to me one hot Saturday afternoon by a woman living in Walnut Creek, California, who told of the sudden sense of isolation she felt when she left her job to stay home with a new baby: "It was as though I had suddenly been sealed off from the world, and all the days took on a gray sameness. I felt as though I was actually becoming stupid. As though I was turning into some nightmare version of myself. I spent that year cooking wonderful meals, cleaning house, sitting in front of the TV and getting fat. It took me only a few months to get achy and depressed. I finally got scared of what was happening to me and decided it was time to get out there and back to work."

Many suburban women I have talked with also told me that they feel they have outlived their usefulness. After a busy period of housekeeping, childrearing and community service, they may come to feel that their lives have become purposeless. One Hollywood, Florida, woman described the monotony of her affluent existence: "There I was sitting in that magnificent house in a golden cage, as I used to think of it, and I had nothing to do. No reason to get up in the morning except for the children. But they went off to school and were busy with other activities all day. The question—what was I going to do for the rest of my life?—began to haunt me."

That same sense of aimlessness often described by suburban women may have strong emotional consequences that eventually force the women to take decisive actions to change their lives. A North Shore, Chicago, woman with two small children told me that she finally decided she must return to work because she finally understood that it was only when she was working that she felt she was a "real person." Once a nun, now married to an attorney, she returned to work part-time as a social worker two years ago. One night she explained to me the effect full-time housework had had on her: "I decided to go back to work to get over the feeling of not being valued. For when I was at home, I came to understand that society values people for what they can do and what they can earn. We talk in this country about motherhood and family as being very important, but in reality we really don't think much of them. If we did, there wouldn't be mothers on welfare and latchkey children. I love being a mother and I love my kids, but I've come to recognize that in this society, it's the almighty dollar that's important."

It goes without saying that power has become a familiar word to many working women today. More and more women are coming to understand that by engaging in paid employment, they have the potential to create or dispel power in the marital relationship and the home. As Caroline Bird observed, "Most wives didn't go to work for the power of the paycheck, but they liked it when they tasted it and they are not going to give it up."

Even when we consciously choose to ignore the relationship between money and social power, most middle-class suburban women come to feel powerless in their unpaid status as housewives. Typically, though, many couch their expressions of psychic unease in other terms. When asked why she worked, one energetic young woman from southwestern Miami with three children put it this way: "I just got bored at home, that's all. It just wasn't my style. So I decided to get out of the house and make some money. Why not? I mean, how much housework can you do? So I went into business with my brother and sister-in-law. My kids watch themselves after school. My husband helps with the housework and the laundry. Don't get me wrong, though, I'm certainly not a feminist—I just couldn't sit around the house all day. It would drive me nuts."

Where did that pervasive sense of boredom, worthlessness and restlessness, or the psychological importance of earning the dollar, come from? Probably they were always there, judging from what we know about women in earlier periods of history. But our threshold for enduring such emptiness has been lowered. Why? How much has contemporary feminist philosophy had to do with lowering that threshold? Does work and the immediate status it seems to confer upon women have its own kind of tyranny, making us feel that a job is the only way to achieve respectability?

I personally believe it has done just that—particularly among women who have the luxury of deciding whether or not to work. As the sociologist Lillian Rubin observed in *Women of a Certain Age,* middle-class women characteristically experience more difficulty with self-identity in their middle years than working-class women. "'I have a job and it feels good.' These are words more likely to be heard . . . from women with a high-school education than from those with a college degree. . . . The problem of finding their way into the work world and the problem of what they'll do when they get there are considerably more complicated for [educated women] than for most high-school educated working-class women."

Why should the middle-class suburban woman work if she doesn't have to? And if she does have to make money, what kind of job should she take? What kind of a job could she realistically expect to find if she has been out of the work world for a decade or more? After all, the mere fact that she is a woman means she is already operating under a handicap—that she will probably earn only sixty cents to every dollar a man will make with the same skills. Compounding those difficulties is the difference between the traditional male career timetable, which dictates that the years between twenty-five and thirty-five are crucial in establishing a career, and the fact that most women spend those years bearing and rearing children. When the suburban woman returns to the workplace at age thirty-five or forty, it is often "too late" for her to bloom professionally. Typically, she is classified as a reentry woman and placed on a lower rung of the corporate ladder than either those young women just out of college or her contemporaries who have spent the last ten years of their lives at work. She is usually slated by the personnel office for a position with little career potential.

If her husband happens to be a business executive or a professional, there are additional worries. Will her new low-status job be demeaning to his own position? Should the wife of a vice-president of a major oil company, for instance, take a job as a secretary in another corporation? Should a doctor's wife accept a job as a sales clerk in a department store? And how easily will her husband accept the idea of her employment in such a position? Agonized thinking, all of this, but remarkably common among today's suburban women. It paralyzes many middle-class suburban women in a never-never land of indecision and frustration about the proper way to use their free time.

Middle-aged women may have an especially difficult time,

because they were brought up in an era when women were still expected to stay home. "Many of them had not planned for or been aware that there would be social pressure upon them to make something of their lives career-wise once their children were grown," says Dr. Maj-Britt Rosenbaum, a psychiatrist who has a large practice in Westchester County, New York. "There's a feeling of being caught up in a different system from the one they grew up in, a different world. Suddenly they're expected to work. This is where so many middle-aged women feel squeezed by the movement."

Other counselors observe that many middle-class suburban women are unable to express their dissatisfaction with their housewife status directly, but manifest behavior symptomatic of underlying psychological conflict. Dr. Joan Robertson Cross, a Texas psychologist who treats many suburban wives in the Dallas-Fort Worth area, says: "They don't explicitly state, 'I'm unhappy living through my husband and children,' but rather come to me with complaints like, 'I cry all the time,' or 'I yell all the time,' or 'I'm obsessive.'"

Underneath all those symptoms and excuses, Dr. Cross maintains, many of those women are changing, and striving for change quicker than their husbands. Even while many suburban women don't officially embrace the tenets of feminism, nearly all are beginning to accept the idea that they need an identity for themselves beyond that of wife and mother. "Fifty years ago, they wouldn't have dared ask," Dr. Cross says. "But today there's a sense that they know they're missing something. The sad part is they still can't ask directly. They can't give themselves permission to demand something beyond serving others. So instead they get mentally ill, so that somebody has to step in and help them and finally give them permission to find something for themselves, to go back to school, to get a job, to get involved in something beyond their families."

There are many other valid reasons why middle-class suburban women return to work. My own feelings as a young wife and mother surface. After moving to the suburbs of New York City in Westchester County and giving birth to a second child, I spent the next six months wondering at my new position. Suburban wife and mother, I kept repeating to myself. I kept pinching myself, trying to get used to my new role. But despite the "adultness" of that role and my delight in having two young daughters, I also found myself wondering whether this would be all. Was this what my years of school, college and graduate school were all about? I began to fret, as I changed diapers, planted tulip bulbs in the garden and baked bread. Was this what Chaucer, Modern Poetry and Victorian Literature courses that had kept me up till three in the morning with their interminable reading lists were all about? Was this what all the term papers, editorials in the school newspapers and painful poetry I published in the college literary magazine were meant to teach me? Somehow it seemed like an awful cheat—both for me and for my family.

How much Old English and Contemporary Fiction, after all, would I end up imparting to my two young daughters? And even when they were of an age to appreciate it, how much would they be interested in it? An even more distressing question was: How much of it would *I* remember by that time anyway? I thought better of those difficult years in college and graduate school, and of myself. Too much effort had gone into those years to see them go to waste. Finally, one particularly dreary winter night, I decided I would have to get a job. I began part-time in a Manhattan publishing house.

Education—and the expectations it has raised among women to engage in worldly, disciplined tasks—is the key to women's relationship to the working world and has had a profound influence on the formation of their adult sense of self. Elizabeth Janeway writes that as women's education and vocational skills increasingly parallel those of men, their self-concept is more likely to be based upon occupation rather than upon attainment of a husband.

Just as it was meant to do, education has served today's women as the prelude to meaningful life work. Once educated, most young women today exercise their skills in a paid vocation. When women disengage from that vocation to bear children, there may be a painful transition. While there may be other reasons for their discontent at home—including the suddenness of the transition itself—perhaps the most important is that their sense of self has almost inevitably been forced to contract. If modern woman has gained at least a modicum of self-confidence in her worth as a human being beyond her reproductive function, she may likely experience an erosion of that identity when she suddenly finds herself occupied twenty-four hours a day in a housewifely and motherly role.

If she is lucky, she may be perceptive enough to realize how intricately her identity is tied up with her educational or vocational achievements, and make appropriate adjustments. A 33-year-old Greenwich, Connecticut, attorney who remained home for the first three months after her daughter was born and began to suffer from bouts of acute depression suddenly came to that understanding. Realizing just how much her self-confidence had eroded in the time she had been home, she resolutely returned to work. Another year and a half has passed, and now she has two young children—one not quite two years old and the other an eight-month-old baby. She juggles the demands of motherhood with those of a fledgling law practice, but the rewards of enduring these difficult years are worth it, she says, because she has discovered that work is necessary for her personal sense of well-being. And as she walked her gurgling baby back and forth in her family room, she explained why: "Maybe it's just that I have a very strong work ethic and maybe that's even a kind of problem. But I've just got to go on working because I studied too hard in law school to let that all go now. I'm a woman with a need for self-fulfillment and I'm very honest about it. My feelings about having a career are very important to me. I want my children to grow up well adjusted, and that's also very important to me. But I couldn't deal with the narrow environment of motherhood indefinitely day in and day out. I know I'd be a lousy parent if I were there with them seven days a week."

Job Realities

In purely economic terms, higher education is also a powerful determinant in who attains jobs. In fact, it is even more important in predicting employment patterns among women than it is for men. In 1976, a report of the Bureau of Labor Statistics found that the number of working women ranged from about 40 percent for those who did not complete elementary school to about 70 percent for those who were college graduates. The strong correlation between education and employment was particularly evident among married women, as the report noted, because education increases wage potential and benefits.

Not only does the suburban family have a higher income level than the urban or rural family, it also has a slightly higher educational level. Census Bureau figures for 1979 indicate that almost 30 percent of all suburban men had a college education, compared to 27 percent of those living in central cities. Figures for suburban women were virtually identical to those for city women—20 percent of all suburban women were college graduates and 19 percent of all urban females. Given the fact that they were as educated as their city sisters, it was likely that the suburban women would seek work.

But what kind of work can the woman living in suburbia do? What kinds of jobs are realistically available to her? Strained as she already is in her duties as household manager and chauffeur, and anxious to work for personal or economic reasons, she is faced with a limited work market—limited as well by her lack of access to public transportation and the automobile, and by her unwillingness to spend inordinate amounts of time commuting. Where should she look for a job? Here is another dilemma of suburban women.

I think of a 35-year-old woman I know who was slowly wending her way through the arcade of a shopping center near my home one bright summer morning when we happened to meet. Despite the beauty of the morning, she seemed remarkably sad, her head bent and her shoulders slouched as she walked toward me.

"Hi, how are you?" I asked as we stopped near the entrance to a donut shop to chat.

"Oh, I'm depressed, terribly depressed," she sighed. "The kids are in camp and I'm so bored and lonely at home that I just can't stand it. To be honest with you, I'm just counting the days till they come home. And at the same time I'm dreading it. I wish I had a job."

"Well, why don't you look for one?" I asked her.

"It's just too hard," she sighed again, as if she had had this discussion with someone before. "What kind of a job could I get out here anyway? I haven't worked in years and I'm prepared to do nothing. What kind of training does a B.A. in French literature get you anyway?"

"Maybe you can find something in the city," I suggested.

"Never! I would never consider it, at least not at this point. What would happen to the kids after school? What I really need is a part-time job, something that would be professional and something that's right here in the county. And that kind of a job is about as easy to find as hen's teeth."

Her problem is a real one. Responsible professional jobs for women are difficult to obtain at best, and part-time positions are even more scarce. Most part-time jobs are in sales, secretarial and clerical positions. Most women are also still employed in these traditional "pink collar" jobs—the clerical, secretarial, sales and factory jobs that are often associated with women's work, characterized by low status, low salaries and little opportunity for advancement. Only 20 percent of the country's working women are employed as managers or professionals, and such jobs are still relatively rare in suburban communities, even though the suburbs are becoming more urbanized.

Clearly, the old distinctions between city and country are disappearing. Commercial congestion is often a continuous fact of life from city to suburb today; even from suburb to country, the boundaries are becoming less distinct. Businesses have moved out from the city centers to suburban areas and beyond, into exurban ones. Green space has dwindled or is imitative, coyly arranged to resemble what was once open countryside. It is now the age of the campus-style corporate headquarters, the age of the suburban industrial park. Increasing numbers of suburbanites now work in or near their residential communities rather than traveling to the cities to work as they did years ago. Counties such as Santa Clara, California, Cook and DuPage counties, Illinois, Fairfield County, Connecticut, and my own Westchester County are prime examples of that trend and have witnessed a dramatic influx of major corporations, manufacturing plants and service industries where once only homes, churches and shops stood.

On first glance, the corporate migration to the suburbs might seem to be a boon for suburban women. And in a way, of course, it has been, because it has meant an influx of new jobs. But while there are indeed more jobs in the splendid chrome-and-glass suburban business centers, there is also an overabundance of new low-level jobs for women, for whom their sole attraction is their proximity to home.

The suburban job market often resembles a pink-collar ghetto even more than that of the central cities does. About 25 percent of all suburban working women held part-time jobs in 1980, while only about 20 percent of the women working in the central cities held such positions. Labor studies show that part-time workers tend to make only about 80 percent of the hourly wage given to full-time workers for the same job, and rarely receive the same health plan coverage, pension plans and other company benefits. Of the 441 occupations listed in the Census Occupational Classification System, 80 percent of all women were concentrated in only about twenty jobs—sales, clerical, services and factory work. Because more women seem to work part-time in the suburbs than do women elsewhere, their chances of engaging in such work are especially high. Joan Goodin, who at this writing was Executive Director of the National Commission on Working Women, suspects that the percentage of all working suburban women holding pink-collar jobs may be as high as 85 percent.

A second indication that the suburban business climate is more conservative in its attitude toward women than that of the cities is the fact that the pay scale for almost all traditional female jobs is lower. Employers can afford to keep it substantially lower, too, because they know that suburban women are eager to work near their homes. As women have become increasingly interested in working outside their homes, suburban employers have come to think of them as viable members of the potential labor pool; in some cases, companies have decided to move to the suburbs because they felt they could draw upon the clerical and secretarial skills of the suburban housewife just as effectively—if not more so—than those of the inner-city resident. While that decision itself may be a measure of progress, I suspect chief executive officers rarely think of suburban women as potential candidates for management slots while contemplating their moves.

The trade-off that most women who live and work in the suburbs seem to make is one of time—convenience to work— versus money. But it may also be one of job versus career—a dangerous trade-off for all women, but one which may be particularly tempting to suburban women struggling with double duties of household and children. "What women often do is settle for a job instead of a career," says Mary Tobin, regional administrator of the Women's Bureau of the Department of Labor. "They tell themselves they'll take this low-paying job that's nearby just for this year to help their families financially. But then before they know it, twenty years have gone by. And there these poor women are, working in the same dead-end jobs with little chance to get ahead, and suddenly it's become too late to do anything else." Given the suburbs' rapidly rising divorce rate and the financial status of most divorced suburban women, it seems especially important that women should not settle for a "convenience job."

The suburban job market may be elusive for the highly trained professional woman, too. More often than not, if the new woman of the suburbs is searching for a job in which to develop her career potential, she must travel to the city where innovative work policies, stricter equal employment and affirmative action surveillance and a more liberal attitude toward female professionals and managers usually exist.

I remember talking with a woman from Park Ridge, Illinois, one hot summer day during a NOW barbecue we were both attending. At first, we discussed suburban living and feminism, but then the subject finally drifted to her own attempts to find a suburban job. Newly widowed and still anxious about leaving her teenage children alone for ten or more hours a day while she worked and commuted to Chicago, the woman had spent several months looking for a managerial position in the North Shore area. After a painstaking job search and finally locating one job reasonably close to her home, she found the wages were substantially lower than those offered in the city. Even more distressing, the opportunity for advancement in that office seemed slim. "It wasn't that I would never be promoted," said the woman. "It would have to happen eventually, I suppose, but it certainly would have taken a lot longer here than in the city. The atmosphere was so conservative there, you could almost taste it. As a woman in that office I would have been an anomaly. All the other women there were secretaries. They would have thought a good long time before promoting me any higher."

Equal opportunity laws and affirmative action quotas have done much to correct this imbalance, especially in the nation's largest and most visible companies. Major corporations, whether they are located in the cities, suburbs or rural areas, usually comply with such regulations, if only because they have been awarded government contracts, or are nationally prominent. But federal mandates for equal opportunity are being taken far less seriously today under the aegis of the Reagan administration which, at this writing, is making concerted efforts to deregulate big business.

Given the uncertainty of our economic climate and an administration which clearly favors economic health over equal opportunity, it seems unlikely that conditions for women working in the suburbs are likely to improve dramatically. Nor should we forget that many small suburban companies, which have always been notorious for employment practices that keep women in low-level positions, will continue to attract women to jobs in these uncertain times because of their proximity to suburban homes. Given these conditions, it seems likely that social conservatism and the traditional exploitation of women will continue to characterize the suburban workplace, even if they no longer do in the central cities.

Sometimes, because the pace of the suburban business community is slower than that of the cities, women may also lose sight of their own potential for career advancement. A 34-year-old bank vice-president living in Westchester County recently told me how, after taking a maternity leave to have a child, she requested a transfer to a suburban branch of the bank. Management quickly accommodated her, and before long she was working as a loan officer in a local company bank. "But it was boring—especially after working downtown in corporate headquarters," recalled the woman. "I just couldn't get used to the slowed atmosphere of suburban banking. Finally, I grew quite unhappy there." She dropped out of her job for a while and considered changing careers. Today, she has transferred back to her old banking job in Manhattan and has recently been promoted to an even more responsible position. Now she regularly commutes on the 7:50 A.M. train to New York City—and takes occasional business trips to London, Paris and Rome.

A Bergen County, New Jersey, nurse, who is now the head of a new treatment program at Columbia Presybterian Hospital in New York City, told me how she had spent several years working in a suburban hospital near her home when her children were little. "And oh, how I hated that job and the whole stultifying atmosphere of the place," said the energetic mother of two. "The money I earned there was really blood money. I wanted to work in the city, in a university hospital, in a place where intellectual stimulation was paramount. So when the opportunity came at Columbia, I grabbed it. There is an excellence expected of you here that pervades everything else you do in life. If I'd stayed in that suburban hospital passing out pills, I never would have grown intellectually or professionally the way I have here. And I certainly never would have had the chance to set up a program like this one."

Some suburban business communities with special interest economies present additional problems for working women. The San Mateo County peninsula south of San Francisco commonly known as "Silicon Valley" because of its high concentration of computer companies and high-technology research firms is one dramatic example of such an economy. Countless women I met and interviewed living in that area commuted to San Francisco in order to work, because they claimed the job opportunities on the peninsula were poor for women. Factory and assembly work jobs were plentiful, as were jobs in computer science, mathematics, engineering and aeronautics—professions women have traditionally avoided. But for the young woman trained as a business executive, retail sales manager or health professional, the job opportunities were far more limited. A 30-year-old commercial designer, who commutes over three hours a day from her home near San Jose to a job in downtown San Francisco and back, describes the frustrations of her suburban job search on the peninsula: "When we first moved here I contacted thirty firms on the peninsula, feeling pretty sure I'd get a job. But the employment situation was much worse than I thought for women, and the competition for whatever jobs there were in my field keen. As it turned out, I was the one who ended up commuting an hour and a half each way, while my husband has just a five-minute drive to his office."

Child Care

Women in high-level positions often find that they cannot manage a commute to the city, a demanding work schedule and a suburban home and family at the same time, and may move back to the city. Some of the more ambitious suburban working women I have interviewed restrict themselves to having just one child; other mothers resign themselves to low-responsibility jobs or part-time work in the suburban community. The last two options are the most common. Labor studies indicate that most married suburban mothers tend to work closer to their homes than do their husbands, worrying, as my shopping-center acquaintance did, "about what will happen to the children."

Child care has always been a concern of working women regardless of where they live. In 1980, 47 percent of all mothers with preschool children were in the labor force, and several national studies, and my conversations with women, indicate that child care remains one of their most pressing problems. In 1978, a study in *Family Circle* magazine on 3,000 women found that over 30 percent were so dissatisfied with child-care arrangements that they had changed care services within the last two years. Another study by the National Commission on Working Women revealed that of their 80,000 employed female respondents, over one-third with dependent children cited child care as a major problem.

For those women living in the suburbs, child care is an especially difficult issue, exacerbated by the vast distances between home, school and the workplace. Bus and taxi service is frequently inadequate in the suburbs, leaving only the automobile and the mother behind the wheel. The logistics of caring for children and working full time can be awesome. How can the working mother commute to her job and arrange for her one school-age child to get to the same child-care center where her younger sibling is in the after-school hours? If there is no school bus transportation—as there often isn't in suburbs where children live less than a mile from school— how will the child get there? Can he take a public bus? Should his parents hire someone to drive him to the center? Should he be placed in a cab alone? Will transportation eat up his mother's salary? Would it be easier for her to hire someone to sit in her home, someone, preferably, who could also drive? Can she find someone to baby-sit in the after-school hours— and on school holidays?

It was a problem I could never resolve in our own family after we moved from the city to the suburbs. For years, I vainly experimented with all kinds of child-care arrangements. The cab I hired to take my daughter to dance class never seemed to come on time. That gem of a baby-sitter I finally found couldn't drive. Or if she did, had no access to a car. The only day-care center I felt suitable for my youngest child was a half-hour drive from my home. My personal solution was to work as a free-lance journalist and author from an office in my home. But few women have careers as flexible as those of writers.

More often the problem arises that a low-paying job out of the home may be difficult to justify if the woman must also pay a high fee for private child care. "Why," she may ask herself, as a woman from Upper Arlington, Ohio, once asked me, "should I work as a department store clerk in Lazar's, if I have to pay someone else almost as much to watch my child after school? It simply doesn't make sense." Like the suburban job market for women, the child-care issue is tangled and highly competitive. Good child care is often expensive and almost always difficult to find.

With few exceptions, child-care centers and providers are more plentiful in the cities than in the suburbs, if only because the need for child care was felt there much earlier. Many city and federally funded programs were established a decade or more ago through public funds to help low-income working parents. Some have continued, others have evolved to include middle and upper-middle income families, still others have cropped up as private institutions. While a few publicly funded programs were also established in the suburbs in low-income communities, the growth of child-care centers and providers was slower there until quite recently, and with recent federal cuts in child-care programs is likely to shrink.

With the massive influx of young mothers into the work force the demand for such centers and services rose sharply by the mid-1970s, even in more affluent communities. Suburban nursery schools began to expand quickly to accommodate children at younger ages and for longer periods of time each day. Cooperative playgroups and new nursery school programs

mushroomed. Private schools announced after-school programs and extended the age downward at which they would
accept young children. Churches, temples and other institutions developed child-care programs, "mother's day out" services and child drop-in centers.

Yet the need still far exceeds the supply in most suburbs
and waiting lists for child care have become the rule rather
than the exception. It is not uncommon for young suburban
parents to put their children on waiting lists immediately after
birth, knowing that it will take several years for a preschool
program to have a vacancy. Some center directors have even
reported to me that they have received phone calls from
prospective parents who are contemplating starting a family,
but want to assure themselves of a place for their child shortly
after birth.

Even in states known for their high level of social services,
like California and New York, suburban day-care councils and
day-care referral services are just beginning to come to grips
with the demand. "In the last three years alone our requests
for day-care services have doubled," says Arlyce Currie, one of
the directors of Bananas, a state-funded day-care referral
service in Berkeley, California. "Lately we've been getting a
number of calls from places we never heard from before,
women in affluent communities like El Cerrito and Ken-
sington who suddenly find they must go back to work." Even
in San Mateo County, the second richest suburban county in
the state of California, fewer than 30 percent of all children in
need of child care are currently being served. And costs there
are high—ranging from $65 to $95 a week for infant care and
$25 to $35 a week for school-age children.

In Westchester County, New York, Marilyn Selig, assistant
director of the Day Care Council of Westchester, Inc., estimates that only about one out of every three children in need
of day-care services is receiving them, and that the situation
for infant care there is "absolutely pathetic." She adds,
"There's an across-the-board need for care at every level in the
county, and it's only going to get worse as more women return
to work." In Fairfax County, Virginia, perhaps the wealthiest

suburban county in the United States, where 59 percent of all women were employed, day-care needs have gone up by more than 50 percent since 1974, but services have lagged far behind.

One factor in the current squeeze on suburban child-care services is the fact that day care has become an acceptable concept to middle-class women. "Day care," as Marilyn Selig says, "is no longer a dirty word. Middle-class women no longer think of it as just something that poverty-level families have to use." As a result, women have begun to look at group-style day care as a more practical alternative to privately hired sitters.

Those who are able to find or afford such facilities are certainly not always happy with them. Some, like the Walnut Creek woman cited at the beginning of this chapter, find that the center hours are strictly limited, and that if they do commute to the city, there is always the worry of arriving late. Others may feel, as did one North Dallas woman, that a large group atmosphere just isn't appropriate for her particular child. "There the center was, wedged between a Taco Time and a Pizza Hut, and somehow that didn't seem like the right atmosphere to start with. Too many times I got calls from the center that he was crying or that he hit somebody or that he didn't seem happy. Maybe I just should have insisted that he stay and stick it out. Maybe it was my own feelings of guilt. But whatever it was, I pulled him out and got a private sitter."

Another woman, living in Hollywood, Florida, was horrified to discover her sister-in-law had placed her new baby in an infant day-care center. After visiting the facility, the woman offered to care for the child herself. "I just couldn't bear the thought of having the baby there even though my sister-in-law didn't seem to mind," said the woman, a soft-spoken brunette in her early thirties who was herself the mother of two school-age children. "All those cribs lined up in little rows, somehow it seemed unnatural. My first instinct was to get the baby out of there, and I'm glad I did."

These feelings are not unique. Most parents, according to the National Day Care Study, place their children in family day-care situations, small home-based operations usually run by another woman. Some of these centers are licensed in accordance with local or state regulations, but the majority are not and are instead highly personal neighborhood operations. Whether the day-care center is licensed or not, the quality of care often fluctuates and the price is often quite high. An informal comparison of prices in Upper Arlington (a suburb of Columbus, Ohio) conducted by a single mother revealed little difference in price between licensed centers and those that were informally run. "Given the larger licensed center that charged $50 a week or the unlicensed one at $43 a week with a caregiver I could get to know and trust, there was no comparison. For me the personal atmosphere wins out every time," said the woman. But then, as her children grew older, the woman had to struggle with the issue of transportation for her oldest son, who had to be transferred from the school to the day-care center in the after-school hours.

The location of the day-care provider or facility seems to be a particularly thorny issue for the suburban woman faced with a commute to work. Lack of a convenient day-care location may even discourage her from seeking work altogether. A recent survey found that in a three-month period during 1980, over 57 percent of all parents who had been looking for day care were unsuccessful; the most commonly cited reason was "lack of a convenient location." Because of the continually rising price of gasoline, driving distances between home, the workplace and the day-care center or provider have become an increasingly serious issue for the working mother to consider. Some women work out cooperative arrangements, carpooling their neighbor's children in the morning in exchange for afternoon transportation to a day-care service. Others switch caregivers after being on waiting lists for months. Some send their children to private schools with special after-school programs.

Many do without child care altogether, finding it simpler to leave their children on their own. As with the young North Palm Beach, Florida, family portrayed at the beginning of this book, many children have learned, with varying degrees of success, to care for themselves in the after-school hours. Other women arrange for traditional baby-sitters, or house-keepers, but once again the mounting suburban demand and the decreasing supply have taken their toll. Nobody, it seems, wants to be a household worker today. Recent figures compiled by the Bureau of Labor Statistics indicate that household workers—baby-sitters, cleaning help, launderers and servants—continued a steady decline in numbers in the 1970s and will become increasingly scarce in the 1980s. At the beginning of the 1970s, there were 1.5 million household workers in the United States, or 5 percent of the labor force; by 1979 that number had declined to a million, only 3 percent of all employed persons. At the same time, the growing scarcity of these workers and the undesirability of the job have increased demands among household workers for better wages. And while organizations like the National Committee of Household Workers have worked toward legislation to improve conditions for household workers and to help them secure at least the minimum wage—at this writing $3.35 an hour—the going rate for household work is often as high as $5.00 an hour or more. In the suburbs, where household workers are even more difficult to locate than in the cities, salaries can range from $130 a week to $250 or more. Transportation costs can inflate the real cost of hiring such individuals even more.

Some women, like a schoolteacher I interviewed in Coral Gables, Florida, have endured the frustrating experience of rapid household worker turnover, and may finally become so upset by the experience that they give up their own jobs. Describing the horror of her last few months at work, the woman said: "It just got to the point where I couldn't stand the anxiety anymore. The last spring I taught, I ended up having five different baby-sitters in about eight weeks. The house was in constant disarray, the kids were confused by having so many different people caring for them and I was always a nervous wreck worrying as to whether these women would be reliable or not. A few times they simply didn't show up. That's when I decided that I had to stop teaching for a while and wait until my children were both in school full-time."

Another woman, who worked as an assistant buyer for a department store and lived in Teaneck, New Jersey, came home from work one day to find her housekeeper drunk and her 11-year-old daughter terrified and hiding in her room. After unsuccessfully trying to hire another housekeeper, the woman resigned from her job and remained home for the next three years. "I just couldn't pay a high enough price to find somebody reliable," said the woman. "Between commuting expenses, her salary and our taxes, we figured out it was costing me to work."

Unless a suburban woman is in the relatively rare position of commanding a high salary, and is able to find and afford top-quality child care, she may find herself in a no-win situation. She can neither advance herself easily in the suburban job market nor find enough child care to help her do so. Is it really worth her while to work? the suburban woman often asks herself. Given her very real problems, it is little wonder she agonizes over that question. Even so, the tenacity of the suburban woman in finding such work is significant. The migration of suburban women to the workplace means that better day-care, preschool and after-school programs, as well as better public transportation, must ultimately appear in the suburbs. It also means that the expectations the suburban woman has for herself are changing. Instead of regarding herself as a powerless, dependent creature, the suburban woman is beginning to see herself as a vital and autonomous human being.

And yet the question of whether she will develop new ways of climbing the corporate or professional ladder remains. If the suburban woman's participation in the work force continues to mean "all taking and no giving" from her employers and her family, will she succeed in correcting that imbalance? Perhaps she must disregard the traditional male career pattern and try to develop new work options for herself that will be more in tune with her own natural rhythms.

Suburban women have already taken a first step. Within the past decade, the movement of women out of the home has brought profound changes to the suburban way of life. Like her gas-guzzling station wagon, the chauffeuring, caretaking suburban matron of the earlier era is fast becoming obsolete.

4

The Circuit Breaker: The Divorced Suburban Woman

The prince—a resident prince, an elusive prince, even a prince who can dance—does not seem to be the promised key to living happily ever after.

So, we must figure out another way to live happily ever after; interim guidelines suggest that people— men and women—might more successfully pursue happiness if we are free, each of us, to define happiness for ourselves.

Jane O'Reilly, *The Girl I Left Behind: The Housewife's Moment of Truth and Other Feminist Ravings*

Whether I marry again or not is immaterial—my hegira to the Fourth Stage of personal fulfillment has developed a momentum of its own. I have experienced incomparable joy from the full investment of myself in my work, progressively expanding

my capabilities and the attendant rewards by achieving goals that I have personally set for myself.
    Maxine Schnall, *Limits: A Search for New Values*

"IT NEVER ENTERED MY HEAD that we might be
divorced someday. We were going to be married for life, until
death do us part. I will never forget that night. It was a
Sunday, the week after Denny had been on a business trip,
and he sat next to me on the living room couch with his arm
around me and suddenly said that he wanted a divorce. I
couldn't believe it. He lived with me until July but after that I
was crying all the time. I couldn't even go to the grocery store.
I lost thirty pounds in forty-five days. I was smoking three
packs of cigarettes a day. I started drinking. I was just barely
functioning for the children. I couldn't leave the house. I
mean, I felt like it was stamped across my forehead. FAILURE.
I couldn't say anything to my friends, and I kept trying to play
the game.

"The frightening thing is that what I see out my front
window today is a vast wasteland of women in their homes
who literally do nothing all day but bitch about sitting in their
homes and being bored. I'd still be like that if it wasn't
for what has happened to me. That's the worst thing of all, the
not being prepared, because you simply don't contemplate
divorce. You don't think about it as a possibility, until all of a
sudden, there it is one day and you have nothing to fall back
upon."

Except for yourself. But the 33-year-old woman from Libertyville, Illinois, who had lived as a suburban housewife for a
decade, hadn't known about her inner resources at the time
her husband announced his decision to leave her. All she
sensed was that his abrupt demand for divorce was a devastating personal blow, one which would immediately isolate her
from everybody she knew and everything she had always

expected. With her husband's surprising words, she suddenly lost her identity.

Like many other suburban housewives who have weathered the storm of sudden divorce, this pretty young woman spent the next several months torn between anger and self-pity. Depression quickly followed. In time, the help of a professional counselor and her own desire for self-mastery helped her come to grips with her plight. Today, she still lives in the fashionable subdivision that has been her home for a decade, but has returned to college. Life is brighter now, she says, and more exciting than she had ever imagined. Eagerly she looks forward to graduation, her first job and the chance for economic autonomy. If only she had realized years ago what might happen, she never would have slipped into a full-time routine at home with her children, she says. If only . . .

How many have said the same thing? But somehow it was easy. The suburban setting had lulled her into a somnolent state of security. When she awoke from her dream, it was to a tormenting aloneness. Prince Charming had not only failed to kiss and awaken her in time, but had run off with the title to the kingdom. She should have known better, should have remembered to awaken herself, even though that wasn't part of the fairy tale.

The profound psychological devastation that often follows divorce has a special poignancy in the suburbs. People simply aren't supposed to get divorced—the old myth goes, one which is still believed—in the happy bedroom towns of the American dream. That is only for city folks. The divorced woman who remains in the suburbs seems out of synchrony with the two-parent nuclear family. Dinner party invitations stop. Married men and women seem uncomfortable in her presence. Friends drift away. All too often, the newly divorced suburban woman finds herself very much alone.

It isn't only the ill-kept front lawn that brands her as different; it is the implicit paradox of the single-dwelling home she continues to maintain, her solo appearances at school and community activities, her rapid migration to the workplace or the university, the strange car parked overnight in the driveway of her home that stigmatize her as an outsider, the sexy suspect of a subtle new order.

But why should divorce carry that stigma in the suburbs? Divorce is common enough in America, appearing in the suburbs just as it did in the rest of the nation, on the heels of the prosperity of the postwar era. Divorce was the sinister underside of the good life, suddenly looming up at the same time as the campus protests, the race riots and the antiwar demonstrations of the late 1960s. With the social turbulence and political uncertainties of those years, divorce broke out like a new strain of Asian flu: middle-aged couples who had been married for years were divorcing; young couples with new mortgages and infant children were breaking up families; newlyweds were abruptly divorcing.

By 1970 everybody was doing it. Divorce had become an increasingly conventional variation on the married pattern of adult America, a symptom of the "new individualism" that characterized the social climate of the decade.

As census figures later revealed, the divorce rate skyrocketed between 1970 and 1980 by 113 percent, swelling from a ratio of 47 divorced persons per 1,000 married individuals with spouse present in 1970 to 100 per 1,000 in 1980. In 1976 alone, there were more than one million divorces. In 1980 there were almost 1.2 million divorces.

The new national trend was not only reflected, but was actually highlighted in the nation's suburbs, where divorce had previously been rare. In 1960, slightly less than one million female-headed households existed in suburban communities, but by 1979 that figure had risen to 2.7 million families, and more than half of those women were either separated or divorced. Between 1970 and 1977, the number of female-headed households in the suburbs grew by more than 71 percent; at the same time the rate grew by only 41 percent in the central cities and 51 percent in the rest of the nation. Households run by single women appeared more rapidly in the suburbs than anywhere else in the nation in the last decade; their recent proliferation in places they rarely existed before makes them all the more disconcerting. Conservative estimates place the number of divorced suburban women at about 1.5 million, 900,000 of whom are believed to have children under 18 years of age.

Why Should Divorce Be a Problem?

Divorced women have become an important new addition to the suburban matrix. So why the fuss? Despite their growing prevalence and despite the publicity about divorce, therapists maintain that the distress these women experience is often more acute than that of their city sisters. Matrimonial attorneys commonly characterize the suburban woman as helpless and lacking in sophistication. Government and school officials cite divorced suburban women as among their most troubling and least-acknowledged social problems. What is there about the suburban experience that makes divorce such a difficult experience for its women? Why are divorced women still perceived with horror in the nation's suburbs today—more than a decade after divorce became common?

I believe that one clue to the difficulty lies in the tranquility of the suburban setting—the deliberate separation of the working world from the community of homes, schools and churches that has always been one of the prime virtues of the bedroom towns, but has also effectively cloistered women from the stresses of the marketplace and the "real world." I have also noted the psychological dependency that the suburban setting almost invariably foists upon women in their relationships to men—a dependency that has historically been the accepted norm of female suburban behavior as expressed by Catherine Beecher, Christine Fredericks and other early shapers of female opinion. While psychological subservience to men was expected of urban women as well, and indeed became the preferred model of womanhood after the Industrial Revolution, it was exaggerated in the suburbs, where many women have continued to remain at home. The lingering effects of that role are still apparent today even while the social realities have changed. As the psychiatrist Dr. Maj-Britt Rosenbaum recently observed, whether women today are leisured and family-oriented in the suburbs or not is almost beside the point: "The fact is that suburbia still has the appearance of being couple-oriented and family centered. Whether it's true or not, we've internalized that image. Much of the sense of loss suburban women experience when they go through a divorce relates to their own sense of self-esteem and how they will fit into that society."

Other professionals who have worked closely with divorced women also say that suburban women seem more traumatized by divorce than their urban sisters. Lester Wallman, a Manhattan matrimonial lawyer with a clientele including both urban and suburban couples, says of the contrasting life-styles of the urban and suburban environments: "Urban women must continually contend with the noise, crowd congestion and crime of the city which make them immediately more adaptable to human vicissitude."

There are also wider job opportunities, career training programs and distractions in the city. Even if the urban woman doesn't work, she has a constant array of museums, shops, lectures and displays at her disposal, a broad spectrum of activities to keep her aware of alternative living arrangements and roles. In contrast, as Lester Wallman notes: "Suburban women often spend the better part of their adult lives living on a child's level, arranging carpools and chauffeuring, or spending their time at the bridge table or country club. Many who arrive at our office suffer from a distinct lack of a sense of reality. Often they appear frightened, and yet haughty. Some of them seem almost infantlike in their understanding. Some of them don't even know how to balance a checkbook. It's unusual to see the same naivete in city women—they're usually much more street-wise and independent."

While not all suburban women fit Wallman's description, I have noticed that many do seem crippled by their dependency—the vast number of suburban divorces are instigated by men who have, after all, the economic independence to break out of an unhappy marriage. Women who have given up economic independence for the comforts of a suburban life-style, but who have unhappy marriages, often find themselves in a frighteningly dependent situation.

It strikes me that the very isolation of the suburbs may contribute to the breakdown of the marital relationship. For when suburban women live a consistently cloistered life while their husbands are engaged in the impersonal demands of the working world, it is likely that the couple's interests and perceptions of life will begin to differ. Since those differences tend to widen with the years and are often compounded by the different sex-role duties of the suburban mother and father, the frequent result is a breakdown in the couple's ability to communicate.

As sexologist Dr. Jessie Potter, herself a wife, mother and one-time suburban resident near Chicago, observes, women who remain exclusively within their communities often develop a distorted picture of life beyond it. "Suburban women are at least as ghettoized in their understanding of the real world as the low-income welfare mothers who live in publicly funded high rises in the central cities. The husband and kids may take on an overexaggerated emphasis if she has a distinct lack of life satisfaction or challenge in other areas."

Suburban home life often not only becomes a substitute for ongoing contacts with the working world, but also increasingly narrows a woman's ability to adapt to that world. In a recent study of 200 newly divorced adults living in central Pennsylvania, family sociologist Dr. Graham Spanier discovered four especially important factors in the adjustment of women to postdivorce life: the length of time a woman had been married, how long she had been unemployed before the divorce, how much financial dependency she had upon her husband, and how much psychological reliance she placed upon him. The more extreme these factors are, the greater her difficulty in adjusting to divorce.

· The divorced suburban matron is suddenly tossed out on her own, beyond the community she has always known and has come to think of as her due, into a world of human heterogeneity and uncertainty. The result is often panic, for she suffers a special kind of culture shock. Frequently, the financial arrangements of the separation or divorce necessitate her immediate reentry into the labor force—a world she may have encountered only briefly, if at all, before her children were born.

Once the dependent suburban woman is divorced, she may become an unwitting threat to other dependent women. For in her plight others see the shadow of their own precarious position. Sometimes the divorced woman finds herself suddenly ostracized. The pain she then experiences is doubled, not only because it follows immediately upon divorce, but also because it inflicts additional blows to her self-esteem and her feeling of community. The once-protective aspects of suburbia become hostile and threatening to the newly divorced woman. Divorce is often a harrowing experience for city women as well, but the impact of community censure upon divorced women there is harder to measure, as the sense of community is more diffuse in the city. Urban friendships are more likely to be based upon similar interests and appetites than those formed in the suburbs, which are often founded on geographical proximity.

Dr. Sheila Kessler, a divorce expert and the author of *The American Way of Divorce*, says that the suburbs are a double-edged sword for divorced women: "The relative social homogeneity and its tendency toward conformist attitudes may make the suburbs a good place to raise children and develop a peaceful home life, but the same tight social mores of suburbia can also work against women once they're divorced. Suddenly they don't fit in anymore. All too often, divorced women end up feeling very isolated in a sea of marrieds."

Many divorced people flee the suburbs. But increasing percentages of divorced women now remain there—rooted in an environment they once perceived as nurturing, but now find cold and even inhibiting. Many stay on simply because they can't afford to move. Others do because they still consider suburbia a symbol of stability for themselves and their children. "I'm planning to remain in this community because I've already made enough drastic life changes," the divorced women of the suburbs often tell me. Some say that at the time of their divorce, they just couldn't bear any other adjustments. Others claim that they prefer the suburban life to that of cities or small towns, but in the next breath many of them acknowledge there are tensions when they decide to stay.

Finances

One of the main problems of the divorced suburban woman is her sudden loss of financial security. What was once a social amenity of the suburban life-style rapidly becomes a luxury. The annual dues for a summer pool club, a new pair of designer jeans, the gardener who cut the front lawn for years, summer camps, new bikes and weekend ski trips: all are major financial issues for the divorced suburban woman. Inevitably a tug-of-war between the ordinary suburban life of married couples and the fiscal realities of the divorced woman's household begins. She has a hard time keeping up with the Joneses. Like the White Rabbit, the divorced suburban woman seems always to be late, seldom able to catch up. Having fallen down the tunnel of marital dissolution, she becomes part of a suburban underclass.

Government studies show that divorced and separated women have significantly lower family incomes than those of married couples. The 1980 median income of female-headed families was 55 percent lower than that of married couples: $10,408 compared to $23,141. And while divorced women workers earned a median income of $12,899—slightly above the average income earned by married women—their earnings are often the sole means of support for a family with several young children. In 1980, a Census Bureau study on child support and alimony among divorced women found that of the

7.1 million American women with children and absent fathers, only 49 percent received the child support payment originally awarded by the courts or arranged in the final separation agreement. Only 14 percent of the 14 million divorced or separated women were awarded or had an agreement to collect alimony. As of spring 1979, less than half of the 12 million women who had been divorced had received some form of property settlement.

The shaky fiscal status of the divorced suburban woman puts her at an immediate disadvantage among her married peers and often has disturbing repercussions for her children. If she remains in the same house she lived in while married, she may find her ability to maintain her former life-style seriously impaired, a situation made all the more painful by the memory of what once was. One such woman faced with that dilemma is a school psychologist from Chicago's North Shore. Remaining in the family home with her two daughters after she became divorced, she found that not only was she unable to keep up with the small amenities of home mainte- nance such as lawn care and fresh paint, but that the foundation of the house was in serious need of a major overhaul. The woman, anxiously contemplating a move to a nearby condominium but reluctant to do so because of the high mortgage rates, said: "My biggest worry is money. I'm literally afraid that some day the house will fall down. I mean that honestly. There's a lot of interior structural repair that should be done, but I simply don't have the funds to do it."

The suburban home often becomes the focal point of many divorced women's financial struggles. As the primary repre- sentation of her socioeconomic status before divorce, the house sometimes takes on a distorted symbolic value. Dr. Rosenbaum explains: "For many women, the house seems to be an important reflection upon themselves, an extension of their personal identity. But while the house may be a comfort to the divorced woman at first, it can also become a dinosaur, one that seems to have a life of its own, one that drains her of energy and money. At some point divorced women must contend with the house. I encourage my patients to hang onto their homes as long as they can, but not when it becomes self-destructive."

While divorce courts frequently award women the right to remain in the family home until the children are grown (at which time the house is usually sold and the proceeds split between husband and wife), the fervency with which some women insist upon that arrangement in predivorce negotiations sometimes borders upon the irrational. "Even when we sit down with our clients at the time of the separation and say, 'Look, you simply can't afford to run this house. You're going to have to sell,' many of them simply refuse to believe you," Lester Wallman says. "Some women hang onto their homes almost to the point that they are financially drowned by them."

One glimpse into the symbolic importance attached to the house was provided by a Hollywood, Florida, woman I interviewed. An energetic woman in her late thirties, she explained that even after her nine-year marriage to a young doctor had failed, she felt entitled to the same standard of living she had enjoyed when wed. An important part of that standard, she insisted, was the kind of home she inhabited. Silently I gazed at her handsome four-bedroom house and wondered how she was able to maintain it: she had not yet found a job, although she mentioned that one recent possibility looked promising. Apparently my interviewee sensed my curiosity. She confessed that in order to meet expenses, she had rented out one of the bedrooms to a boarder. But even so, she said, "After all the years I suffered through my husband's difficult training, I feel I ought to live relatively well. I've got three more years of financial help from my ex-husband and then I'm on my own. I'm adamant about trying to retain this house. It represents a life-style I feel I've earned."

Some women make different arrangements, like one Palo Alto mother of a 10-year-old son, who realized that she would not be able to support the family home on her new entry-level job. Rather than uproot her son from school and his friends, she agreed to a joint custody arrangement with her husband. She rented a nearby apartment in the back of a farmhouse while her son and former husband remained in the family home.

For some women, the realization that they may not be able to retain the family home and support children comes later, after years of fiscal struggle and anguish. A petite 30-year-old housewife living in Upper Arlington, Ohio, near Columbus, told me of the trauma she endured in the first years following her divorce: "After the divorce, I tried staying in the house with the kids for the first year and a half, but I just couldn't do it. My ex-husband made much more money than I did, and with women's liberation, the courts only gave me one year of alimony. I'd gone back to work, of course, but it was a new experience. I'd get home after eight hours on the job and try to spend time with the kids, helping them with their homework, getting dinner and doing the laundry. But I was a wreck, always tired, always yelling at the kids and hating the world. I couldn't keep up with the bills on the house on my salary, and before a year had passed, I was in serious debt. The creditors began to hound me. Finally things got so bad that I began to realize it didn't make sense to be a martyr just because I was the mother of the kids, and just because that was what society expected. I couldn't take care of the kids financially anymore and the emotional strain was wearing on all of us. So at last I asked my ex-husband to move back into the house with the kids. I'd be the one to move into rent." The woman sighed, looked sadly at me, then around at the sparsely furnished apartment that she shared with another woman and added: "I wish I'd done that before, wish I'd been able to understand from the beginning that I couldn't swing it all by myself. Now I've got a bad credit rating. I can't afford a car, can't afford to borrow money. And it's going to take me years to pay back the money I still owe."

Other suburban women who have whittled down their lifestyles to match their shrunken incomes claim that money remains an ongoing concern. The loss of financial security from pension benefits, life insurance and stock dividends resulting from divorce seems to have a particularly devastating psychological effect upon middle-aged women. In a longitudinal study of middle-aged divorce among ninety adults living in metropolitan Pittsburgh, the sociologist Gundhil Hagstad found that the one striking characteristic of the divorced women in her sample was a profound sense of betrayal, a sense that an important social contract had been violated. "There's a common sense of surprise among these middle-aged women that they have been cheated out of a life-style they had earned—financial security as a reward for years of diapering babies and cooking meals which were part of the unspoken expectations and unwritten contract of their marriage—and which they will never have. What they suggest and sometimes even explicitly state is, 'I've had a whole set of goals and rewards in my life that have suddenly come crashing down. Now time is running out for me and it's too late for me to start another script.'"

I noticed that same sense of time slipping through the hourglass in a 59-year-old divorced woman from Berwyn, Illinois. After twenty-two years of marriage, she had left her husband and moved from the southern Illinois community that was her home to suburban Chicago. Within a short time she found a full-time secretarial job in downtown Chicago. That was four years ago, the woman said, and she hadn't regretted her decision to divorce for a moment. But, she said, "Sometimes I get chills just thinking about the fact that at my age, I only have four years of social security, no pension plan and no benefits at all from the years I stayed home and my husband worked. I'm just hoping that my health will remain good so that I can work another decade and accumulate some benefits."

For younger women there are other, more immediate worries. The day-to-day demands of supporting children in the suburbs, coupled with the runaway inflation of recent years, often bring additional fiscal pressures upon divorced mothers, and may wrack them with serious doubts about the kind of parenting they may be able to provide. A divorced woman living in a HUD-sponsored apartment near Dallas expressed it this way: "The money issue causes divorced mothers all kinds of guilt. For instance, you know that you can't really afford to take your kids to the nearby amusement park very often. The schools nickel and dime you to death. And the children of married couples continually seem to get new toys and new clothes. Intellectually you realize it's silly, but you can't help feeling bad if you can't provide the same things for your child, feeling that you can't be as good a mother."

The divorced woman's sense of guilt—as well as her culturally conditioned sense of inferiority and her own sense of disillusionment with love—often comes back to haunt her in the mirror of married suburbia. To compound these problems, her family and friends are often less supportive than she had expected before the divorce. Suddenly she may find herself isolated—and puzzled by the abruptness of that reaction. That sense of abandonment was evoked poignantly by a 36-year-old divorced woman living in a Westchester apartment house with her infant son. Although she claimed that her neighbors and married friends were attentive to her during the day, during the evenings and on the weekends they were busy with their own families and husbands: "At 5:30 every night, they would say good-bye and leave. And so there I was night after night, left alone looking at my baby, with nobody to talk to and nowhere to go. It was even worse on the weekends. You'd get up early Saturday and Sunday and then the whole day would loom before you. All you could do would be to go to the beach and sit on a blanket by yourself. But you would feel uncomfortable even about striking up a conversation with the couple on the next blanket."

Another divorcée, living in Hempstead, Long Island, recalled that when her son finally entered the first grade, she had assumed that she would meet a young group of mothers with whom she could become friendly. But despite her willing participation in school activities and her eagerness to meet others, the married mothers seemed reluctant to befriend her. "It wasn't anything outwardly hostile, nothing you could put your finger on exactly. But the fact was that the other young mothers were becoming friendly and I was never getting any invitations."

Other women have reported more pointed signs of exclusion. A young mother of two living in a primarily Catholic neighborhood of suburban Columbus, Ohio, found that several of the teenage baby-sitters she had used while married refused to sit for her once she became divorced. An attractive divorcée from Menlo Park, California, reported that once her marriage had ended, her name was dropped from a neighbor's annual Christmas party list. "I never knew I had so few friends until I was divorced," bitterly remarked another woman from Fort Lauderdale, Florida. "Intellectually, I knew my friends were bound to change after divorce because we no longer had as many common interests. But once the divorce went through, some people seemed to drop me like hotcakes. Suddenly I was *persona non grata.*"

Neighbor Ambivalence

Many suburban women have reported a noticeably ambivalent attitude in their neighbors once their divorces became known. "They regard you with a measure of disapproval, but also a certain envy," said a 35-year-old divorcée from Winnetka, Illinois. "There's even outright curiosity about your dating habits. It's as if you've done something that many of them would like to do, but don't dare." One woman, living in Plano, Texas, told of her female neighbor's constant scrutiny of her comings and goings and her inquiries about the strange cars parked in her driveway. A divorced woman living in San Mateo County, California, observed that while her next-door neighbors had assiduously avoided her for the first year after her divorce, eventually they began to make tentative inquiries about her dating habits. After a time they even invited her to dinner to meet several of their single male friends.

Neighborly ambivalence is often seen in the behavior of married men. Some become very protective of the new divorcée when they first learn of the breakup and may offer to help with financial advice, snow removal or other tasks traditionally performed by the man of the house. An attractive dark-haired woman living in Highland Park, Illinois, told how a male neighbor suddenly appeared on her doorstep one Saturday morning in early summer with extra grass seed, fertilizer and a spreader. "Your grass looks like it could use some help," he told her. When she explained that her husband had always been the one to tend the lawn and that she had no expertise in the matter, the neighbor offered to teach her the rudiments of lawn care. He even volunteered to seed and fertilize the lawn himself. "To this day, I can't figure out whether he volunteered because he thought my lawn looked so bad and it reflected on his own property values, or whether he was truly interested in helping me, but the lawn certainly looks better and he seems pleased. Now it's become a little joke; every spring and fall he reminds me about what I should do."

More often, however, divorced women note that many married men appear uncomfortable in their presence. A Park Ridge, Illinois, divorcée told me that several months after her divorce she had found a job in downtown Chicago to which she commuted by automobile every morning. One rainy day, she passed a male neighbor waiting at a local bus stop and asked him if he would like a ride. Instead of accepting her offer, the man blushed, stammered indecisively for a moment and then awkwardly refused her offer. Her reaction, even as she recounted the story some months later, was one of intense hurt.

The flip side of that ambivalence is outright hostility, sometimes outright sexual aggression. Suburban divorcées tell me that it is not at all uncommon for the husband of a good female friend to make furtive sexual overtures to them once the divorce is official. An attractive 41-year-old blond living in Richardson, Texas, who characterized her transition to divorce as a surprisingly smooth one, had an even more startling encounter with a male neighbor. Waking one night at 2:00 A.M. to the sound of a slamming door, she was shocked to discover the husband of her next-door neighbor standing nude in front of her, ready to offer her sexual solace. "It was an unforgettably traumatic experience, one that resulted in a terrible alienation, but the strange thing was that the man had no provocation for his behavior. It turns out that his own marriage was failing at the time and he was acting out on the basis of his own needs and fantasies. But at the time I had no way of knowing about his unhappy relationship with his wife."

While her experience may have been unusual, it does shed light on the fears and fantasies married suburban couples frequently have about the divorced. Divorce kindles something powerful in unstable personalities; it has the potential to bring other volatile issues and emotions to the surface of seemingly stable people.

I have discovered that happily married couples who are secure in their own marriages may not find divorced women a threat, but those with glaring weaknesses in their own marriages—and those who have entertained thoughts about divorce themselves—may find the divorced woman a challenge to their own unresolved conflicts. A 37-year-old woman who had lived in an exclusive community near Columbus, Ohio, during her marriage said that after enduring years of physical and psychological abuse from her husband, who was a millionaire and offered her fur coats and diamond jewelry after each abusive incident, she finally fled to an abused-spouse center. Shortly thereafter, she filed for divorce. News of her defection spread throughout the community quickly, and her friends expressed perplexity, curiosity and criticism: "Some of them said they just didn't understand how I could have left that beautiful house, no matter what my husband had done to me. Some of them who are very unhappy told me they envied me that I had gone through with the divorce. Can you imagine that? I laughed at them. I mean, I live in a small apartment, nothing at all fancy, and I have to work full time to make ends meet. But even so, some of them said they were jealous because they didn't have the guts to do what I did. They said they just couldn't leave the material things behind. I guess I made some of them feel uncomfortable, because I don't see much of them anymore."

Many divorced women come to understand the diffidence of their old married friends as a reaction to a perceived double threat. A divorcée from suburban Chicago said: "There's no question that once you're divorced, you appear to them as a carefree member of the singles crowd whether you are or you aren't. Married women don't want any part of you because maybe they would like to taste a little of that freedom themselves. Men don't want you around because you might put ideas into their wives' heads. And the women don't want you near their men because now that you are a free woman, you might be after their husbands."

Tracing the three stages that newly divorced individuals frequently encounter in the dissolving of old friendship bonds, the sociologist Robert Weiss notes that it is not at all unusual for them to lose most, even all, of their married friends. While the individual may feel saddened by the dissolution of old friendship bonds, it is the *network* of married friends rather than specific relationships that often become the "casualty of marital separation." Nowhere is that network as obvious as in the suburbs. As a suburban divorcée living in Dallas said: "People in suburbia simply don't look at you as individuals, but only as couples, with your stomachs tied together."

Weiss tells us that the sense of desolation and loss of self-esteem that come from the loss of such a social network can lead to a further retreat for the divorced woman from social interchange. She may draw back further into herself, setting up a vicious circle of loneliness. When invited to a dinner party with couples she and her ex-husband had formerly been friendly with, she may beg off, rationalizing to herself or even to the hostess that she "just feels out of place," or that being with other marrieds makes her feel even more lonely. Or she may feel, as a Short Hills, New Jersey, divorcée did, that she has more in common with other single women. "It's just an attitude toward life, an expression, a way of looking at something or someone that is different, that makes you feel more in tune with other single women."

Meeting Men

Compounding that isolation is the fact that many more divorced suburban men leave for the city than do divorced women. A frequent lament of the divorced woman is that the suburbs are "no-man's-land—no man, that is, who is unmarried."

It seems to me that there are obvious reasons for the departure of the divorced suburban male. Many have jobs in the city and may, after their divorce, decide to live closer to work. And because the vast majority of divorced women still retain custody of the children and remain in the family home, ex-husbands have fewer ties to their old communities. As a result, some men who are anxious to begin a new life for themselves gravitate to the cities, where they believe the opportunities to meet other singles may be better. As one divorced man from White Plains once told me, "The last thing you want to do is be seen in the community where you once lived with your former wife. It's okay for her because she's got the kids and the house. But if you're the breadwinner and don't have custody, you're free! Sure, you drive up on weekends to get the kids, but then you get out of there fast. What's to keep you around in a community where everybody else your age is married?"

A predictable pattern emerges. Once a suburban marriage ends, the man drifts toward the city center, while the woman remains in the family home with the children and attendant responsibilities. For her, the once-proud possessions of home and hearth become shackles after divorce, preventing her from access to the singles world, grounding her in the coupled matrix of suburbia.

If she is lucky, she may find a job, meet other singles and begin to carve out a new life for herself. If not, she may remain isolated or flounder in self-pity as she tries to adjust to her new life station. She may begin to visit the singles bars, although that often means finding a baby-sitter and incurring additional expenses. And unlike her ex-husband, whose daily contact with women in the working world has provided him with an instant group of acquaintances and experience in casual flirtation, she may feel intimidated by the prurient appraisals and cruel competition of the singles scene. For her, whose life has centered around the home and whose friendships have taken root slowly and naturally in the community, the flashing lights, driving disco music and frenetic sexual scrutiny of most singles clubs may be overwhelming. For many suburban women the suburban discothèque is as unsatisfying and alienating as socialization with old married friends.

A petite divorcée from Columbus, Ohio, said: "Walking into a singles bar is like having loneliness echoed back in your ears. You always feel like you're on display, like you are a part of a meat market that can be bought and sold. It's just not the right atmosphere to meet men. Finding somebody to go to bed with, yes, but a meaningful personal relationship, forget it."

Sex must be contended with. The old double standard of sexuality may have gone the way of the 45 LP, but it still confounds many suburban women when they enter the singles world. After spending years in the home, or even on the job, as married women, relatively few have had the opportunity—or the courage—to experiment with the open sexual mores of the 1970s and 1980s. As the Libertyville housewife explained, she was fighting old traditions and finding the transition difficult: "I'm still operating by the standards of the fifties. I'm still the me that was formed when there was a difference between casual and meaningful sex. The sexual revolution may be old news to today's young singles, but for me, who spent the last ten years married, it's still a new concept."

The suburban woman who wants to engage in the singles scene may travel to the city, where singles bars and clubs are more numerous, only to discover that her status as a suburbanite is a disadvantage. Sitting in the air-conditioned expanse of her living room to escape the scorching summer heat, one Plano, Texas, woman smirked as she described to me the reaction of men she had met in singles bars when they learned where she lived: "'You're geographically undesirable,' they'd say, just like that. 'It's impractical to have a relationship with you because you live so far away.' At first I was shocked when I got that reaction from them. There you would be dancing with them, or maybe talking a little, and then when they'd ask where you live and found out, they'd walk away. In a sense, I suppose you can't blame them. After all, it takes about forty-five minutes to get here from downtown Dallas, and for some of these men, it's a big nuisance. They figure, why should I bother, when I can find someone who lives closer in?"

Disenfranchised as a member of coupled society, and yet intimidated by the glittering singles life of the city, the divorced suburban woman often wanders from one unfriendly environment to another. It is no coincidence that the suburban suicide intervention centers and mental health associations report that the largest number of calls come not only from women, but from those who are separated, divorced or single parents. One such center is the Suicide Prevention and Crisis Center of San Mateo County, just south of San Francisco. As in many other affluent suburban areas, the suicide rate there is high, 21 per 100,000 population, considerably higher than the national average of 12.5 per 100,000. A recent survey of the San Mateo high school population revealed that only 38 percent of all students had both natural parents at home. Director Charlotte Ross told me that the nature of the calls at the center has changed considerably in the fourteen years of its operation. While many calls used to come from unhappy housewives and pregnant teenagers, a disproportionate number now comes from single and divorced women. A similar phenomenon has been observed throughout the nation.

I was shocked to discover that at the time of this writing, no suicide studies have yet been conducted upon suburban women, even though the rapidly increasing number of female-headed suburban households indicates the urgent need for such scrutiny. Government agencies, schools, social service organizations and self-help groups must begin to address the special problems of the divorced suburban woman.

Children of Divorced Women

Child care is another difficulty. As a single parent with the obligations of homemaker, breadwinner and authority figure for her child, as well as her own new social needs, she may feel persistently torn between her various roles.

Although most of my studies support the notion that children reared by one emotionally healthy parent are apt to thrive just as well as those reared by two—and certainly better than those raised in a household with marital strife and emotional tension—the myth of the superiority of the two-parent family prevails. "Is Johnny doing as well as the other boys his age?" the suburban divorced mother constantly asks herself, her friends and her doctor in a quest for personal validation. If the child performs badly in school or displays deviant behavior, she is more likely to blame herself. After all, she doesn't socialize with Bill Jones's parents anymore, and that may be why the boys are no longer friendly. She may no longer be able to chauffeur her children around after school, if she works. Besides, there were all those years of fighting before the divorce that must have disturbed her child.

Of course, if her child has difficulties, there may be external factors that account for them, such as the school's attitudes toward children from divorced families and the number of such children in the youngster's peer group, as well as the kinds of transportation, after-school programs and community support groups offered in her neighborhood. But few divorced mothers feel secure enough about themselves and their identities to explore these inequities.

Fortunately, the growing number of single parents in America has begun to kindle interest in such information. A recent survey queried 1,237 single parents in forty-seven states (over half of whom lived in suburbs), and found that most schools do not have programs that take into account the growing percentage of children from single-parent families. According to the study, about two-thirds of single parents did not believe school personnel considered the one-parent family to be a normal family style. Nearly half of those interviewed had heard school personnel use the words "broken home" or other damaging stereotypical language when referring to the single-parent home. Over 50 percent of all single parents said they were compelled to take time off from work for teacher conferences because such meetings were rarely scheduled for single parents in after-work hours.

In another study of children and after-school programs, conducted at the Wellesley College Center for Research on Women, codirectors Jim Levine and Michelle Seltzer estimate that more than 2 million children with working parents have no place to go after school. Although their data is not yet complete, Ms. Seltzer believes that a disproportionate number of "latchkey" children, so called because they wear keys around their necks so they can let themselves into the house after school, come from single families. I met with the directors of three after-school programs in Brookline, Massachusetts, and the single-parent home was repeatedly mentioned as the family with the most pressing needs.

Lately there has been cost-cutting state legislation, such as Boston's recent Proposition 2½ and California's Proposition 13, which threaten to curtail these social services, and federal legislation, such as the proposed Family Protection Act and the Human Life Amendment, which suggest a dwindling of federal support for most social service programs, and a national reactionary backslide toward privatism. Nevertheless, there are hopeful signs of increasing recognition of single-family problems. As the single family continues to grow in numbers and becomes a permanent fixture of American life, there is little doubt that its members will seek each other out.

New Suburban Networks

There are already such suburban networks in existence. Single-parent councils, self-help groups, programs sponsored by the national Y's and the churches are just a few. Most of these groups, it should be said, are privately or individually funded.

Parents Without Partners, a national organization for single parents in the United States, is one of the most successful of these organizations. Begun in New York City in 1956 with a handful of single parents, the organization has grown to a membership of nearly 195,000 people and nearly 1,100 chapters. Although the group is open to anyone who is single and a parent, about 80 percent of its members are separated or divorced; about 65 percent are women. Entry requirements are strict, to insure the authenticity of its membership; anyone who wishes to join must show proof of his single status, either through legal documentation or a letter from his doctor, lawyer or clergyman. While the initial growth of the organization during the 1950s and 1960s was primarily in the major cities, Executive Director Virginia Martin says that most of the organization's recent growth has been in the new suburban chapters.

At a recent orientation meeting of Parents Without Partners in Mamaroneck, New York, the appeal of this nonprofit, privately funded organization became immediately apparent to me. It was a frosty, snow-covered morning in early January, and as I walked up the path to the apartment house of a host member, I realized I had my own set of anxieties. I was not, after all, single, and I had come as a writer and observer. This was a place where singles had come to meet each other; I wondered whether it would be as cold and abrasive as a singles bar. Some women I had interviewed had denigrated it; others had praised it, saying it was the best thing that had happened to them since their divorce.

The door was opened by a cheerful young woman who took

my coat, ushered me into her living room and offered me coffee. As I slipped quickly into a chair in the corner, I felt the silent scrutiny of about a dozen solemn faces. What was the emotion behind those faces that made them turn out so early on a cold Sunday morning?

Predictably, over half the initiates were women, from their early twenties to their mid-sixties. Anxiety, tension, disappointment, even suspicion colored the expressions of the men and the women in that room. Some had come, I later learned, after months, even years, of loneliness and desperation. Others had joined the group immediately after separation from their spouses, hoping for an immediate antidote to their loneliness. Most had remained single for a while before coming to the meeting. Some were tall, attractively dressed, obviously affluent; others were casually, even carelessly attired. But the pain in their eyes and the initial wariness of their expressions marked them as a group with similarly unhappy experiences.

Within moments, the meeting was called to order by our hostess. Her candor put us immediately at ease. "We were all nervous when we first came here, just as you are today. When you have to start over again in a new social setting, it's natural to feel like you're sixteen again. That's something that happens to all of us. But you're among friends—others who've had experiences like yours. That's the most valuable part of PWP. You may not be interested in getting thrown back into the dating scene right away, and that's all right. The beauty of the group is that it offers much more." Our hostess added that while the organization did sponsor dances and house parties for its members, the emphasis was on the development of mutually shared interests—especially the common problems and joys of single parenthood.

Regularly scheduled events are held both for the adults and their children. The adult-only activities include photography workshops, theater parties, financial seminars, tennis competitions and art groups. There are also family-style barbecues, trips, outings, skating parties, holiday events and picnics.

From the description of group activities, it was obvious that there were more events scheduled than any individual, no matter how lonely, could possibly pursue in a given week.

Other veteran members of Parents Without Partners got up to talk about their experiences. One told about a weekend she and her children had shared with other PWP singles at a dude ranch—a trip she never would have taken by herself, or even with another single woman and her children. A third said that children's clothes were passed through the group as one child outgrew a pair of slacks or a ski parka, "just like in an extended family." Those were the words we heard over and over that day: family, friends. These were people you could feel comfortable with and relate to without feeling apologetic about who you were.

The initiates' faces began to brighten perceptibly. These suburban singles were discovering for themselves that they weren't so different after all—there were many others like themselves. By the end of the formal presentation, people began to act more relaxed, as though a burden had been lifted. Unlike the anxious people in the singles bars, these adults realized that they were under no obligation to compete sexually if they didn't wish to. They could just be themselves—singles who found themselves displaced in suburbia, eager to meet others who might just as easily become friends as lovers.

People began to mingle by the dining room table, sipping coffee, nibbling cake and chatting quietly. A young woman stopped to talk with me. She had been divorced eight years, she said, and had a young child. It was lonely being divorced here, and she was glad she had decided to come to the meeting today. She had tried to come to a Parents Without Partners meeting seven years ago, but she had felt intimidated. She was only twenty-two then; the group had seemed small, too small, and she had never come back. But she was older now, and besides, she thought there were more divorced people living in the suburbs now than there used to be. She also hoped to make some good female friends in the group. In some ways, she said, having a good female single friend was more valuable than anything else. She smiled, as we wished each other luck.

I left the meeting with a warm feeling about the people I had met, turning over in my mind how they appeared at first and how different they seemed later. My thoughts drifted to some of the divorced suburban women I had interviewed around the country: women who had languished over endless cups of coffee in their empty homes for months after their divorces, women who had cried themselves to sleep every night, women who had battled creditors and utility companies when the lights had gone off, women who took sleeping pills on Christmas morning or Thanksgiving to avoid facing the barrenness of those holidays.

But most of all, my thoughts returned to those women who had gone to school or work, who had rediscovered the sense of self-worth they had lost along the way.

I realized that despite the onus of divorce that continues to burden the women of the suburbs, and despite the fact that social institutions have not kept pace with their needs, many divorced women have acted as catalysts for change. The necessity for them to become fully realized individuals in the face of adverse social and financial conditions has rattled the complacency of many married suburban women. Without realizing it, the divorced woman of the suburbs has set an unprecedented standard of independence that married women are just now beginning to emulate.

5

Liberation and Backlash: The Suburban Woman Who Stays at Home

∞∞∞

Today more women are going into the workplace and those at home see what they think is glamorous and independent. Then they look at themselves and it's children, laundry and cleaning. It's boring. Their husbands come home and quite often don't share with them what's been happening. A lot of these women don't have the courage to make decisions that will effectively put them into a whole different life-style, nor are they willing to opt out. So they stay and take what they have to take and therefore they escape into soap operas, drinking, medical problems, neurosis, whatever is an escape . . .

> Muriel "Nikki" Beare, Florida feminist and
> founder of National Association of
> Women Business Owners

Now I do see some women who definitely want to pursue a career and they feel unfulfilled at home. But I'm not so sure that they really do. I think that women have really been intimidated and sold a bill of goods by the feminists. There isn't a way in the world that I could lead as exciting a life as I do here if I worked in an office.

Paulette Standefer, president of the
Texas Pro-Life Committee, June 1980

"I WONDER, is it really inflation that drives so many women out of the house and back to work? A lot, I think, has to do with people wanting to live too high and wide. Just look at the amount of clothes we buy. And it always amazes me how often people think they have to go out for a pizza or a hamburger, when they could probably fix something at home a lot cheaper. Is that really necessary, all this extra expense we're bringing upon ourselves? The problem is that our values are all screwed up. Women's lib really hurt the homemaker—it made us feel like we're nothing, like we're second-class citizens because we aren't working. What people don't realize is that by staying home, we may not be making money, but we're not spending any either. By bringing up good kids, we're saving society money in the long run. But the working women look down their noses at us, and meanwhile there we are, picking up the pieces for them, being the unofficial neighborhood baby-sitters or the ones who give time to community activities. Don't bother me, they say, don't ask me to do things in the community, because I'm holy—I'm working."

Mary Tedrow sits in the cluttered living room of her gingerbread-trimmed nineteenth-century home, and as the summer night closes in, looks intently at me as she speaks. In the deepening twilight, her voice rises and falls in surprising bursts of emotion, betraying the bitterness of her thoughts, a bitterness so deep she can no longer contain it. Talking to me is a kind of relief. Outside, hard by Route 317, which has brought me just minutes ago from downtown Columbus, Ohio, there are still the reassuring cornfields—remnants, it seems to my eastern eyes, of another time, when the values of home, family and community were central to the lives of women. But the cornfields, as I soon learn, have been rented out to another farmer. The farmlands are rapidly disappearing, to make way for the tract housing that is the new face of Groveport, Ohio.

A thin, gentle-looking woman, Mary Tedrow is surrounded by the things she loves most: her desk crammed high with information for her Girl Scout troops, bookcases lined with records for the church where she is an elder, and a table piled with papers for the Groveport School Board, of which she is a member. In the next room, two of her teenage children sit reading books, watching television and chatting, vibrant young people, the magnetic center of her life.

Mary Tedrow is a serious, committed women, and like millions of suburban homemakers, she is deeply disturbed by what she sees as a progressive societal devaluation of her role. Motherhood and devotion to home and family seem no longer to be enough. More than half the women in her community work outside the home. And even though she is a prominent leader, Mary Tedrow feels excluded from the mainstream of American womanhood, even, in some subtle way, slightly less than respectable. Understandably, Mary Tedrow is surprised and hurt by these changes, but she would never think to confront them—or the women who epitomize them—directly. Instead she contains her sense of indignation quietly inside.

Galvanized by rapid social and economic changes, wounded pride and anger are common among many suburban women remaining at home, but the depths those feelings reach are as varied as the women themselves. Some feel anger and outrage, leveling their attacks on the women's liberationists in direct action. Many have aligned themselves with such pro-family groups as Stop ERA, the Pro-Family Political Action Committee, the Eagle Forum, the National Right to Life Committee and the Moral Majority. Others identify themselves apolitically, but personally, with that well-publicized hyperfeminine stance of the "Total Woman," or the "Positive Woman" of the Schlafly/Morgan order, leading their lives in a traditional female-dependent role. Still others have tried to bring a new respectability to the ranks of the homemakers by becoming involved in such groups as Homemakers' Equal Rights Association, Displaced Homemaker organizations, Mothers' Centers or other female-support services. Many have shunned political identification altogether and set about conducting their own lives in accordance with highly personal or religious codes. Most hold fervently their chosen role of homemaker as superior to that of the career woman. Ask a suburban homemaker which life course she believes preferable for the improvement of society. Chances are, while she will make exceptions for the woman who is forced to work out of economic necessity, she will contend that the raising of children and commitment to the family unit are the most positive and natural role she and all other women can pursue.

The apotheosis of that defense can be seen in the antifeminist movement headed by Phyllis Schlafly, whose anti-ERA efforts gained a vocal constituency in the late 1970s. In *The Power of the Positive Woman* in 1977, Mrs. Schlafly set forth the core of her beliefs: "After twenty years of diapers and dishes, a mother can see the results of her own handiwork in the good citizen she has produced and trained. After twenty years of faithful work in the business world, you are lucky if you have a good watch to show for your efforts." Work, Mrs. Schlafly contends, is often a thankless task for women because most of it is menial in nature, and offers women little opportunity for personal growth. Why slave away at some colorless job when you can reap the rewards of home and hearth by pleasing a man with your sexual and maternal prowess—a man, Mrs. Schlafly points out, who will be easier to win over than most bosses in the workplace? "If you complain about servitude to a husband, servitude to a boss will be more intolerable. Everyone in the world has a boss of some kind. It is easier for most women to achieve a harmonious working relationship with a husband than with a foreman, supervisor or office manager."

And as Mrs. Schlafly later reiterated in a telephone interview: "Most women are happier with motherhood and a good marriage than with any other career. The feminist ideology has made for a lot of unhappy women. When the years begin to run out, many of them end up wishing for marriage and motherhood." The intent of the anti-ERA, pro-family movement, she says, is to impress upon young women the lasting value of the family unit and of leading a chaste life. "Why," Phyllis Schlafly asks sharply before we hang up, "do we have to apologize for embracing those values today?"

That question is the crux of the anger behind the so-called backlash movement. For while the Schlafly-headed Eagle Forum, which opposes the Equal Rights Amendment, claims to have over 50,000 members today and draws its constituency from an increasingly vocal segment of the population, theirs is a defensive position rather than the effortless embrace of the "natural course of womanhood" it once was.

The very fact that the traditional life has had to be formalized with rhetoric is significant. It is a symptom of the vast social and economic changes that have occurred in America within the last decade.

Backlash was an inevitable counter-reaction. By the late 1970s, the feminists had felt the tremors of this conservative defense and become painfully aware that a negative image of them as man-hating radicals had permeated the popular mind, with serious repercussions for the cause of female equality and, especially, the passage of the ERA. By the end of the 1970s, the feminists openly deplored this new characterization, insisting they did not mean that every woman should go to work or forgo the bearing of children, but rather that each woman should have the opportunity to make that choice for herself.

Betty Friedan clearly addressed that issue in June 1980 in a speech to the National Association for the Commissions on the Status of Women. Speaking of women's right to have free choice to embrace traditional matrimony and to become a mother, she said: "I think the choice to have children is of profound value, and as a feminist who approves the full treatment of women, I approve that role. Any sense of the women's movement opposing that value was wrong and it came from a time when there was no choice, when women were only patterned for that one destiny."

As Judy Goldsmith, executive vice-president of the National Organization for Women, explains: "We know that active identification with feminism still remains threatening to many women today. The image of us as wild-eyed, bra-burning radicals is something we've labored under for a long time. But the fact is we're not those things at all. We continue to work through conventional political channels to effect change. And our goals are not radical—unless you consider equal opportunity for women to make choices an extremist position."

Acknowledging the dangers of an extremist interpretation of feminism, Roxcy Bolton, the founder of the Florida feminist movement, expresses concern that many women really want to stay home with their children, but that feminism has somehow made them feel guilty when they do so. "We were right about liberation in the late 1960s when the corps of women were still in the home, but I'm concerned that in our struggle for equality we may have implied that every woman must work. We have talked a lot about liberation, but the truth is that not all women *want* to be liberated."

Despite ardent assurance by the feminists of the true intention of the movement, a kind of siege mentality has set in among many women remaining at home in the suburbs today, leaving them increasingly angered, wary and even militant. A young North Dallas mother who was searching for a part-time job explained: "The suspicion is that if you stay at home you're either lazy, not too bright, or there is something else wrong with you. The idea, at least as it presses upon most women today, is that you should be out there working."

Incensed with the disapproval she experienced when she identified herself as a homemaker at social gatherings, one suburban Philadelphia mother, who later went on to become president of her local NOW chapter, resorted to describing herself as a "graduate student" when introduced to strangers. "It just made getting to know people easier at parties. They treated you differently if they thought you were doing something worthwhile. When I introduced myself as a housewife, you could see their eyes glaze over before they found a way to gracefully slip away. But I don't say I'm a student anymore. Now I tell them I'm a homemaker because I'm proud of what I've chosen to do."

Increasingly, a sizable proportion of women who have remained at home have begun to rail against this diminished social image of themselves, against what they perceive as unjust discrimination, the tyranny of the working women. Some have begun to wear T-shirts or to decorate their cars with bumper stickers that read "Every mother works" or "This is no ordinary housewife you are talking to." Others limit their friendships to women who remain at home like themselves. Some are hesitant about letting their children associate with those of working mothers. A 35-year-old woman I interviewed in a fashionable suburb just west of Chicago admitted that she not only held such a parochial attitude, but that she had pragmatic reasons for doing so: "All of my children's friends have mothers who are at home. We all have the same views about children and so our kids get along well. I think that the kids of working parents grow up differently—they are more independent and street-wise. But the kids with mothers at home seem happier and better adjusted."

The woman was openly stating a feeling that many women privately think but seldom express, which manifests itself in the distance and distrust that often seem to exist between the working women and the housewives of the suburban communities. At the heart of the dissension is the question of how much "mothering" a child needs to develop as a happy, successful human being, an issue seldom raised among the devoted mothers of traditional suburbia, but which now occurs with increasing urgency among the new women of suburbia.

Given the intensity of the feeling beneath the issue, it was only natural that the pro-family, anti-ERA, antiabortion forces in our country would surface, closely aligned with the economically conservative forces of the far right which rode Ronald Reagan into the presidency. The very forces that have shaped the American family and the mother's place in it were thought to have been damaged by feminism. It was the 1973 Supreme Court decision legalizing abortion that was the linchpin for that opposition—and its repeal remains a major goal of the New Right today. Symbolic of the excesses of feminism, abortion was a powerful, emotionally charged cause that galvanized groups as disparate as the Catholic Church, the Christian fundamentalists, the John Birch Society and the Women's Christian Temperance Union. As Faye Wattleton, executive director of the Planned Parenthood Federation of America, observes: "Although improved birth control methods such as the pill and the IUD gave women unprecedented control over the decision to bear children, it was the legalization of abortion, more than any other recent social or technological change, that gave women their ultimate reproductive liberalization." While abortion remains a disturbing issue for many Americans today, it is merely the tip of the philosophical iceberg; the larger question remains: what should a mother's role be today in the childrearing process?

Does a mother's working hurt a child's mental and psychological development? Or does working outside the home represent a positive factor in the mother's mental health, as many social scientists have conjectured, thus benefiting the child's psychological development? Does day care serve a positive function by making children better able to imitate adult tasks, as Harvard Professor Jerome Kagan has discovered, or is the intermittent presence of the mother in the child's early years harmful to his psychological development, as Cornell professor Urie Bronfenbrenner and other social scientists suspect?

The debate continues to rage, and still no one knows for sure. I believe that children and their parents fare better when they allow each other personal space as well as love, that the burden of absolute maternal devotion to a child carries with it a heavy price tag of subconscious anger and resentment, often fostering a set of implicit return demands which may surface neurotically in the later relationship of the child and parent. Slavish devotion to another, the relentless sacrifice of one's life, whether the person is a young child or another adult, it seems to me, is not only an unjust expectation but a setup for poor mental health.

I believe sound mothering is that which recognizes the special needs of the young child but also honors the human needs of the parent—a delicate balance, in anyone's book, and not one easily settled by emotionality.

It is this issue, perhaps more than any other, that has divided women in the late 1970s, and that threatens to forestall their future growth as a united voice in the 1980s. For many middle-class Americans, weary of high taxes, inflation and unemployment, frightened by youthful drug abuse, the rising teenage pregnancy rate and the soaring divorce rate and baffled by the subtle questions of the modern mother-child relationship, there has been a return to the things once thought safe—a breadwinning father, a home-centered mother, the fundamentalist church and political conservatism.

Political expression is, however, only one manifestation of that underlying social unease. The 1980 presidential election was decided on the basis of so many complex factors that it would be presumptuous to attribute its outcome simply to a backlash against feminism. The New York Times/CBS poll on the national 1980 election showed that women voters were split rather evenly between Reagan and Carter, while men favored Reagan 54 to 37 percent. And there is little doubt that Carter's uneven presidency, along with his callous treatment of female government appointees, seriously harmed his credibility among liberal voters. As Gloria Steinem observes: "When the oil crisis, inflation and Carter's semi-incompetence produced more and more free-floating anger, where else was it to go?"

At this writing the outcome of the ERA is still unknown—mired as it is in the larger question of women's rightful place in our society—though it looks bleak. All signs point to a conservative ending to the twentieth century. For most of us living our lives as ordinary citizens in the private sector, this reaction is usually expressed quite subtly. In the suburbs, where it has always been considered poor form to show outright hostility to one's peers, it is often covered with a thin veneer of amiability. The question of where women belong, if it is raised at all, usually appears in ambivalent neighborly behavior, sparking unseen tension and contributing to the relentless fragmentation of the suburban neighborhood.

Avoidance is a typical attitude among suburban homemakers I have observed or interviewed, when faced with such issues. Often they profess at least surface indifference to those women in their neighborhoods who are careerists. When asked whether she had friends who worked full time, a Northvale, New Jersey, woman considered the question carefully for a moment before admitting that her closest friends were those at home. Then, with just a suggestion of triumph in her eyes, she added, "Both of my friends did work for a while after their children were born. And you know what? They both decided that it was just too hard, so they quit." She had made her point. Some personal battle had been privately settled, some victory gained against an unseen enemy.

A 38-year-old homemaker living in Great Neck, New York, a former health planner for a New York hospital, expressed her disapproval more haughtily: "And where would you meet these working women who live in the community? And when you do meet them, they are usually so busy there is no time for socializing. They get home late in the afternoon, and on the weekends, they are running around like crazy trying to get their errands done. One working mother I know tells me she'd like to be friends, but honestly, she just doesn't have the time for me. So I don't really see any point in calling her."

A 51-year-old homemaker with two teenage children spoke of the harm she perceived working caused to the family: "A few years ago, many of my friends went to work because they were getting bored at home. But what I saw was that while they returned to work and seemed to enjoy it, it was at a tremendous sacrifice to their children and their marriages. Of course, I never said a word to them because I knew it was a sensitive issue. But after that there were a number of divorces and cases of kids getting into dope. Once through my volunteer work, I even ended up counseling a friend's pregnant teenage daughter. It was only then, when that happened, that this friend and I could sit down and talk about what went wrong when she went back to work."

By the same token, many of the working women I have interviewed respond with a similar coolness toward their at-home peers. Like the homemakers, they often insist that their friendship patterns have to do merely with where they spend their time. A 43-year-old bookkeeper from West Palm Beach, Florida, who was the mother of three teenagers, said: "Most of my good friends are now among those I work with here in the factory. I just have more in common with these women now. It's not that I like my homemaker friends any less. Of course, some of them make me feel a little bad. Some of them are hurt that I don't have much time for them anymore."

Friendships, of course, normally arise among people with similar interests; we might expect that people who spend their time in similar pursuits will become friends. But remarkably, in the suburbs today, as fewer people do remain at home, the split between these two groups of women grows more extreme and seems to extend well beyond simple explanations of where they spend their daytime hours.

A Voorhees, New Jersey, homemaker articulated that division well. Comparing her memory of attending wedding and baby showers in the late 1950s and early 1960s with those she recently attended, she observed: "The problem is you simply have less in common with other women living in the suburbs today. Even when you go to a shower or a luncheon, it has become increasingly difficult to find others who are at home and who have the same ideas as you. The tendency, when faced with so many unknowns, is to remain quietly polite and cautious. Whatever I do, I don't mention the words 'abortion' or 'day care.' For all I know, the woman sitting next to me might be violently opposed to both."

Many homemakers do wish they could return to work, but don't see how they could find a suitable job and good child care. Others scoff at the concept altogether and write off career women as unhappy, poorly adjusted women. Others wistfully express the need for outside stimulation and a little cash on their own, but feel that their husbands would disapprove. But amid these various stances, many women, like Mary Tedrow, maintain that a pernicious reverse discrimination has taken hold of their communities.

A 30-year-old woman from Great Neck, New York, who elected to stay home with her children because she believed it the most healthy approach to childrearing, analyzed her own insecure reaction when a friend with a two-month-old infant suddenly announced she was returning to full-time work. "It wasn't anything she said directly to me about my own choice that made me feel so bad. It was just the way she put it—that she was getting a housekeeper. The implication was that parenting, and especially mothering, could be done by just anybody just as well as her. After we hung up, I began to fret. Is what I'm doing really that important? I found myself wondering is what I'm doing every day really so easy that anybody else could bring up my children just as well? It sounds funny, but her decision made me feel threatened."

For a surprising number of homemakers, a personal sense of anger lurks beneath the surface, eroding the foundation of the suburban social structure itself. I think of the young Larchmont, New York, woman I met at a conference in Harriman, New York, at Columbia University's bucolic conference center. A bright energetic woman in her early forties, she was working, as was I, as a conference reporter for the nonprofit organization sponsoring the meeting. For ten years she had remained at home, but now that her children were older she had decided to return to work. After months of searching for a job, however, she still had not found a full-time position as an economic writer. Late one night we sat up talking on a deserted back staircase in the luxurious old mansion once owned by Averell Harriman. Curled up in one of the niches of the graceful arches, where pictures of young women in flowing gowns of an earlier era graced the walls, we chatted about work, children and men. To my surprise, she began to complain bitterly: "You can't even go to a cocktail party anymore without someone asking you what you do. It makes me sick. And if you say, 'Well, I'm just a wife and mother'—as I do sometimes when I get annoyed at the question—they look at you funny. Why can't they accept you as a human being? Why do you have to *be* something all the time?"

I was to hear her words repeated by dozens of other women around the country, women who remain home through a fierce sense of commitment to their families, but feel disquieted by that decision all the same.

I remember two lively League of Women Voters leaders I interviewed in Daly City, California, one foggy afternoon. They had given unselfishly of themselves to the community and to many volunteer organizations. When the subject of the scout troops they were heading became a topic of conversation, an uncharacteristically harsh tone appeared in their voices. It was the working mothers that made them angry, they said, the mothers of many children they had in their scout troops. Many of those mothers refused to volunteer their services, even for an occasional Saturday meeting, because they claimed they had little time. "It's a perfect excuse, a great way for them to get out of doing anything extra for their children," one woman told me with grim assurance, while her companion nodded her agreement beside her. "These mothers even instruct their children in what to say when I ask for help or assistance on trips, for snacks or for extra supplies. 'My mother works and she can't do anything,' the kids say automatically, and that makes me furious. A few times when that has happened, I've just decided, 'Okay, we just won't have this field trip or extra activity since none of the working mothers seem willing to help.'"

The sense of personal discomfort often applies to both sides. A Richardson, Texas, entrepreneur, a well-known figure in the Dallas business community, was repeatedly set on edge by the behavior of the other women in her community when she went to a PTA meeting or attended a sports event in which her son was a participant. As soon as she greeted her homemaker acquaintances, she sensed an uncomfortable shift in their behavior. "It was as if my appearance triggered some special signal. As soon as they'd see me, they would actually begin to talk differently. The entire thrust of the conversation seemed to change. Instead of discussing laundry detergent or grass seed, they'd start talking about what they read in the papers or about local politics. Gradually I came to realize that I was in some way a kind of threat to them."

This is not to suggest that there is no cooperation between different groups of women in the suburbs. Countless working women do share carpools, children's play arrangements and neighborhood activities with those mothers remaining in the home. And many women work part-time. Often a working mother will arrange to do a morning shift of the carpool, for instance, while the mother at home will do the afternoon shift. Nor is it unusual for a mother unable to participate in daily activities in the home or at school to try to make it up to her friends by taking the children along with her on weekend trips and outings.

Yet even with these exchanges, resentment often runs through even the most benevolent of these relationships. The rift between these two groups of women is a new and ominous social phenomenon, extending to the core of the suburban experience. It is symptomatic of the increasing social fragmentation in today's middle landscape which threatens to render tomorrow's suburbs as anonymous and inimical as today's modern cities. Unless they can work together, as I believe they can.

Mother Support Groups

The air was languorous as I drove down Green Bay Avenue on Chicago's North Shore in July 1980, heavy with the heat of midsummer. By noon I felt myself sliding into a near-hypnotic state, caught up in the seductive splendor of the towns passing into view from my car window: Winnetka, Lake Forest, Glencoe, Wilmette, Northbrook, their small tidy village centers well manicured and established, the buildings constructed in the English half-timbered style, the clusters of brick-front shops as charmingly designed as hand-decorated cookies at tea, and everywhere on the streets attractive women dressed in pretty sports clothes. Here, in the heart of the Midwest, I found myself thinking, suburban women must surely be more content than they are elsewhere in traditional roles. Here it cannot be changing as rapidly as on the East and West coasts.

There was a special aura to these North Shore women. The same placid faces found in only a handful of Westchester County and San Mateo County communities: serene faces set against the muted backdrop of tree-shaded streets, mesmerizing the casual observer into a belief that all is comfort here, all is well, all understood, all accepted. Even the North Shore shops seemed to perpetuate that vision—hairdressers, hardware stores, luncheonettes, drugstores, cleaners and kiddie shops, replicated in a dozen grand architectural variations down Green Bay Avenue.

But on Wilmette Avenue, up a creaky flight of stairs, sat Henry Owen, the Executive Director of the Family Service Center of Wilmette-Glenview-Kenilworth and Northbrook, who daily witnesses the personal anguish and self-doubts that often confront the women of Chicago's North Shore. The central theme, he says, is confusion about their roles. About feelings of worthlessness in being "just mothers." About their overwhelming loss of self-esteem in being home.

Where did this negativism about something so natural come from? From the women's movement? From the economy, which drove women out of their homes? The answers are difficult to determine, but the symptoms persist with alarming frequency. Henry Owen tells of alcoholism, depression, drug abuse, psychosomatic diseases, mental breakdowns, even child abuse and spouse batterings in the seemingly tranquil communities of Chicago's North Shore.

This is a relatively new phenomenon, Henry Owen says. For the first time in our history the women at home get no support for being there. It is worrisome; so troubling, in fact, that he and his staff hope to start a mother's drop-in center for homemakers, where they can find others like themselves. For the neighborhoods are lonelier now with so many women at work. It is more difficult for women at home to find each other, and motherhood is a stress for all women. But the money to start such a group has not appeared; in fact, aside from the mental health professionals, a handful of League of Women Voters members and a scattering of community volunteer service groups, no one else seems to care much about the women at home.

Why? Is it the economy? Or the perception that women in suburbia really have little need for this sort of thing? After all, everyone knows they are affluent, sophisticated, educated. They should be able to resolve this sort of thing on their own. Henry Owen turns to me and expresses his doubts that they can.

It is the next year, a bright March day, the kind of morning that hints of spring, and I am sitting in one of the sunny classrooms at the Unitarian/Universalist Church of Central Nassau in Garden City, Long Island. I am not there for worship but for education, as an observer of a church-based Mother's Day Out program—the kind that Henry Owen would like to see organized on Chicago's North Shore. But even within the vast thicket of homes that characterize the suburbs of Long Island, such programs are relatively unique. Mother-support groups are still hard to find here, the cutting edge of a new, barely perceived need among the women at home. And because it is one of the few existing programs on Long Island, the Unitarian/Universalist Church program has grown well beyond the church community where it began in 1972. Today, the day I am visiting, it includes forty-five women who come together for classes once a week from half a dozen communities in northeastern Nassau County. At the same time the women attend classes, their children are watched over by baby-sitters in another part of the church. For many homemakers, these few hours of group baby-sitting represent the only respite they have from child care all week—a service they welcome, which eases the monotony of the long, lonely week ahead.

The program is understandably well regarded by homemakers. It is so popular, in fact, that program codirector Carol Reiss reports that mothers often have to wait a year or more before they can be accommodated. Its purpose is purely social, in contrast to the therapeutic one Henry Owen hopes to design; this one was designed to help young mothers meet and engage in activities beyond child care and homemaking, such as photography, bridge, arts and crafts, and dance. Inevitably, as I suspected but was to witness more clearly by the end of the day, the group also serves as an informal support group and a forum for the interchange of ideas.

At the invitation of the program directors, I move at first from room to room before finally settling in the arts and crafts class. The conversation among the women there is light and disparate, as cheery and innocent as the hand-crafted silk flowers they are carefully pasting onto branches and baskets in anticipation of the new season. There is an underlying sense of excitement in the air: with the approach of spring the children will soon be able to play outside, instead of remaining indoors as they have done all winter. Before long, school will be over and the long bright summers of Long Island Sound will begin in earnest. It will be the best part of the year for these women. On Long Island, summer means frequent excursions to the lush parks and beaches. It is a good life, the women tell me, that of being home as wives and mothers, and in many ways, far preferable to paid employment. They speak with authority. Some tell me they had held jobs for as long as a decade before becoming pregnant with their first child. Others cherish hopes of returning to school or work when their children are older. But not now. Being a mother and wife is their first priority, they say with undisguised pride. Tenderly, they maintain that it is essential for them to be home with their young children. And they get satisfaction and pride in that nurturing role.

"I used to scoff at the housewives when I worked myself," a

trim mother of twins says, "but that was before I became pregnant and had the experience of trying to run a house and bring up kids. It's a lot harder than it used to look." Another woman describes her own transition from working woman to suburban housewife: "At first, when we moved here, I felt like I was in shock. There I was, suddenly, with two kids and a station wagon. Could that really be me? It was a joke. But now I've accepted myself in that role. Recently I filled out a credit card application and where they said 'occupation,' I listed 'unemployed.' Where they asked for salary, I wrote in big bold letters, 'You couldn't pay me enough!' And I meant it. I even underlined it with a black Magic Marker!"

"But don't forget, that's not what the rest of the world thinks," retorts a dark-haired woman sitting in the corner, who had just completed a basket of dainty violets. "There's an attitude among people and especially among working women that holding down a job is much more admirable. Almost like there's a moral obligation for women to work. They don't see how staying home can be a fulfilling role, mainly because they can't stay home themselves. When these career women finally do have kids, they go right back to work. Frankly, I begin to wonder why they have children in the first place, if someone else is going to bring them up."

Several women start to answer her at the same time. "People just don't care about anybody but themselves today," says a woman sitting across the craft table in a voice louder than the rest. "It's all me, me, me. What I want and think is important, not what is right for the family or the kids. Some of these women even go and have amniocentesis to find out the sex of their child. Then, if it's not the right sex, they have an abortion."

The other women immediately become silent. "And there are other examples of that selfishness," persists the same woman, in an increasingly angry voice. "They don't stop to think about what they are doing to their husbands and kids. Worst of all, it's the kids who suffer."

"There's a working mother just like that on my street," says another young woman. "Her attitude is, 'The baby can wait.'

She comes home after a day's work and puts the baby in a carriage with its bottle propped up against it. 'I need my time alone to unwind after work,' she tells me. 'When I'm relaxed in another hour, I'll be able to play with the baby.' I've tried to explain to her that kids can't wait like that—that when she gets home, she's *got* to pay attention to them immediately. But still she doesn't seem to understand. It's the career women like that who really bug me—who infuriate me, in fact!"

"But you can't make generalizations," protests a pregnant woman bent over a delicate spray of cherry blossoms. "Some mothers who work are better with their kids than we are, and some who stay home all the time are wretched. It's not fair to categorize them all the same way."

"Okay, I suppose there must be exceptions. Some working mothers do manage to turn out great kids, I suppose, but I've never met any of them. Why is it that the working mothers I seem to meet are always so bad?"

Why, I have often asked myself, does this critical attitude occur among women and why does it surface with such intensity in the suburbs? Because the suburbs have long been known as friendly places, the split between these groups is a particularly painful one. A frequent lament heard among many women I've spoken with who have moved to the suburbs is that their communities are often much less friendly than they had expected. "With half of the women at work and many others in school, it's harder to find people at home anymore," a White Plains, New York, homemaker says. "Today nobody seems to have time for anybody else. Years ago, there was always somebody out in the yard or down the street you could talk to, somebody you could share your problems and ideas with. And while you didn't want to be in each other's homes all the time, it did give you a warm feeling about your neighborhood."

Today, that warm feeling seems to be gone. Women, even in the most affluent suburban communities, have scattered. "All you see around here are housekeepers taking care of children and youngsters pooled together in private play groups. It's surprisingly difficult to meet other mothers at home," observes a woman who was participating in a Great Neck, New York, mother's support group.

It was not always that way. There are persistent memories of the suburbs of the 1950s and 1960s where many of us grew up. I remember the Boston suburb where I was raised and where, in the 1950s, just about everybody on my street had a mother at home. In fact, of the twenty-five children who were part of our neighborhood gang, not one had a working mother. Mothers remained at home, and because they did, there was constant socialization among them. There were, of course, some disagreements among women just as there are today, but with such a large pool of women to draw from, there was a ready-made opportunity for women to find others like themselves.

I believe that the tension stems also from the very visibility of people in the suburbs, set off by the low population density and greenery of the suburban neighborhood. The family is remarkably transparent there, as transparent as its split-level windows. Its comings and goings, its changing size and shape are on view to the entire neighborhood. Such dramatic emphasis of the individual and family unit are seldom as apparent in the crowded central cities. Suburban visibility often carries a steep price tag—the likelihood of being judged by one's neighbors.

Dr. Bobbie McKay, a minister and psychologist in Glenview, Illinois, and author of *The Unabridged Woman,* says that suburban women inevitably seem more caught up in the image of themselves in the community than do city women. As a practicing psychologist who treats women both from Chicago's North Shore and from the central city, she has been in a position to make such a comparison. "The city women who are my clients seem better able to get down to wrestling with the basic, internal issues that are troubling them. But as a general rule, suburban women seem to get caught up in a lot of externalizations, like what will the neighbors think if I return to work, or what kind of mother will they think I am if I leave my kids alone after school? Somehow, the proximity of people to each other in the suburbs seems to have a kind of inhibiting influence upon their behavior."

Today, despite the explosive social changes among our youth and the increasing emphasis on individualism, the conformist tendencies of the 1950s still seem to be operative. Dr. Richard Gelles, a sociologist at the University of Rhode Island and coauthor of *Behind Closed Doors: Violence in the American Family,* found in his 1976 study of 1,100 families that suburbanites consistently displayed lower rates of physical violence than did families in the cities or in the rural communities. But the lower rate of physical abuse in the suburban family did not imply a greater degree of harmony in those families. "Instead," Dr. Gelles explains, "there's less of a feeling of privacy in the suburbs. If there is a family argument involving physical force, the neighbors are more likely to become involved. So people think twice before using physical expressions of anger. In a certain sense, neighbors and friends serve as agents of social control in the suburban communities."

Even if one doesn't know one's suburban neighbors, one can always observe them. So for the woman at home who watches her female neighbor dressed in smart office clothes leaving for work every morning, there is a highly visible, and perhaps irritating, reminder that she is being left behind. With today's media glorification of the working woman, such a reminder may be particularly painful. To the homemaker, the working woman may be perceived as glamorous and worldly, and like her male counterpart, who leaves for the racy world of the city, she may be suspect. She may be thought of as irresponsible, sexually promiscuous and even an unfit mother. Distrust, envy, anger, resentment may be intertwined in this view of the working woman, and these feelings become difficult for the homemaker to sort out.

A Redwood City, California, full-time homemaker expressed the confused emotional responses she had to the working women in her community: "Sometimes I feel like a real dud when I'm in my shorts and all, and I see those women with their smart business clothes, with their hair all nicely coiffed. They look great. I think to myself, and I bet they have a great job. Then the next thing that happens is I begin to think, well, what's wrong with me that I can't be like them? Then, I tell myself they probably all have jobs as secretaries, and aren't I lucky that I don't have to do that, that I have a husband who can support me."

The affluence of the suburbs compared to the central cities also contributes to the intensity of the negative feelings experienced by many homemakers. More suburban women do have the luxury of deciding whether or not they should work. The existence of choice, however, also places a heavier psychological burden upon the suburban woman than upon her poorer peers: whatever decision she comes to she must somehow be able to justify. If she feels that the sacrifices she must make in order to work are simply not worth it, it follows that her decision to remain at home must be sound and well reasoned—at least well rationalized. So it seems that many suburban full-time homemakers adopt a defensive attitude toward their roles. "Often," Bobbie McKay says, "if you can't achieve something that others may be able to attain, then your denial of its worth has to be strong, very strong, to bolster the reasons why you can't have it too."

The Value of Motherhood

It cannot be denied that society now places a lower value on motherhood than in previous generations. There are many reasons: the vastly improved medical techniques that permit most babies to live through infancy and grow to maturity, thereby making serial childbearing less necessary than it was years ago; the increased educational options for women, and hence wider job opportunities; the increased control over youth education by the schools and the media rather than the family structure itself; the unstable economy which has forced many women back to work; improved birth control methods; the increasing depersonalization of our highly technical, highly mobile society; and the fact that children have become an economic burden rather than an economic advantage as they once were on the farm. Last but not least is feminism, which stresses that women are human beings with individual talents and abilities, rather than merely reproductive vessels.

The devaluation of motherhood, like the devaluation of femininity, has been gradual, beginning at the time of the Industrial Revolution and reaching its peak in the late 1970s. Consistent status erosion of any social role makes a person feel ashamed, and rage is a natural sequel. Some of the anger expressed by the suburban women at home may be understood as a knee-jerk reaction to the declining value of motherhood. But there is some justification for that reflex. Conventional child-development theory, for instance, supports the belief that the child's earliest years are crucial for his subsequent development, and that the mother, as the biological bearer of the child, is the most logical and natural one for primary care.

Yet our society transmits a double message about motherhood—that it is both sacred and worthless. The myth that motherhood is holy endures in our national consciousness, epitomized in Mother's Day cards and presents promoted by greeting card companies and department stores, but the harsh practical reality, as feminists often point out, is that it is worth nothing. Nancy Siegle, president of the New Jersey chapter of the Homemakers' Equal Rights Association, and Teri Wedoff, president of the national HERA, both suburban wives and mothers, maintain that while the official belief supports "apple pie and motherhood," the reality of our tax and inheritance laws dispels that myth. Currently, the law doesn't allow homemakers to establish IRAs for their retirement; nor does it enable them to obtain disability insurance for themselves. A homemaker must still be married at least ten years to collect social security benefits from her husband's estate if she is widowed or divorced. In some states, a homemaker who has worked with her husband on a family farm is still ineligible to inherit his property after his death. "These laws certainly don't encourage any of us to have respect for the full-time home-makers," says Nancy Siegle. "Until our legal status changes, our economic status won't be any better. And until both those changes occur, our social status won't be greatly enhanced, for they are intricately tied together."

According to Sandy Wolkoff, a psychiatric social worker who heads a mother-support group in Manhasset, Long Island, for many women who do become full-time suburban home-makers, the break between career achievement and mother-hood is often a traumatic experience. Part of the problem, she maintains, is that most jobs offer employees some form of feedback, if not outright support for their work. "When you go to an office, even if you're feeling terrible, if somebody says, 'Hey, that was a great piece of work you did the other day,' you feel better. But if you're at home, nobody praises you for keeping your house clean or for making good coffee. Even if somebody says, 'You're a good mother,' you think to yourself, 'You should see me at three in the morning when I get up with the baby.' You just don't get the same consistent support and feedback being a mother that you do in a job. Most women who do become full-time suburban homemakers after working at a job aren't prepared for the shock of going from feeling competent and in control of things to feeling very much less significant."

Many women I have interviewed who stay home report that they don't even get that sense of support from their hus-bands—despite the fact that their men are genuinely glad to see them at the conclusion of a day's work and eager to enjoy the comforts of a well-run home. "It was not so much that my husband didn't appreciate the fact that I had a hot, home-cooked dinner waiting for him, that the baby was dressed in a clean playsuit and that I was wearing makeup that used to bother me," says a young mother from Walnut Creek, Califor-nia, who recently returned to work. "It was just that he had no real understanding of the difficult day I'd put in. The house looked clean and the baby was quiet. But so what? Housework and child care are ongoing tasks that seem to require little comment—except of course when they aren't going well and life becomes chaotic."

Patsy Turrini, a psychoanalyst who began a Mother's Center in Hicksville, Long Island, that has served as a model for other such groups, notes that the peculiar atmosphere of the suburban environment and a woman's early ideas about being a perfect mother often come into direct conflict with each other. "We assume an inborn competence at being a mother that begins to fall flat at the moment of delivery. If you combine that with living in the suburbs, which is already isolating, and the trouble young mothers have getting small children around, it can be a shocking experience." The perception that many women have of their roles as a twenty-four-hour-a-day commitment and the horror of discovering that it may be a boring and even thankless task at times can wreak emotional havoc. As a result, the homemaker may become depressed—or direct her dissatisfactions outward as anger.

Women have ambivalent feelings about dependence and independence. Colette Dowling feels that while achieving personal or career autonomy, many women still cling to behavioral dependency patterns learned in their childhood, as for instance, crying when confronted with a crisis, or leaning heavily upon the advice of others while making a highly personal decision. Dependence comes from earlier notions of being feminine. She writes, "Caught in transition between two vastly different concepts of femininity, women are still emotionally reluctant to commit themselves to independence." As Dr. William Tooley, a McKinney, Texas, psychiatrist and chairman of the board of the North Central Texas Mental Health and Mental Retardation Center, points out: "We still encourage women to be tender and vulnerable because we believe it will make them good mothers, but then we turn around and devalue them for being soft and sensitive. We're putting women in a real bind. We want them to be sensitive, but at the same time, we aren't giving them enough of the support they need."

According to psychologist Dr. Joan Cross of Dallas, the angry housewife engaged in political or religious backlash causes often feels devalued by her husband, with whom she has had to assume an unequivocally subservient role. Often, beneath the facade of a pretty face or a smart wardrobe, she tries to assuage her bruised sense of self by channeling her energies into activities that will reinforce the validity of her role—the anti-ERA, pro-family forces that serve to bolster her position as a dependent member of society. In psychological terms, this is a kind of "reaction formation," an attempt to make the other women she knows similar to her so that she will feel more comfortable in her position. "Often, the woman doesn't even realize she's angry," says Dr. Cross. "If her position in the marriage is at all tenuous, she's simply got to find a way to rationalize her position so she can continue to hold onto it."

One striking feature of the women who join conservative groups is that among those who joined in adulthood, a pervasive sense of unhappiness and discontent often preceded their "conversion." One 28-year-old woman living in Rahway, New Jersey, told me how that underlying sense of unhappiness provoked her transition from liberal to traditionalist. The editor of a nationally prominent magazine, she surprised her boss one day by walking into his office and announcing she was planning to quit her job. Her reason? Not that her pay was too low or her position too difficult, but rather that she had been "saved," and now planned to devote herself to her family and church. She was, as she explained to me, disillusioned with feminism and many other contemporary values she had once espoused. In her search for happiness she had joined the Christian Fellowship, a charismatic Christian church founded several years before in suburban New Jersey. After her conversion, she spent considerable time in prayer and had come to the realization she had erred in her ways; she now decided she must devote her time to her husband and the home. "In the world's view I had everything: an exciting job, travel and prestige. So why was I still unhappy, I used to ask myself? And why were people around me so unhappy? Through the church I learned that God has a perfect order and that the basic unit of life is the family. I came to realize that feminism was too self-centered. In order to be the kind of wife I wanted to be and offer my husband the kind of support he needs, I couldn't continue to work full time anymore. The peace I have now is beyond anything I have ever known."

Like the women who have been drawn to conservative religious organizations, many who identify with pro-family political organizations also experience a visceral sense of discontent, an emotional response to the social changes of the last decade that eventually prompts them to action. That action is often fervent, they say, because it is a heartfelt response to what they perceive as alarming symptoms of moral decay in the nation.

One such activist is Phyllis Graham, the New York State director of the Eagle Forum. A suburban Long Island wife and mother, she maintains that she had remained quietly apolitical all her life until 1973, when she became so upset at the Supreme Court decision to legalize abortion that she felt she had to speak out. "I love more than anything else the domestic arts and keeping a house and I wish the world would leave me alone so I can do it. But when I read the Supreme Court decision in 1973, I couldn't believe it. This catapulted me into the political arena and I haven't stopped since. I don't know now that I ever can." Most of the other women she has met and befriended in the pro-family movement, Mrs. Graham says, have come from similar circumstances, having initially followed a pattern of political noninvolvement and an adherence to a traditional way of life as a wife and mother. But then some court decision or legislative proposal set them off— abortion, school prayer or the appearance of alcoholic beverages in the supermarkets, to take three common examples— and they find themselves entering the political arena as angry "grass-roots" activists.

Ceil Herman, a Levittown, New York, wife and mother of five children, and the past president of the New York State Pro-Family Federation/Operation Wake-Up, who helped spearhead the defeat of the New York State ERA referendum proposed in 1975, says: "The women who fight to uphold the importance of the homemaker role are tired of being told they are unproductive and not worthwhile because they don't have a dollar sign to their name at the end of the week. The idea of being regarded as nonproductive because you're a homemaker either gets you so damn mad that you join a movement like Pro-Family, or you get so convinced that you *are* nonproductive that you join a feminist organization."

Lamentably, the issue of the full-time homemaker and her significance for the well-being of society seems to have polarized contemporary women. Much of that anger seems to have begun in the suburban neighborhoods, where the flight of young women into the workplace has had such a shattering effect. And so we find ourselves divided today, as we have never been before, about the rights of women. Today it has become difficult to talk to one's neighbors. Today, in an economy crippled by inflation and social dissent, it has become even more difficult to find out who those neighbors are.

Sometimes, the divisions between us run deeper than we care to admit. Often we have to go on pretending to avoid the pain, as a neighborhood friend and I once did. It was a memorable Thursday in June 1979, a morning when the sky glistened a pale robin's-egg blue, when the spring mud had disappeared and the azalea, rhododendron and dogwood blossoms had begun to appear in Westchester County in bright bursts of fuchsia, purple and white. The children in my daughter Elisabeth's second-grade class fairly bubbled over with excitement as we arrived at the Muscoot Farm in Katonah, New York, pushing their way eagerly off the bus with laughter and squeals of delight. The teachers, the other mothers and I exchanged knowing looks. It would be a trying morning: we would all have to work hard to keep the children with us as we toured the sprawling farm run by the county of Westchester.

The field trip was to be my one contribution to my daughter Elisabeth's class that year, and as a working mother I felt vague twinges of guilt that this was all I had done. But the teacher had heard about the farm through a newspaper article

I had written for the *New York Times,* so I reasoned that my contribution, although slight, had at least been noticeable.

Yet even on this day that I had promised to my daughter and her classmates, there were other distractions. The night before, I had received a phone call from my parents in Boston. My mother, who had long been waiting to have elective surgery, had been notified by the hospital that they now had a bed available for her. The operation, she was told, would be performed on Friday, and she should appear at the hospital on Thursday to be admitted. Weeks ago, I had planned to fly to Boston to join her at the time of surgery. But I had hardly expected it would coincide with my daughter's field trip. Now, the night before the school outing, it was too late to find another parent to substitute for me. What was I to do? How could I honor both obligations?

To make matters worse, I hadn't even arranged for a baby-sitter for Thursday. After the school field trip, I had planned to be home to meet my youngest daughter when she returned from nursery school. Now, even if I could take a plane to Boston after the field trip, I had no one to watch my children until my husband returned from work. I was in a terrible bind.

"Maybe Susan could help," my husband suggested. Quickly I called my friend and asked her if she would be able to watch my children. She was one of my best friends, who lived a few doors down from me. We had both moved to New Rochelle at the same time, and for the past three years had shared house decorating schemes, carpooling and baby-sitting. Our children had become fond playmates, too. And yet Susan and I were quite different. She was a full-time homemaker; I, a working journalist. She had tired of the working world and had gratefully "retired" when her first child was born. Yet she approved of my life-style, accepted my often unpredictable hours as a free-lance reporter and often applauded my work when it appeared in the newspaper. In turn, I admired her fun-loving ways, her easygoing manner and her keen aesthetic sense. We saw qualities in each other we wished we had in ourselves.

"Sure I'll watch your kids," Susan said when I explained my

dilemma, and I slept easier that night knowing she would be able to help me. But the next day was destined to go badly. After the field trip had ended, I drove home, changed from my dusty jeans into a fresh cotton dress and awaited the arrival of my younger daughter. She was supposed to arrive at 3:00 and her bus was usually on time. But the minutes ticked away, and still her school bus failed to arrive. At 3:15 the cab I had ordered for my trip to the airport arrived and began honking madly. Quickly I ran to the curb and explained my dilemma to the taxi driver. "You're going to miss the four o'clock plane," he warned me solemnly.

I called the school. The bus had been delayed. Panic-stricken, I called Susan again. "I'll come over and wait at your house until she arrives. You'd better go. The plane won't wait." Hastily I jumped into the cab and braced myself for what I knew was going to be a long, anxious drive to La Guardia Airport.

Three days later when I returned home, I called Susan to thank her for all she had done. But her voice sounded tense on the phone, in fact, almost angry.

"I'm not angry," she said, "just a bit put out with you."

"With me? *Why?*"

"I don't want to get into it over the phone. It's too complicated. Sometime when you have the time, we'll have to straighten it out." There was a distinctly sarcastic edge to her words.

"Well, why not now? Can we talk?" I asked.

"Why don't you come over here then?" she snapped. "Maybe we'd better have this out now." It was after 9:00 P.M. and my husband looked at me with curiosity when I announced where I was going.

Still perplexed, I arrived at her doorstep in the darkness. As she turned on the vestibule light and opened the door, I saw that she too seemed nervous.

"But what is the matter?" I asked her again.

"Everything and nothing," she said, after a long awkward silence. "Sometimes you really make me angry. Or maybe it's not you. Maybe it's just me and my problems that make everything seem so bad lately. You really got my goat the other day. Just because you work doesn't mean you're more important than me!"

"I'm not. Whoever said that?" I responded, feeling suddenly very uncomfortable.

"Well, no one did. But it's just the way I feel. It's the way you make me feel sometimes."

"But how? Are you angry about the other day? I'm awfully sorry. Really."

"No, it's not that," she protested, "or at least that isn't the primary cause. It was just the straw that broke the camel's back. You've taken my kids plenty of afternoons, too. It's just that you always seem so busy. That makes me feel real bad, insignificant. Like I'm not important because I'm at home."

"How can you say such a thing?" I gasped with surprise. "I don't feel that way about what you do. In fact, I wish I could do what you do—stay home with my kids all the time. But I'm just not cut out that way."

Then, in a calmer tone, I explained the chaotic series of events that preceded my trip to Boston and my own jumbled feelings of guilt. As she listened, tears welled up in her eyes. Before long she told me of her own worries, her growing boredom at home, her ambivalence about returning to work and her anxiety about what she would do when both her children were in school full time. Golf and tennis are fun, she said, but not really enough. Club work didn't interest her. "I think deep down inside I really envy you," she said. "I wish I could find something I liked as much as you like to write."

By this time we were both laughing. "But look at how complicated it gets for me," I reminded her. "Look at what a mess that day was. If I stayed home full time, I never would have volunteered for that field trip in the first place. It was my way of making things up to Elisabeth's class. If I'd been home, I would have been involved in other school activities throughout the year. Sometimes I think your decision to stay home with the kids is far more sensible than mine."

We were both startled by our mutual confessions and saddened by the rift that had grown imperceptibly between us.

Her life was no easier than mine, and in many ways more frustrating. And my guilt was no small issue for any working mother.

"We're friends again," she said simply.

"I'm glad we talked," I told her. "We should do it more often."

"Between deadlines," she said with a giggle.

We looked at each other across the space that separated us as we sat near each other on the handsome couch in her antique-filled living room. For a moment we moved a step closer to understanding women's dilemma today.

If only we hadn't harbored our resentments against each other in silence for so long. If only we could really talk with each other in the future, the differences that separate us would no longer be threatening.

6

The New Pioneers: Single and Childless Suburban Women

∞∞∞∞∞∞∞∞∞∞∞∞∞∞∞∞∞∞∞∞∞∞∞∞∞∞∞∞∞∞∞∞∞∞∞∞∞∞∞

> Main Street may be reborn in the suburbs, and if it is, it will be peopled by a new and diverse population.
>
> Andrée Brooks, "Single at Midlife,"
> *New York Times Magazine*

> I've been a bridesmaid six times, but now I hardly see any of my married friends. There's something that happens to friendships when women get married.
>
> A 27-year-old single broadcast journalist from Franklin Park, Long Island

"I'M ONE OF THOSE PEOPLE you would categorize as the forgotten of suburbia, because I'm single—one of those women who never made it to the respectable part of town where there are free-standing homes, marriages and children. Over there, in the apartment building I live in, we're a world apart—a separate community with our own swimming pool, tennis court and parking lot, and a social life that has nothing to do with the quiet residential streets around us.

"Most of the people who live in my building are young; many of them have never been married, or married only briefly. There's a lot of comings and goings in my building and you only get to know a few people well. But my friends are like me, reasonably content with their lives, busy with their jobs and leisure activities, interested in meeting men, but only if they're not duds or a waste of time.

"Sometimes, though, when I drive home after work at night, I look at those streets near my building with their ranch homes and cars parked in the driveway and wonder what it would be like to be married and living there. What would it be like to have kids and be cooking dinner for my husband at that hour? The idea kind of appeals to me for a minute, but at the same time it terrifies me that I could be tied down like that. In the next breath I'm thankful that I'm still free."

She was only 30 years old, but the dark-haired computer saleswoman I met in a suburban Dallas coffee shop had given up on the idea of ever getting married. She had dated so many men, had been infatuated so many times and then disappointed, that she had become increasingly wary with the years. Like so many other single women, she had come to accept her single status as a healthy condition, had come to prize the freedom of her single life as a unique opportunity for personal growth. That was one of the advantages of her job, she explained: the fact that she traveled to other cities and continually met new people in new surroundings.

Yet the idea that a better life might still await her somewhere, beyond the tall brick wall that encircles her apartment building, haunts her. For the tranquil home-lined streets of northeast Dallas near her apartment building serve as a reminder that married life is still the dominant mode, that to be single in the suburbs is still an aberration.

"Oh, we've enjoyed living here in a private home for the past four years. It was a sensible financial investment, especially in terms of today's mortgage rates. But sometimes it's so lonely here and so quiet, you could go nuts. We hardly know any people in our neighborhood. You can wander around here on the weekends—which is about the only time we are home—and there's never anybody around. Where are all our neighbors? I used to ask my husband and he would just shrug his shoulders because he didn't know either. After living here for a while, we've concluded that the married couples with kids are always busy with their families on the weekends.

"But we're the type of couple who enjoys living without any responsibilities to anyone but ourselves. Last summer we were so bored here on weekends we finally bought a sailboat. Every second weekend we traveled to Southampton where we had a share in a summer house and where there were other couples like us. But here in Westchester, it seems so settled and so conventional. The suburbs seem to be designed for people with children and with very little thought to nightlife and entertainment. You can't even get a pizza at one o'clock in the morning if you want to. At least in the city and in resorts like the Hamptons you can always find something interesting to do and other lively people to be with."

It was with considerable surprise that I heard these words spoken by my 32-year-old neighbor—surprise because my husband and I were one of those neighborhood families she was referring to who were always so involved with their children and family on the weekends that they were seldom around. Suddenly, through my neighbor's eyes, I saw my husband and myself as she viewed us: as a married, child-oriented couple well settled in the conventional suburban mold. At the same time, I came to understand that our neighbors, whom we had perceived as a footloose and fancy-free young couple, felt themselves excluded from some mysterious rite of the middle landscape.

And indeed, they had some justification. For the past several years, my husband and I had greeted this couple on the street, exchanged community information and chatted politely at infrequent neighborhood gatherings, but had never made any attempt to mix socially. Why should we become friendly with them? my husband and I thought, since they were a childless couple with a great deal more freedom and financial ease than ourselves? What did we have in common with them except proximity? We had, after all, our own set of married friends with children of their own—friends who, like ourselves, often had to be home before two on a Saturday night for the baby-sitter. How could we socialize with this carefree young couple on weekends if we were worried about getting home on time? What if they wanted to go out on the town until four in the morning and boogie? It was the marked contrast in our lives as suburbanites, the difference between having children and not having them, that kept us and our neighbors far apart, as if we spoke different languages.

The growth of a permanent singles population and the increasing appearance of childless couples have been widely touted by the press as urbanized phenomena, but they have found their way to the middle landscape as well, symptomatic of irretrievable social change. What was once the conventional suburban matrix—the two-parent, two-child family—is no longer a dominant form, having been replaced in the last decade by a new untraditional mixture of household types. Single men and women, who might have hastily fled suburbia a generation ago for the protective anonymity of the city, have appeared in the suburbs during the seventies, after having graduated from college, having separated from their spouses, or having made a deliberate decision to retreat from the crime and clamor of urban life.

At the same time, thousands of young couples, who have either postponed or rejected the idea of childbearing, have migrated to the suburbs, where they have carefully pooled their paychecks to buy homes and condominiums. A sizable number of these young couples, less certain of their jobs or relationships, have also rented apartments or houses in an effort to avoid the cost and the pace of city living. Some of them are married; others are not. The sexual revolution and individualism spawned by the protests and riots of the late 1960s and early 1970s have splintered the once unified suburban pattern: the childless couple, the swinging single and the fun-loving, sexually sophisticated career girl are social types that have become as ordinary in the suburbs as the matron herself, as acceptable as her new foreign, gas-efficient automobile.

Yet the old myths linger on. The notion that the suburbs are composed of peaceable, two-parent household units nibbles at the heels of the young, uncommitted population who, as relative newcomers to the socially conservative suburbs, still feel uncertain about their single or childless status. As part of a new population subgroup, many single women have come to feel, as did the computer saleswoman from northeast Dallas, that they are somehow less acceptable than their married, childbearing counterparts of the ranch-home communities. Or, like my married but childless neighbor, they may openly express a deep-rooted dissatisfaction with the suburban life itself, which they suspect may be related to their own childless state that somehow prevents them from fully savoring the fruits of the middle landscape.

Unlike the social fragmentation resulting from the civil rights and feminist movements, the single and childless woman's detachment from the traditional suburbanites has deeper roots, difficult for both the mainstream and new populations to confront. The truth is that the single and childless women enjoy a glamorous sexual aura that serves at once to attract and repel the married, childbearing women, an aura heightened by their proximity to the traditional households.

Sex, once limited to the marital relationship and the occasional extramarital affair allowed men, has become a legitimately expressed need among all men and women today, regardless of their life stations and marital states. And with the maturity and new affluence of the baby-boom generation and the "liberated" life-style they have espoused have come changes in social behavior and cultural mores that have permitted a more open expression of sex.

How-to books, sexually explicit movies and sex-therapy clinics have become ordinary parts of daily life. Magazines like

Screw, Hustler, Penthouse and *Oui* regularly appear on neighborhood newsstands; group sex, casual cohabitation and homosexuality no longer have the same shock value they once did in polite society. The new myth of everlasting ecstasy says that sex without commitment leaves one a freer and happier human being.

"My mother openly admits that she is jealous of the life I've led," says one unmarried 27-year-old woman. "I honestly don't see what is so exciting or enviable about my life compared to hers, but she is convinced that she missed out on a lot by getting married at such an early age."

"As soon as they hear you're single, there's a different attitude among the women you meet," says another young woman who rents a home in Lake Forest, Illinois. "There's a whole range of emotions people display, ranging from curiosity and pity to suspicion, disapproval and jealousy. Just because I'm single, they assume I'm either lonely or promiscuous. And the promiscuity bit often takes precedence."

The myth of the sexual revolution has ripped through the old Puritan ethic, confounding the traditionally monogamous population of our nation and leaving many wondering what they have been missing. Like all myths, there is truth in it. People in general, and women in particular, are freer today than ever before. Sexual activity outside marriage no longer necessarily elicits the guilt it once did. Should a woman invite a man she is attracted to out on a date? Should she buy him dinner? Should she invite him to her apartment? Should she sleep with him on the first date? These are questions that would have been unthinkable for most middle-class women fifteen years ago, but have now become ordinary considerations for many.

The easier life-style facilitated by the new sexuality is reflected in all aspects of modern life—not only the popular press, movies, records and nightlife of the central cities, but also in the heart of the suburbs. In the traditional sanctuary of the happily married, there has recently been a proliferation of singles clubs, bars and apartments.

If the new sexuality has left any physical emblem of its

presence in America, I think it may be most dramatic in the suburbs, where there has been a sharp change in the type of living accommodations now being built: witness the growing number of apartment houses, condominiums and cluster-type housing that honeycomb the hills of California, the flatlands of Texas and Arizona and the plains and prairies of Ohio and Missouri—and all over the country. These buildings are often located right next to the conventional strips of free-standing homes built just a decade or two before in a flurry of family-oriented developments.

The message implicit in these buildings is unmistakable: singlehood has come of age—even in suburbia. Marriage may be costly, these apartments seem to silently suggest, may even be unnecessary for happiness.

Condominium construction accounted for over one-third of all multifamily units built in 1980. Between 1975 and 1979, the number of owner-occupied condominiums grew by nearly 91 percent throughout the nation, and housing officials predict that the singles population will continue to become an increasingly important part of the home-buying market in the last two decades of the twentieth century. "People are marrying later, and if they are having children at all, having them later. Many people simply prefer to remain single today," says Jay Shackford, assistant staff vice-president for public affairs for the National Association of Home Builders. "In fact, more of the new construction is geared to the single-person household than ever before because singles are becoming a larger segment of our population today and have become more interested in owning their own homes and condominiums."

Government figures verify that observation. According to the U.S. Bureau of the Census, more than 25 percent of the female population 14 years of age and older had never married in 1979, compared to 20 percent in 1960. Even more striking has been the increase in the number of single women who now live in the suburbs: the Census Bureau calculates that the number grew by about 40 percent, rising from 6.1 million in 1970 to 8.5 million in 1980.

At the same time, childlessness has become increasingly

common among those who do marry. Nationally, the number of childless women aged 20 to 24 grew from 24 percent in 1960 to 41 percent in 1979. The changes witnessed in the suburbs have been even more dramatic. Between 1972 and 1979 there was a 23 percent increase in the number of suburban women who had married between the ages of 15 and 44 who remained childless, amounting to an additional 783,000 women!

Like all intruders upon formerly sacrosanct property, the 2.7 million married, childless women and the 8.5 million single women of the suburbs have been met with varying expressions of protest and disapproval. Some women, like the one from northeast Dallas, live in a world apart from the mainstream community in which their apartment complexes were built. Another woman, from Cedarhurst, Long Island, who lives in a private house, found that there was minimal interaction with her more traditional neighbors and that her close friends were other single people who lived scattered through the neighboring towns in western Nassau County. Others, like one childless married woman who had lived in West Palm Beach, Florida, found that her neighbors barely talked to her. "I don't know whether it is because we are considered curiosities on the block or they think of us as a wild hippie type of couple, but the fact remains we hardly know our neighbors well enough to say hello. Sometimes I have the feeling that I'm living in a kind of split-level island."

Nevertheless, intrigued by the tranquility of the suburbs or by the lower cost of apartments and homes, these women have continued their flight from the central cities to the suburbs in ever-increasing numbers. But for the single woman or childless married woman there are costly trade-offs: she often finds that the potential for a social life she took for granted in the city has been diminished by her move, that there is less opportunity to meet others like herself. "I love the beauty and quiet of living in the suburbs, but I think I'd do a lot more dating if I lived in the city," concedes a 34-year-old single woman living in an airy condominium in Lafayette, California. "I think, for instance, I'd feel a lot more comfortable going into a singles neighborhood bar in the city than I do here, where I have to drive fifteen or twenty minutes to get to one of those suburban singles watering holes. Also there is probably a greater selection of men in the city. But the atmosphere of the city unnerves me so much that I'm not willing to make that move."

Yet the city does offer many advantages to single women, not the least of which is social indifference to singlehood and a protective anonymity. As a 33-year-old single health-care administrator living in Norwalk, Connecticut, after having lived in Manhattan, explained, the urban centers do provide people with a greater variety of ways to mask their loneliness. She contrasted her decade of single living in New York City with living in Fairfield County: "In the city there are always movies, shops and museums you can visit by yourself and never feel odd for being there alone. But in the suburbs, it's a different story. Everything there is couple- and family-oriented, and it takes a brave person to go it alone. In fact, the only times that I've felt frantic about being single, now that I think of it, have been in my years living here in Fairfield County."

The Bar Scene

One of the problems with being single in the suburbs, as a 28-year-old woman sitting at a bar in suburban Garland, Texas, told me one evening, is that the circle of people one meets in the suburbs is usually quite limited. "After you've been to the five or six bars you'd even consider going to, you start to see the same faces. It begins to get a little discouraging. You are suddenly faced with the absurd notion that these are truly the last remaining men on earth. And they might as well be, too—unless you are willing to spend all your time traipsing back and forth between your home in the suburbs and the city."

Another single woman, who works in Manhattan as a journalist for a major radio network but commutes to Franklin Park, New York, said: "The suburban bars are usually a downright disaster. I do give them an occasional try, because by the end of the day or the week, I've had enough hassling in the city. I've gotten to the point, though, where I've practically given up meeting anybody decent in those places. So why do I continue to go there? Just to have fun, I guess. Many nights there are more women than men. Sometimes my girl friend and I just end up dancing ourselves rather than sitting around and feeling sorry for ourselves."

For single women who work in the cities and live in the suburbs, there are other, subtler problems. Some, like the ones I have mentioned above, claim they experience an abrupt sense of discontinuity in their lives, that they lead one type of life and adhere to one set of social expectations in the city, but are faced with a different set of values from the men they meet in the suburbs. The contrast between their suburban social lives and the social opportunities provided in the city is often demoralizing for these women—particularly for those who are career-minded, engaged in building an identity as success-oriented professionals.

They may feel, as did the woman from Franklin Park, that the caliber and quality of social life they have to choose from in the suburbs is second-rate compared to what they witness daily in the cities. "There I was, sitting with my friend in one of those bars with music and dancing, and suddenly this outrageously obese man comes over to ask me to dance," she says, herself an attractive young brunette. "This man was about 45 or 50, completely bald, really quite grotesque looking. While I'm not one to put someone down because of his looks, I immediately refused him. He became insistent, though, incredulous that I wouldn't dance with him. At the same time I was horrified that he thought, assumed in fact, that because men were so scarce, I would dance with him. My God, surely I could do better than this, I thought. Is this what living in the suburbs reduces you to?"

Another young single woman, who had become the general

manager of a prominent San Francisco restaurant but had opted for the leisure-oriented life and milder climate of Marin County for her home, noted a growing disparity between her value system and those of the single men she tended to meet in the suburbs. So jarring had those differences become that she had finally decided to move into San Francisco. Sitting one night in the back of a bar in Sausalito and surveyed by the flinty eyes of a single man at the next table, she said: "The problem is that I'm beginning to feel that my life is very fragmented. The city is only fifteen miles away from here, but it might as well be a hundred. There's definitely a slower pace here. People are more relaxed and laid back—too laid back, I guess, for the direction I'm headed in. There's a different mind-set here. I won't call it antiestablishment, because there're plenty of establishment types here in Marin among the singles, but there's a frivolity, a lack of seriousness that I'm not able to relate to very well. In the city my friends have high expectations for themselves and the people they seek out. Here there's only a fast sexual hustle. If you are a woman serious about becoming a success in the business world, you can probably forget it. Lots of men out here can't relate to that."

A 28-year-old attorney who was single and living in Lyndhurst, New Jersey, observed similar disparities between her personal and professional expectations and those of the single men she often met in the suburbs. "Once they learn that you're a lawyer, they often become terribly intimidated. One man I met through local politics and subsequently dated finally told me how relieved he was to find out I was just a regular gal. 'What did you think I was?' I asked him, and laughed, even though, if you think about it for a minute, it's probably not a laughing matter. But it was the mystique that surrounded the role that frightened him. He explained he had never dated a female attorney before—or a female doctor or college professor for that matter. You'd probably get less of that type of reaction from men in the cities, where professional women are much more common."

*   *   *

It was an incandescent summer night in July 1981, with the sun gradually settling over the glass-and-chrome buildings of White Plains, New York, lighting up the sky with crimson hues before sinking—the kind of night on which a woman might well imagine meeting that tall, handsome stranger. And yet, sitting in a chic restaurant and bar known as a nighttime haunt of the singles population of Westchester County, there seemed little chance for such an encounter, despite the friendly atmosphere of the place. Seated beside me at the handsomely fashioned bar were two young women, pretty girls engaged in a heated discussion about men and their intractability in personal relationships, sexist attitudes in the workplace, and feelings of vulnerability and inferiority. As we shared a bowl of pretzels together, the three of us talked about men, dating in the suburbs, career hopes and aspirations. But the women, both of whom were graduate students at Cornell and working in White Plains on a corporate internship program, told me they were disappointed with the social life they had experienced so far in Westchester County, which they found appallingly bleak and stereotyped.

"What you seem to get is just two types of places to go to in the county," the perky redhead said. "Either there are the dive-type bars with the sleazy men or there are hangouts like this—safe enough places, but where the men are full of themselves and seem to be posturing. The classic story is that they are executives and earn handsome salaries. But once you go out with them, you find out they really aren't in such high-powered positions after all. Or they turn out to be married, which is even worse."

"The point is that if any man had his act together and was still single, he probably wouldn't be working here in the suburbs," said the other woman, a brunette, bluntly. "He'd probably be working in the city. Unless, of course, he was that married impostor who had moved to the suburbs with his wife and kids for the good life."

"Excuse me, but what are you two girls doing in a place like this, anyway, if you think suburban single men are so lousy?" the man sitting to the left of the redhead asked my acquaintances.

"We work quite near here at IBM and it's convenient. It's a good place for us to have a drink or two after work and get a chance to visit with each other," the brunette said in a defensive tone. "We've pretty much given up the idea of meeting Mr. Right in a place like this, though. What about you? What do *you* think of the social life here in White Plains, anyway? You look like a native."

"I don't know whether that's a compliment or an insult after listening to you girls talk," replied the man jovially, "but the dating scene is pretty bad here. I do most of my socializing in the city."

"Then why are you here?" the brunette persisted.

"I happen to work down the street too, but in the other direction. I'm a broker, and I've come in here for a drink after work because it's been a long, hot day."

The two girls sitting next to me broke into knowing smiles.

"A likely story," smirked the redhead, now obviously enjoying the banter. "I bet you come in here all the time."

"Not really. I seldom come here. I work right over there," insisted the man solemnly, pointing through the window on the other side of the bar. "But even when I do come here for a drink after work, it's not usually to meet women. I have a busy social life. And I still spent lots of time with my married friends."

"Oh, you're divorced," said the brunette with a quick look at her friend.

"Yes, I am," the man replied in an even tone. "Now, let me guess. You've never been married."

Two nights later I visited the bar again, this time somewhat later in the evening. By ten the place was crowded with people standing three-deep around the large square bar, some engaged in lively conversations with members of the opposite sex, some talking to the friends they had arrived with, some sitting or standing alone, some slowly wending their way through the crowds of people standing at the bar, almost all of them with drinks in their hands.

"I honestly don't know why I put myself through this," murmured one curly haired young woman sitting on a bar stool and looking decidedly bored. "I actually hate drinking."

"But you like men and this is the only way you're going to find them," said the woman standing next to her, a tall sparkling-eyed brunette who was surveying the scene with a majestic turn of her head, "unless we go to the city, which I just wasn't up for on a hot night like this."

"Yeah, with my car broken down, I'm really stuck, really limited in my options," muttered the curly-haired woman as she sipped a Bloody Mary from a tall, nearly empty glass.

"You mean, you're lucky I could give you a ride. And we're fortunate to have gotten in here tonight," her friend said as she continued to scrutinize the crowd. "Some nights they have a line outside and you have to wait to get in. It's about the only good singles place around. But still, you've got to make your own good time in a place like this—nobody's going to do it for you."

"Hey, can I buy you girls a drink?" said a voice behind me. At the same time I felt a hand placed momentarily on my shoulder.

I turned around to see who it was. The girls standing in front of me were smiling weakly at him.

"Sure," said the tall woman. "Why not? I'm drinking gin and tonic."

The man who had placed his hand on my shoulder and I stared at each other with embarrassment before I turned to walk away. It was the stockbroker I had chatted with just two days earlier.

Sometimes single suburban women avoid the bars altogether, feeling that they are the worst possible place to meet men, especially the type of men with whom there might be the possibility of a long-term relationship. "The moment I step across the threshold of a singles bar, I begin to feel like I'm advertising that I'm available to all comers," a pretty young woman from Worthington, Ohio, says. "The truth is that I'm not. I'm pretty selective in my friendships and even more so in the men I date. Why should I put myself in an artificial setting like that to meet guys, I ask myself? It just sets up unrealistic expectations for me that are doomed to failure."

"When you walk into a singles bar in Marin County, you can almost predict what will happen," says another woman, who works in San Francisco but lives in San Anselmo. "I call them the Mr. Plastic Men, the ones who haunt those plastic places. The most profound bit of conversation you might hear the whole night is, 'Hey babe, what's your sign?' There's a remarkable inability on the part of most men you meet there to be interested in anything but themselves and what you can do to bolster their image. Even the language you hear in those places is an indication of what the mentality is—words like 'focus in,' 'let's be mellow,' and 'let's play it by ear' tell you that the bars are no place for sincerity."

Sociologists, therapists and psychologists often maintain that the atmosphere in singles bars almost demands that the interchanges there between people be superficial. "Practically all the singles in my practice tell me they are dissatisfied with the people they meet in bars and clubs," Dr. Joan Cross, who has a large suburban practice in Dallas, says. "The problem I keep hearing is not so much that singles have trouble meeting people, but meeting people of quality. At the same time, I do know that people of substance occasionally go to the singles bars. But something must happen that twists and warps the kind of social interaction that takes place, so that the only goal is a quick sexual encounter."

According to Dr. William Tooley, however, the bars themselves attract certain types of individuals who are by nature narcissistic and superficial, who will be likely to judge people on their external appearances, type of dress and ability to engage in cutting repartee. Dr. Tooley maintains that the *raison d'être* for the singles clubs and bars—dating and mating—endows them with a distinctly feverish ambience which distorts all social interchanges likely to take place. "The best place for singles to meet each other is through mutually enjoyable activities, such as special interest groups, sports, hobbies, leisure pursuits and community service work," he says. "Then, if a relationship does begin, it grows naturally out of common interests and shared experiences and stands a chance to blossom into a healthier interchange."

Studies do show that bars and discos are the least favored

places for singles to meet each other—despite the popularity of movies like *Saturday Night Fever* and *Urban Cowboy* that depict true love blossoming amid the bands, beer mugs and electric broncos of discos. A study conducted by the University of Texas at Dallas on 1,000 singles found that bars and discos were placed well down on the list of preferred ways of meeting—long after dates arranged through friends, social groups, parties and the workplace.

"Nobody ever seems to meet people they've had long-lasting relationships with in singles bars," observes Sharon Lyons, publisher of *First Person Singular,* a monthly tabloid for singles in the Dallas area. Once a single woman herself living in a suburb north of Dallas, she had initiated that study with the University of Texas. She went on to say, "But still the dream, or the hope, that you will meet someone in that setting persists."

For singles living on the predominantly married streets of the suburban communities, there are few other practical options. The light issuing from that beckoning bar may be too tantalizing to ignore. Single suburban women often awaken the next morning only to discover that illusion has given them the slip once again.

New Options

One fortunate solution to the problem of meeting single men and women in a healthier atmosphere has been suburban church and community-group singles organizations. These have begun to appear increasingly, as evidenced by the growing number of churches that list singles nights on their outdoor announcement boards, in the notices for singles events appearing in community newspapers and heard over the air on local radio stations.

One of the most popular and successful of these groups is

the Westport Unitarian Singles Group located in affluent Westport, Connecticut. Thought to be the largest such group sponsored by the Unitarian churches in America, this one was initiated five years ago by Stephen Coiné, a silver-haired divorced businessman, then a board member of the church, who had perceived an unmet community need. Within the last five years the group has blossomed from twelve individuals to over 3,000 members, drawing its population from Connecticut, Westchester and Nassau counties in New York, and Bergen County in New Jersey. Today the group includes singles, divorced and widowed people ranging in age from the early twenties to the late sixties. It no longer has an official affiliation with the church, other than its use as a meeting facility. Membership is $10 a year, entitling single men and women to the monthly newsletter, reduced rates for meetings, parties and group outings. Groups are also divided by age into those over and under 35.

Despite descriptions of the organization, I still had little understanding of what had made this particular group work when so many others like it in other suburbs had failed. "What is the secret of your organization's success?" I asked Steve Coiné one hot July night as we stood on the crowded terrace of the church's central entrance amid several hundred people. He answered that the meetings are carefully engineered to enable people to meet each other in a low-key, nonthreatening way. The organization operates on a highly professional basis: volunteer group leaders, for instance, first have to pass through a series of training sessions with a professional psychologist before they are allowed to lead a discussion; other volunteers who help with office work and travel arrangements are also expected to perform with a high degree of commitment. "Our aim was to operate this with sensitivity to the many needs that single people have. That includes companionship as well as the opportunity to date. And by running this in a careful way, we have continued to attract an intelligent, discerning membership. We didn't want the group to get a reputation as another careless pickup place, but rather as an organization where people could come and feel comfortable about meeting each other, could even use it as a way to meet others of the same sex with whom they could be friends."

The next two nights of observation provided me with many insights. Evening meetings started at 7:30 with an informal opportunity for men and women to talk with each other before dividing up into various discussion groups. The first night I arrived at the church during a heavy downpour, with the ominous crackling of a summer thunderstorm, only to discover that the large parking lot outside the church was already filled with cars. I ran through the rain and into the church meeting hall where dozens of people were drinking iced tea, smoking, talking and laughing. Many of them, I noticed, were still arranged in sex-segregated groups, much as in the singles bars. So far, I could see little difference.

Before long I was talking to a young attractive woman wearing a hot pink blouse and white slacks standing near one of the refreshment tables. "I come here often, ever since my divorce," she said. "This is a wonderful way to meet people, but not feel under some pressure to go to bed with them. I've made some wonderful women friends too. The real key, though, is the loosening-up process that occurs in the discussion group. After listening the first few times, you begin to talk yourself. And inevitably you begin to make decisions about the people around you. If you like what they said, or who they are, you don't feel uneasy about talking with them afterward. If you don't like what they said, you know you don't have to bother with them later."

Another woman I was introduced to a few minutes later, who had been a member of the group for several years, described her experiences: "It can be compared to a peacock who wants to display his plumes to a potential mate—you can show whatever you want to about yourself in the discussion group. If you're feeling sad or depressed about your single status, you can express that. Or if you are feeling pretty good about yourself, you can talk about that too. It's a chance to be honest with yourself and others about who you are, which is exactly the opposite of what takes place in the singles bars."

"And unlike the bars, it gives those people who are not the most beautiful an even chance," said the woman standing next to my acquaintance. "The point is that in the singles bars, all you can do is judge someone by their face, their clothes, their figure and dance steps. That's a hell of a basis on which to try to start a relationship. Here at least you get some inkling of what the inner person is really like."

The discussion group I was assigned to that night was located in one of the church's Sunday school classrooms, decorated with children's art and paintings. As we shuffled through the tiny classroom carrying our folded chairs, I could not help but muse on the irony of our topic, "How do you feel about being single for the rest of your life?" in such a traditionally child-centered setting. The session began with each member of the twenty-eight-member group introducing himself and giving a brief description of his or her feelings about singleness. I introduced myself as a writer-observer. "But are you single?" a dark-haired woman in an orange dress asked me curiously.

"No, I'm not," I replied.

"That's too bad," said a tall man on the other side of the room, and the rest of the group laughed at his apparent disappointment.

But at the same time, a woman sitting closer to me said in a loud, chilling voice, "You have my deepest sympathies."

Later, after discussing the ambivalence many members of the group had about being single, we disbanded, only to reassemble along with the rest of the membership in the large meeting hall on the first floor of the church. This time, the timid groups of young women who had been standing apart at the beginning of the meeting were no longer visible, obviously having been dispersed by the discussion groups and aided by the cold white wine offered at the refreshment tables. The men and women were standing in various arrangements of twos, threes, fours and fives, engaged in heated debate or animated conversation about their hopes, fears, joys. Laughter, loud talk, excitement and a genuine sense of friendliness pervaded the room. Some of the conversants, I noticed, were simply good friends, enjoying a hearty interchange with others like themselves in a setting that was positive and conducive to friendship as well as sexual overtures.

As I wandered through the hall and talked with some of the people in my group, I began to understand what the woman I had spoken with at the beginning of the evening had meant. By this time, I, too, had formed opinions about the various individuals in my group. A sifting-out process had taken place for me, as well as for the others in my group. The rapid growth of the membership here was no coincidence.

One comment, made by the woman in the orange dress who had first spoken to me in my discussion group, lingers in my mind: "I've lived here in Fairfield County for the past three years and for two of these years I don't think I went out more than twice. But since I've joined this group I've been dating frequently. Nothing serious, just lots of good times with other single men and women, other people like me who live alone in what is still a married, child-oriented community."

Of course many single women living in the suburbs do have married friends with whom they socialize and exchange confidences. Almost universally, however, single women have told me that their closest friends are those who, like themselves, are still single—that almost inevitably a barrier springs up between those who are married and those who are not. Is it jealousy? Pride? Fear? The fact that there is a different set of concerns? Or is it something deeper in the human psyche, something stretching far back before rationality, back into our primal consciousness, what Jung called the collective unconscious? The power of fantasy, or a primitive fascination with and simultaneous horror of the glittering snake and his forbidden fruit? Is it our sexual histories, after all, which fragment women, even when they live side by side in a traditional neighborhood setting, even when in this age of improved education and mass media, women are becoming increasingly aware that there are probably more similarities between them than differences?

It is another state, another summer night and the singles bar in Hackensack, New Jersey, is teeming with young men and women. As I enter the long, dimly lit bar, I feel the silent gaze of fifty sets of male eyes upon me, and suddenly a rush of anxiety comes over me. Why are you so nervous? I ask myself, and walk down the long corridor opposite the bar to the central room. It is apparent from my first glimpse at this bar that the rules are different here. This is a more aggressive meeting place than other suburban bars I have attended, a no-nonsense pickup place with colored lights that shed cones of pink, vermilion and indigo upon the customers and give them the same distorted look as if they were in a disco. It is immediately apparent as I walk down the bar corridor that women do not sit at this bar unattended—unless, of course, they are obviously looking for a man. Instead, the more discreet women congregate at tables in small groups in the central room.

Feeling extraordinarily self-conscious because I have entered the bar without even a female friend, I ask a group of three young women if I may join them. They acquiesce suspiciously, but then listen with growing interest and even delight as I explain my purpose for being there. A faint smile lights up the face of the oldest of the three women, who tells me that she is the only one of her companions—the three women are sisters—who is unmarried. "I used to be married, but it just didn't work out. If you're married, men begin to feel that they own you after a while, and that you can't do anything without their permission. I'm living with someone now, but there's no way that I'm ready to get married again. There's too much fun to be had in life for that."

"But the other two of you are married?"

"Yes, and we both have kids," says the woman to my right with a bitter laugh. "If our husbands ever knew we'd come to a place like this tonight, they'd probably kill us. But this is our night out together. We take an exercise class together on Wednesdays and go out for a bite to eat afterward."

"It gives us a chance to get away from the kids and the house for a while and some time to talk together," the youngest woman says, as she munches on a roast beef sandwich and sips a Scotch on the rocks. "It kind of gets to you after a while, being home and feeling like a drudge all the time."

"Last week, after our exercise class we started riding around here looking for a place to eat, and you know where we ended up?" the woman to my right asks. "At a Dairy Queen! A *Dairy* Queen, for God's sake!"

"I'm not allowed in bars, because my husband says there's still a stigma attached to women who frequent them," says the youngest sister softly, "but I figure if it's good enough for my husband, why not for me, too?"

The woman to my right continues, "Can you imagine that! A Dairy Queen is no place for three grown women to eat dinner together just because that's about the only place that's open, or because we're so afraid of our husbands we don't dare venture into a place like this. So this week, we thought we'd give a place like this a try. Have a little fun, not look for trouble or anything, but just see what we've been missing."

Suddenly the conversation is interrupted; the cocktail waitress has appeared at the head of the table. "Excuse me, ladies," she says, "but the gentleman sitting at the back of the room is a friend of the owner and he says he would like to buy you all a drink on the house. Is that okay with you?"

The three women look momentarily surprised. "Sure," says the divorced sister pleasantly and then turns around to try to identify the man. She nods once in his direction, then turns back to the waitress. "Make mine a Vodka Collins."

The other two women and I give the waitress our orders. She leaves as abruptly as she appeared.

"Gee, I wonder why he did that," the youngest sister says, twisting her napkin with obvious discomfort. The woman sitting next to me says nothing, but drums her fingers on the table and murmurs something softly under her breath. The divorcée smiles, explaining that this is simply part of the singles bar scene. "Wonder which one of us he likes best," she says.

Someone turns the music that has been playing over the

speakers up loud. The cocktail waitress returns, serves the drinks around and then asks if there will be anything else.

"No, thanks," says the divorced woman brightly, "but please tell the gentleman thank you for us."

The three women are silent as they start the next round of drinks. "Do you think you'll come back here again next Wednesday night?" I ask the woman at my right.

She turns to me with an insouciant air. "I guess we will. This place looks like it could really be fun. It certainly beats housework and the Dairy Queen. Maybe the young single men and women are right. Why should they get married when they could get anything they want for free today?"

Sexual Suspicion

The myth that the single woman has a happier existence and a richer sex life than her wedded sister troubles the married population of the suburbs, keeping them far apart from their single neighbors. The married woman worries that the single woman is somehow more dynamic. Who is this single woman? the married childbearing woman asks herself. Why does she live in the suburbs, on my block, in the first place? Why couldn't a nice normal family have moved in here instead, one with other children for mine to play with? Does she have an interesting job? Why is she so seldom around? Does she have an exciting social life? Or is she a deviant, unable to form a stable relationship with a member of the opposite sex, unable to make a commitment to matrimony—or to the creation of the next generation?

It is as if the traditional suburban woman is wearing bifocals when she thinks about her single or childless neighbor, constantly shifting her vision from one set of values to another in an attempt to understand who she really is. Sexuality and its well-publicized association with the singles society have made social interchange between the singles and marrieds far more awkward than it was years ago, when the single person was considered a safe, if odd, member of the American small town. Today's single or childless woman of the suburbs is a different specimen altogether, one who often appears alluring in her anonymity.

Therapist Lyn Wabrek, co-director of the Sex Therapy Program at Hartford Hospital who counsels many married women living in suburban Connecticut, illustrates how that awkwardness often begins: "If a young single or childless woman is mowing her lawn on the weekend and the next-door male neighbor is doing the same thing, and they stop to chat, it is only natural that the man's wife may begin to feel anxious because the young single or childless woman is seen as one who is unencumbered, carefree, a symbolic sexual threat. Singleness gets equated with sexual availability in our culture and women reflexively react to it as a personal threat."

Many single women I spoke with in the suburbs are painfully conscious of their status and comment on the marked indifference, even outright hostility they encounter when they first move there. "The day I moved in, there was a flurry of friendliness from my neighbors," recalls a single woman from Northbrook, Illinois, who, after renting for years, finally purchased her own home. "One of my woman neighbors even came over with a batch of cookies. 'I hope you and your family will like these,' she said. But when I explained to her that I had neither a husband nor kids, that I was, in fact, single, her whole attitude changed. 'Well, enjoy them anyway,' she said abruptly before she went out the back door. I've hardly seen her since and that was three years ago."

Another single young woman living in Upper Arlington, Ohio, was planting a flower garden in her small back yard one summer afternoon and stopped to say hello to her neighbor, only to be told that her outdoor outfits were causing a stir in the neighborhood. "You know, you really should be more careful about wearing those short shorts and halters out here while you're gardening," her female neighbor said tersely. "It's bad enough that you're single, but your clothes suggest even more. Seems to me you'd want to be more careful about the people you live near."

Childless Women

Many married but childless women seem to fare little better in the suburban neighborhoods. Some have come to regard their homes as little more than large city apartments against a backdrop of shrubbery, so little do they relate to the suburban community around them.

A married childless woman living in Sepulvedera, near Los Angeles, described her peculiar sense of alienation: "Virtually all our friends live in the city and that's where we spend a great deal of our time. The fact is that I really don't like living in the suburbs, but I do like the idea of owning a home. Maybe I would feel differently if I were involved in the community, but without kids, there's no impetus to meet people living here, no real reasons for me to get involved."

Another childless woman, a free-lance writer living in Irvington, New York, commented on the decidedly frosty reception she and her husband received when they rented a home that had previously been occupied by a couple with young chidren: "You could see there was a distinct sense of disappointment when our neighbors found out that we had no children. It's as if we don't exist here in the community because we don't own our home and don't have children. Even casual acquaintances I meet in the community blithely assume that I have kids. When I tell them I don't, there's an obvious drawing back."

The woman told me that there are other ways that she was excluded from community life. One day she called the local department of recreation to find out where and when exercise classes were being offered in the community and was informed that such classes did exist. However, the classes were announced each season in a newsletter sent home through the public schools with the children. "But I don't have any children, let alone any who are in school," she explained. "Please, can't you send me the newsletter anyway?" She was then curtly informed that in order to be placed on the mailing list, she would have to make a trip to the high school to fill out a special request form.

Such a community attitude is not really that surprising, social scientists and therapists say who have studied the problems of childless women. As Caryl Rivers, Rosalind Barnett and Grace Baruch have written, "The woman who cannot have children is pitied, thought to be shorn of the chance for happiness. The woman who chooses not to have children receives a harsher verdict. She is *unnatural.*"

Ann Ulmschneider, program director for the National Alliance for Optional Parenthood, an educational group supporting the concept of informed parenthood, attributes the disapproval often directed toward the childfree woman to a powerful remnant of the belief that motherhood should still be the center of a woman's existence. "I think there is probably greater acceptance now than there was in the 1950s and 1960s for voluntary childlessness, but there is still the subtle belief that a woman cannot really be fulfilled without being a mother—that somehow she is either selfish or self-absorbed if she chooses not to have children. For the suburban woman without children it is probably more difficult than for those living in the cities, where the singles life-style has always been more acceptable."

Even in suburban apartment houses and condominium complexes where there is, presumably, a more urban atmosphere than on the residential streets with single-family homes, there is a sharp division between those who have children and those who are childless or single. An attractive 40-year-old elementary school teacher living in Mill Valley, California, who had lived in San Francisco for a decade before moving to Marin County, told me that after living in the same town house for the last seven years, most of her friends are single or without children. "There's still a certain amount of segregation that happens to single women in the suburbs. Most of the people who live in this complex are married and very few of them have much to do with me."

A 28-year-old childless married woman living in a single-dwelling home in Rutherford, New Jersey, described the attitude betwen her neighbors and herself as even more hostile: "There's no doubt that they look upon us as crazy because we've had this house for over three years and still show no signs of having kids. And we're seldom around—except to work in the garden. We also keep strange hours, especially compared to our neighbors, most of whom spend Friday and Saturday nights at home watching television. To me, the women on my block are like the Stepford wives. And to them, I guess we seem really off the normal curve. To this day, I only talk to one of my neighbors."

Then there was the almost paranoid feeling expressed by one woman, an office manager for an insurance company, living in a basement apartment in Naperville, Illinois, which she rented from a middle-aged couple living in the same house. "There's always a certain amount of anxiety I feel about bringing a friend back here or even staying out all night. Nobody says anything directly to me, but I have the distinct feeling that my landlady is keeping strict tabs on my comings and goings and has made some pretty negative statements about the kind of life I lead to the neighbors. One Sunday afternoon as I was leaving the house, a neighbor stopped me near my car. 'Out pretty late last night, weren't you?' she asked me. I just smiled at her, but inside I was fuming."

While fantasies about the carefree life led by the single and childless threaten the married population of suburbia from time to time, they are often little more than that—idle projections spun out of unmet needs and frustrations. This was dramatically illustrated by the married women who visited the Hackensack singles bar out of their own unhappiness and curiosity. As Lyn Wabrek reminds us, the idea that singles are somehow sexier or happier than those who are married tells us just as much about the perceiver as the perceived: "I personally think that the fantasies come from the fear that the single or childless woman living in the community will do something so terrific that the married, child-oriented woman will lose her man. The problem is that we've been brought up to regard the other woman as competition for so long that we don't realize how much we probably have in common with her. The woman has got to talk to her single or childless neighbor. She's got to find out whether that neighbor really does it with everybody. She's got to take some of her myths and try to put them into perspective along with some good information."

While other therapists agree with this interpretation and maintain that those who are happily married and content with their own lives are less likely to feel threatened, the myth of the new sexuality still seems to rankle many couples. And the symptoms of doubt about sexual prowess within the married state are pervasive throughout our society. Our passionate attitude toward homosexuality is another good example of our collective insecurity.

Let's consider the murderous anger frequently directed at a schoolteacher when a suburban parent discovers that he is homosexual. Even worse, let us think about what happens when suburban men and women find out that a pair of lesbians are living together in their neighborhood. Often the reaction to them is unjustifiably emotional, our notion of them totally different from the way those individuals actually conduct their private lives. (Many have been married and have children.) Such an attitude was dramatically illustrated by an incident that occurred in Redwood City, where two lesbians were made to feel so uncomfortable by their neighbors that they finally left San Mateo County.

The two women had lived quietly together for several years without incident until one day a coworker questioned one of the women about her sexual status. The woman, a garage mechanic, finally admitted her status to her fellow employee. Before long, she began to experience harassment on the job. One of her coworkers began to follow her home and openly taunt her in the neighborhood about her lesbianism. After considerable public embarrassment, the couple decided to move out of the area. But it was too late. One night the mechanic was physically assaulted on the street.

"It's much safer and smarter to 'go underground' in the suburbs if you are a lesbian than to openly acknowledge it," the woman told me with some bitterness six months later. "In the city, people don't care so much about who you are or what your sexual preferences might be. But in the suburbs you are in for trouble unless you can be very discreet. Suburban men and women get very upset because they feel that if you are a homosexual you represent a challenge to their life-style."

In suburban Dallas, another lesbian couple talked frankly about their love for each other, but admitted they were reluctant to acknowledge the true relationship in the community in which they lived. One of the women, in her early forties, told how she had finally spoken out about her homosexuality in the workplace, although she was loath to do so in her neighborhood. "As lesbians we are in a very precarious position in this society. We can still lose our jobs and our children and get kicked out of our apartments. We tend to be very quiet because, despite all the publicity about gay rights, the community pressures against us are enormous. It's difficult to 'come out' about being a lesbian if you think you might lose your child."

But whatever form sexual expression takes, whether it be homosexuality or extramarital heterosexuality, nontraditional sexuality is almost always perceived as threatening to the married state. This attitude, buried deep within our collective unconscious and denied by liberals, seems to have become a national characteristic.

According to sociologist Sally Ridgeway, assistant professor at Adelphi University's Department of Sociology and the Institute of Suburban Studies, it is the myth surrounding the new sexuality and the myth of what the suburbs should be that have come into sharpest conflict in contemporary America. Adults often project their own negative fantasies about sexuality upon teenage children and attempt to restrict their social activities. Dr. Ridgeway maintains that those same dynamics are often operative in a community's behavior toward the single and childless woman of the suburbs. "What society tends to do is project a kind of carefree adolescence upon the singles and childless. Subconsciously we feel that we've either got to keep them segregated because they are too old to live at home, or we've got to isolate them because we don't want them living too close to us, the feeling being somehow they are contagious, and their sexuality is contagious."

When, however, a suburban community begins to age, when the homes that were new a generation ago are now largely occupied by older couples whose children are grown, when the community begins to feel a loss of revenue from an eroding tax base and owners decide to rent out or sell their homes to singles or new couples, there is often considerable community resistance. The reason behind such reactions, says Dr. Ridgeway, is that community residents are still adhering to the old suburban myth: that the suburbs were designed solely for the two-adult nuclear family with children and that the inclusion of other population groups in the same neighborhood will violate a time-honored way of life, the American dream.

Yet change is unavoidable as the suburbs age and as new social trends make an inevitable impact on the middle landscape. An unprecedented 41 million Americans will enter their thirties, the watershed years for marriage, home purchase and childrearing, in the 1980s. With an extended depression in the building industry, the high interest rates on home mortgages and the lack of apartment space in the suburbs, will come an inexorable demand for the rental of single-family homes by the young, single and childless population of our country in the last years of the century—the end of an era in which the suburbs were regarded as child-centered sanctuaries.

It is precisely in that period, before a community is able to manage that change, to adjust its vision to the new social realities, that a militant attitude among traditional residents is most likely to surface.

Housing Changes

Indeed we seem to be entering such a volatile period today, as the suburbs evolve into mature communities. A look at the recent litigation involving exclusionary zoning ordinances in some suburbs shows the pervasiveness of such resistance, and how it is often manifested in legal action. In 1974, for instance, the town of Belle Terre, Long Island, tried to prevent a family from renting their home to a group of college students on the basis that the students did not legally constitute a "family." The fight went all the way to the United States Supreme court, where the town won the right to prohibit more than two unrelated individuals from living together in a single-dwelling home because, it was judged, they might disrupt the community values indigenous to Belle Terre. Justice Douglas wrote in that landmark decision: "It is said that the Belle Terre ordinance reeks with an animosity to unmarried couples who live together. There is no evidence to support it; and the provision of the ordinance bringing within the definition of a 'family' two unmarried people belies the charge. . . . A quiet place where yards are wide, people few, and motor vehicles restricted are legitimate guidelines in a land-use project addressed to family needs. . . . The public power is not confined to elimination of filth, stench and unhealthy places. It is ample to lay out zones where family values, youth values and the blessings of quiet seclusion and clear air make the area a sanctuary for people."

Yet within the next six years, two others states had grappled with this problem within their own suburban communities so long that their state supreme courts finally overruled that decision. The first case challenging the constitutionality of the Belle Terre decision occurred in Plainfield, New Jersey, in 1979 in *State* v. *Baker*. In that suit, the state supreme court found that the mere presence of a group of unrelated people living in a residential community in no way prevented neighbors from preserving a traditional family life and that exclusionary zoning ordinances actually violated the equal-protection clause of the constitution. The second case overruling the Belle Terre decision was decided in 1980 in *City of Santa Barbara* v. *Adamson* in which the court asked: "Is another assumption behind the rule perhaps that groups of unrelated persons hazard an immoral environment for families with children? That goal would not be legitimate."

Still more recently, New York's Long Island communities have witnessed another go-around on exclusionary zoning, involving the town of Oyster Bay. The issue concerns the rental of a private home to four single men (three of whom, incidentally, grew up in the community), and the municipality's resistance. At this writing, the judgment has not yet been rendered, but the case does point up the persistence of suburban antipathy to the nontraditional family. Curiously, the town of Oyster Bay does make an exception to its own definition of "family." Although the community clearly excludes all people unrelated by blood, marriage or adoption from that definition, it does permit any two unrelated individuals over the age of 62 to live together in a residential neighborhood without penalty. The plaintiff's attorneys for *McMinn* v. *Town of Oyster Bay*, Gerald P. Halpern and Winifred Pasternack, contend that there are no rational grounds for such a distinction, and that such an ordinance is based upon powerful subconscious communal biases. "The town ordinance as it stands now is emotional and irrational and presumably is based on a fear of having the so-called 'groupers' living in the community of Oyster Bay," Ms. Pasternack says. "The assumption is that singles will be noisy, boisterous and will indulge in wild, sexy behavior. The ordinance purposefully makes exception for those over 62. Apparently older citizens are not considered sexy, and are therefore not much of a threat."

But what does it really matter if a suburban home is rented, or bought by a group of single or unrelated people, as long as the property is well maintained? As long as it provides additional income to an individual or couple who can no longer afford to sustain such a home? Such practices may even improve the property, preventing it from being neglected by an impecunious owner. This issue was examined by sociologists Michael Gutowski and Tracey Feild of the Urban Institute in their study *The Graying of Suburbia*. Addressing the fact that by 1976 there were over 4.5 million households headed by people over the age of 65 living in the nation's suburbs, and that there were another 3 million household heads approaching old age, who had, in all likelihood, neither the funds nor the energy to maintain their homes in the suburbs, Drs. Gutowski and Feild proposed several tax annuity schemes whereby elderly people would either be able to transfer title of their homes to banks or to younger individuals who would then purchase the homes and forestall declining property values.

In spite of the fact that the American individual and family are undergoing a rapid metamorphosis, the frequent response to such proposals in many suburban communities is still overwhelmingly negative. Keep the exclusionary zoning laws and traditional real estate practices intact, many towns insist, and we will be sure to keep the neighborhoods healthy, normal, traditionally family-oriented enclaves. But is this so, given the pressing needs of a young, adult, home-hungry generation, a graying suburban constituency and the vast tracts of land still available in the nonmetropolitan parts of our country? I believe that when a community begins to dictate the private lives of its residents, it is spelling out the shape of its own inevitable death.

Money is a primary factor in the single and childless woman's decision to live in the suburbs—one at least as important as her concerns about climate, suburban ambience and urban crime, which have also driven her from the central cities. It might seem that because the single woman is unencumbered by household and child-related responsibilities, she has the greatest amount of flexibility in her choice about where to live. And to a certain degree that is true: she is free; she can move to the Sunbelt, a small town or any major city in quest of a good job without the difficulties encountered by her married, childbearing sisters. But even when she does obtain that coveted position in a large city, the problem of where to live remains. Most of the nation's big cities have become progressively divided into high-rise living zones for the very rich or the very poor. The question for many single women is whether she should live in the city where the social opportunities may be richer but where apartment space may be unduly expensive, or whether she should choose a suburban apartment which will be cheaper and may have more amenities.

The answer—according to recent Census Bureau data about population patterns among youth, the unmarried and the childless—is that she has increasingly chosen the suburbs. In the past decade, she has moved with unprecedented speed out of the central cities, into the suburbs and the non-metropolitan areas beyond, where jobs are beginning to appear and where the living conditions are often better and cheaper.

Census Bureau figures indicate that while single women earn more money than women with husbands, the median income of the single woman today is still lamentably low. The average single woman earned a median income of only $5,059 in 1979, compared to her married sister who earned $3,898; but in 1979, the median income for married couples in the United States was $21,503—more than four times that of the single woman. This means that in order to rent an apartment in the central city, a single woman must share space with several women, face escalating rents, live in cramped quarters or in undesirable and unsafe neighborhoods.

If she lives in the suburbs, however, she is likely to have more space, better surroundings and easier access to leisure activities. And if she has been brought up in the suburbs—as so many young women of the baby boom generation have been—she may not be willing to trade in lifelong patterns for the frenzied pace of city life. She may feel that the suburbs are all she knows. "The city scares me with its rhythms," said a woman in Burlingame, California, like many other second-generation suburban females I have interviewed. "If and when I go to the city, it is for a temporary taste of excitement. But my preference is definitely for the suburbs. I feel at home here. To me the city is foreign, a vast, uncaring and dangerous wilderness."

Typically, when the single, second-generation suburban woman establishes a home for herself in the middle landscape, she is likely to remain there, because she sees the suburbs as an environment she can control. "Sometimes," admits a 39-year-old woman from Highland Park, Illinois, "it is just plain deadly here in terms of social opportunities, but still I wouldn't trade the homey atmosphere of the suburbs for a minute. I hated the city when I lived there. There's something more wholesome, more knowable about living here."

Occasionally the distaste for city life felt by single women is so strong that it takes an exaggerated form, even becoming a phobia. Agoraphobia, for instance, is a well-known syndrome familiar to counselors, therapists and sociologists. Many suburban women perceive the metropolis as a veritable pit of human depravity and crime, a place where their lives may be in constant danger, and as a result refuse to venture there at all. A surprising number of second-generation suburban women have never visited the city at all, or at most have gone there only occasionally. Some of them have unpleasant experiences which only reinforce their initial fears. "But more often than not, it is their body language that gives them away, sending out signals to others on the street that they are frightened newcomers and making them a sure mark for muggers and pickpockets," says Dr. Sally Ridgeway. "Women who have that much antipathy for city life set themselves up for trouble."

Usually single suburban women who choose the suburbs over the city couch their preference in terms of positive characteristics: often they tell me that the suburbs are more aesthetically pleasing to them than the city. A single woman from Woodside who commutes to work in San Francisco put it this way: "I hate the drive, but it's still worth it to me to come back here every night. If I lived in the city, I'd be squeezed into some tiny, expensive closet because that would be all I could afford. I would miss seeing the quail on my front lawn in the early morning, the dew on the grass and the coming of spring."

Compounding those considerations is the new social legitimacy of the single life. I think of a license plate I glimpsed on the back of one sports car in the parking lot outside a Stamford, Connecticut, condominium complex. MYSELF it said in bold white letters, bespeaking the pride of its owner in his singular marital status. And I think of the comments made by countless single women interviewed for this book, who have repeatedly told me they no longer consider marriage and family essential ingredients in their lives. Despite the way these women were raised—and most were still growing up in the late fifties and sixties at a time when marriage and childbearing were considered the only avenues for women— most have accommodated well to singlehood.

With similar faith and assurance in themselves, the childless couples of our era have also journeyed to the middle landscape. "We moved out simply because we could not afford to buy a condominium in the city," says one childless woman from Teaneck, New Jersey. "I hate to commute, but this was the only way we could sensibly invest our money and still have lots of room to spread out in."

Other childless couples maintain that the suburban house, while an important financial asset, is only secondary to a way of life they have come to enjoy. One married, childless woman living in San Rafael, California, explained: "The house is nice and it does mean that nobody can ever say, 'You can't live here anymore,' But to me the suburbs represent something else far more important. More than the city or the country, it reminds me that while we live in a modern technological world, we are still part of nature. Symbolically the suburbs tell us that we must look backward and forward at the same time if mankind is to endure."

It is that same recognition, the thirst for a more natural, leisured existence, that has always attracted families to the suburbs. It is the new breed of single and childless women, who have postponed or rejected matrimony and motherhood for educations and careers, who now stand between the traditionally dependent female population of yesterday and the independent women of the future who foreshadow the populations that will frequent the middle landscape in the years to come. These women, the dauntless new women of our postindustrial society, blending the eternal feminine with the nuclear age feminist, are changing the meaning of America.

7

Charity Begins at Home: The New Volunteer

People say, "You're a fool for doing something for nothing," but I just smile when I hear them talk. I'm not the type to sit by and watch things fall apart.

A Girl Scout leader from Columbus, Ohio

The female volunteer is not given as much respect as the working woman. Take the example of housework. If you don't do the laundry because you're going to work every day, does it matter? But if you don't do the laundry because you are going to your volunteer responsibility, your husband and family may view it differently. That's the kind of subtle thing that happens because you're a volunteer, and not "really" working.

A member of the Junior League of Evanston, Illinois

THE WOMAN IN THE BURLINGAME, CALIFORNIA, office of the American Cancer Society was shocked at what she heard on the other end of the phone. It had been just another routine call, a request for volunteer help to collect money for a fund-raising drive, but the reply had been stinging, so memorable that Francine had repeated it to her colleagues for weeks afterward.

"You're asking me to volunteer to collect money?" the woman on the other end of the phone had said, repeating in a monotone Francine's usual request for help.

"That's right."

The woman drew in her breath sharply, then retorted: "Why don't you ask some of the men?"

"The men?" said Francine, still not comprehending.

"Why not ask some of the *men* to volunteer to collect money for you? Don't get me wrong, I'm all for your cause. I do send money ever year. But stop asking women to volunteer. Women's lives are so full these days already. Why are you preying on us? Our time is worth money too, you know. And so is our energy. I'm not doing any more volunteering unless it's for a political organization to advance women's causes."

"But—"

"Thank you, good-bye."

The woman's voice sounded crisp, almost cheerful, as she hung up the phone. Must have been some kind of nut, Francine concluded. You get them every so often. Statistically it was bound to happen. A feminist. A depressed housewife. Or perhaps someone who just got divorced.

But the woman on the other end of the phone did not fit any of those descriptions. She is, in reality, a happily married 38-year-old Redwood City mother of two who holds a demanding full-time teaching job in the public school system. She is also, as she described herself, a supermom—an energetic, guilt-ridden mother who tries to satisfy the demands of her job and those of her family in accordance with her own high standards. Hers is a regimen that leaves her chronically tired by the end of the week, too stressed to take on volunteer duties. "What I really need at this stage in my life is a little time for myself. How can you think about helping others when your own house isn't in order?"

* * *

Three thousand miles away, 36-year-old Kathy McKnight of Greenwich, Connecticut, measures out the hours of her week with equal precision and within a similarly tight time frame. There are never enough hours in the day or week, it seems, to accomplish everything she has planned to do. At the top of her priorities are her husband, her daughter and her home. Then there are her duties as Girl Scout leader, Sunday school teacher and first vice-president of the Riverside Elementary School PTA—commitments which require phone calls, school appearances and nighttime board meetings. Finally there is the work for the Junior League of Greenwich, where she is vice-president of communications and a management skills trainer.

Kathy McKnight does not have to work out of financial necessity. For her, volunteerism is a central life endeavor that requires a rigorous personal commitment, but which gives back as much as she has donated. Through participation in such long-range League projects as the creation of a Youth Shelter, the development of a community Parental Information Exchange newsletter and the establishment of the League's first Community Advisory Board, she feels she has grown far more than she would have in most paid positions. And she is grateful to the Junior League for the wide range of experiences she has had in the community.

"The things I've seen and had the chance to do probably couldn't be matched in most jobs," Kathy McKnight tells a group of League officers one glistening April morning in the League headquarters on Maple Avenue. "The Junior League has given me professional leadership and management training and the opportunity to put it into practice here in a meaningful way, a way that has made an impact upon our community." Then, thoughtfully, she adds: "It's also a way of keeping my skills sharp and up-to-date, just in case I do go back to work someday."

For 47-year-old Rosemary Petitipas of Chappaqua, New York, working as a volunteer for the Westchester County

Division of the New York Hospital, Cornell Medical Center, was a crystallizing life experience. She had never worked with psychiatric in-patients before, and she considered the volunteer opportunity a necessary step in her search for a career—a second career, to be more accurate, one that followed marriage and children. Although she had recently declared psychology as her major at Manhattanville College, she still had doubts about the wisdom of her choice. Was what she was learning in school applicable to real-life psychiatric practice? Would working with such patients be gratifying for her?

Armed with little more than her doubts and fears, Rosemary Petitipas pledged her services to Ann Eisner, director of the Volunteer Department at the New York Hospital, as an aide—a commitment she has kept for the last three years while completing her degree. "I had heard all kinds of stories about working in a psychiatric hospital, but none of them were true," she said, just two weeks before receiving her B.S. "I ended up learning many valuable things here I hadn't ever anticipated, and applied many of them to my work in school. Serving as a volunteer certainly answered my questions as to whether I could work with people with emotional problems or not. And I found I could, that being with psychiatric patients was not frightening and depressing at all. Now I plan to go on in this field as a counselor or a clinical social worker."

A new pragmatism, born of financial necessity, rising feminist consciousness and changing social expectations, characterizes today's suburban woman. And with that pragmatism has come a dramatic transformation in volunteerism. Once the *sine qua non* of suburbia, the volunteer effort has become an increasingly rarefied activity in the lives of many women, a carefully considered contribution, allocated as thoughtfully as money for the family food budget. The "lady bountiful" type of volunteer and the more plebeian scout, school and church group leader and mother have all but disappeared. They are being replaced by a more specialized and circumspect volunteer who may still be willing to give of herself, but in smaller and more goal-oriented increments than ever before.

No longer is today's suburban woman likely to devote a dozen hours to the local hospital as a "gray lady" or a "pink lady"; no longer is she always willing to head a twenty-five-member Girl Scout troop; no longer is she likely to be licking stamps or folding flyers for an organizational event. Today, like the Redwood City teacher, she may be so busy with her duties as a working mother and wife that she forgoes volunteer service altogether. Or like the Greenwich, Connecticut, Junior Leaguer who still sees volunteer work as a central life commitment, she may see it as a way to develop her personal skills. Or like the Chappaqua psychology major, she may choose her volunteer experience to validate and prepare for a career choice. If and when the suburban woman volunteers today, she wants to make sure it will further her personal or professional growth.

"The idea of the middle- and upper-middle-class woman, who had hours of free time to devote to all kinds of activities while her children were in school, has simply vanished," observes Kris Rees, a staff assistant at VOLUNTEER: The National Center for Citizen Involvement, a group which advocates America's volunteer activities. "There's a new attitude among volunteers today, a demand that what they're doing really fits in with their interests and aspirations. You can't expect volunteers to stuff envelopes anymore and hope to keep them around."

For they *won't* stay. Why, more and more women are asking themselves, should I volunteer when I could be paid for my services? And why, if I do choose to volunteer, shouldn't I gain something in return beyond the feeling of doing well for others? The drift of women from traditional volunteer roles in the schools, hospitals and community service organizations has been noted with justifiable alarm by organization leaders and philanthropic institutions. The Girl Scouts of the U.S.A. reported a 13 percent decline in their adult membership within the last decade. The National PTA witnessed a 33 percent decline in the participation of adult leaders from 1970 to 1980, and not all of that decline, PTA officials say, was the result of the shrinking birth rate. The League of Women Voters also observed the dwindling of its volunteers within the same years—from approximately 150,000 members in 1970 to 117,000 in 1980. And the National Board of the YWCA reports a 30 percent decrease in volunteer leadership over a similar time period.

A 1974 survey on volunteers conducted by ACTION, a federal agency coordinating government volunteer programs, states: "The most typical American volunteer in 1974 was a married white woman between ages 25 and 44 who held a college degree and was in the upper income bracket"—an apt description of the traditional middle-class suburban woman, who was then rapidly becoming a smaller portion of the volunteer sector. For in 1975 the number of women entering the work force exceeded the number of women still at home for the first time in our history. In the same year, suburban women began to join the work force in greater numbers than their urban and rural sisters. The inevitable result was a decline in certain types of traditional female volunteer service. As an article on volunteerism in the *New York Times* noted three years later: "The biggest drop, experienced volunteers say, is in the number of white, educated, middle-class women, who did the most volunteer work in the past. Some former women volunteers are now in school or working."

A national study of volunteer agencies, conducted by VOL-UNTEER in December 1979, indicates that while most volunteer clearinghouses had a stable supply of volunteers, a "significant minority" of those groups had begun to report difficulties finding volunteers. Among the factors the agencies blamed for their troubles were the impact of women returning to the labor force, inflation and the high cost of energy. While some of the recruitment difficulty was in urban and rural areas, the decline was most acutely felt in suburban communities, which traditionally provided the major voluntary organizations with a vast reservoir of educated middle-class women.

A veteran volunteer who serves on six community service

boards in the Columbus, Ohio, suburban area observes: "The young women today by and large sneer at volunteerism. It's sad because volunteerism is the stepping-stone in both social and economic terms to a better community. But few middle-class women see it that way today."

Often they question the validity of volunteer commitment as did a 38-year-old woman from Richardson, Texas. "Why should we continue to volunteer when society looks down on us for doing so? In a way, being a full-time volunteer has even less status than being a housewife. At least if you're a devoted wife and mother, you've got a good excuse for being unemployed. But if you introduce yourself as a volunteer, what's the rationale for working without recompense?"

A 59-year-old ex-schoolteacher from Lawrenceville, New Jersey, said: "I used to volunteer when my kids were small, but I wouldn't anymore. I think women have done most of the work in this world and volunteerism is just another way to get them to do more of it."

While many bitter feelings like these are often carefully hidden from public view, volunteer agencies have felt their sting. One volunteer clearinghouse that has noticed an abrupt change in its client population within the last five years is the Volunteer Action Council of Philadelphia, an agency serving nonprofit organizations in the suburbs as well as the inner city. In past years its principal clients were educated, affluent women. A study conducted by the Council found that in 1975, 59 percent of all women female volunteers were still traditional, white, middle- or upper-middle-class women; by 1980, however, over 70 percent of all female volunteers were nontraditional, lower income and semiskilled people. "What has happened is that the corporate manager's wife is no longer a major customer of the Council," agency director Felix Rimberg says. "She used to be a major customer fifteen or twenty years ago and she was in there for guilt, prestige, upward mobility, hubby or to keep herself occupied. But today hardly 5 percent of our clients are that type."

Another volunteer clearinghouse that has noted the disap-pearance of the traditional homemaker-volunteer is the Volunteer Bureau of San Mateo County, California, a coordinating and placement agency for volunteers in the suburban communities directly south of San Francisco. While the agency witnessed small decreases in its ranks between the mid-1970s and 1980, it has been the changing identity of the volunteers, rather than the decline in number that has been the most radical transformation. A 1979 study by that agency showed that the lowest percentage of volunteer participants now come from the 30 to 50-year-old category—the years when suburban homemakers were historically most active in volunteer organizations. "We've especially seen the disappearance of a lot of well-educated Caucasian women in the last five years," Loyce Haran, executive director, says. "They were very valuable because they used to take the leadership roles in the organization here. Now it's almost impossible to start an auxiliary here, and by auxiliary I mean any type of organization that has a fund-raising component."

To compensate for the loss of that population, the agency has looked increasingly to young single working women, to older people, to the disabled, and to short-term volunteer placements. What this changing constituency has meant for the Volunteer Bureau of San Mateo is increasing paperwork, planning and responsibility for the small professional staff. The pity of it all, Mrs. Haran laments, is that the suburban homemaker was providing a badly needed long-range commitment to social service agencies. "The one thing we do know is that the suburban homemaker still makes the best volunteer. When she was home she had the time and became very involved in what she was doing. Now, even though it is a small percentage of the volunteers we are placing, suburban homemakers are still excellent."

In Westchester County, the twenty-six League of Women Voters chapters in existence in 1973 began to contract, losing membership so rapidly that by 1981 they had combined to form twenty chapters. Today, despite a 14 percent decline in membership, the Leagues still serve a vital function in the county as monitors for local and county government and advocates for legislative reform. But like many other volunteer organizations anxious to attract the new breed of suburban women, the League now holds more nighttime meetings, assigns short-term tasks and has intensified its recruitment efforts. Even in affluent Westchester, the prime suburban county for the largest metropolitan complex in the nation, the socio-economic influences of the decade—finances, feminism and the high cost of fuel—have reshaped the woman volunteer.

"The obvious cause has been the effect of inflation, which made it necessary for women to enter the job market, but some of it is psychological too," says Nancy Craig, council president of the League of Women Voters of Westchester. "We are pretty much still in the 'now' generation of instant gratification. People are more hedonistic today than they were in the past and much less willing to give their talents and services for nothing." With candor, Nancy Craig tells of the community response to her assumption of the League council presidency—how people seemed both perplexed and annoyed at her decision to devote herself to a two-year League commitment without financial recompense. "People would stop me on the streets and the tennis courts and tell me they couldn't believe what I had decided to do. Even now, there's not a week that goes by when somebody doesn't say, 'It's just too bad it's not a salaried post.' I try to explain to them it really doesn't matter, because it's been challenging and fulfilling and can have a meaningful influence on public policy, which, in turn, does affect people's lives. But because there's no paycheck, people don't understand."

In Oak Park, Illinois, Iris Ruffins, executive director of the Lone Tree Area Girl Scout Council, observes that both adult and Girl Scout memberships have declined by almost half within the last five years. The reason, she says, is not only because the Girl Scout programs have failed to keep abreast of current needs (a condition, she hastens to add, that is rapidly changing), but because volunteerism is no longer a priority for the suburban woman. "There was once a time when it was *the thing* for women to do volunteer work but that is no longer true today. Suburban women have finally given themselves permission to say, 'I'm entitled to be my own person, not just Bill's wife or Sue's mom, and to do what I think is most important and meaningful.'"

There has also been a sharp increase in the number of working women in the Oak Park area: about 40 percent of the Lone Tree Area Council volunteers were working five years ago; today that figure is closer to 99 percent. It cannot be denied that working limits the time women can devote to service. And yet, Mrs. Ruffin maintains that there is a new ground swell of interest in scouting, particularly among the young, employed, childless women who wish to have contact with girls. There also remains some interest among working parents. "But we've got to strip down what we expect of those parents," Mrs. Ruffins cautions. "We can't snow them under with paperwork and training."

On Chicago's North Shore, Lois Graller, former president of the Glencoe School PTAs, notes that women volunteers have less time to give to the parent-teacher association, and when they do express a desire to volunteer, they want to make sure their contribution is worthwhile. "Where with one phone call a few years ago you could find a room mother for a school classroom, you might make ten or fifteen phone calls today. With declining enrollment and fewer schools, there are technically more parents per school, but there are also fewer parents available during the day. I used to know all the mothers in Glencoe and now I don't. Many of the women with young children are working."

Without question, the faltering economy, the rising divorce rate and the increase in single-parent households which sent women back to work in the 1970s reduced the time women have available for volunteer effort. There is also a new attitude toward altruism that posits that the individual and her right to happiness are more important than the welfare of the group. This attitude, colored by the feminist thinking of the early and mid-1970s, which encouraged women to work for financial remuneration and to volunteer only to effect social change (as a National Organization for Women conference resolution in 1974 decreed), reflects the philosophical tenets of the age. It was this same emphasis on the self that led social critics such as Tom Wolfe, Jim Hougan, Peter Marin and Christopher Lasch to characterize the 1970s as the age of individualism— the "me" or "now" generation, as it has become popularly known.

Christopher Lasch writes, "After the political turmoil of the sixties, Americans have retreated to purely personal preoccupations. . . . To live for the moment is the prevailing passion—to live for yourself, not for your predecessors or posterity. We are fast losing the sense of historical continuity, the sense of belonging to a succession of generations originating in the past and stretching into the future." The danger of such a narcissistic age lies in the creation of a society of increasing privatism, one that retreats from political and altruistic endeavors and carries the seeds of its own destruction.

That sentiment was expressed in the suburbs, that "hotbed of participation" where the women, who had traditionally devoted themselves to the family and the betterment of the community, had begun to embark on a new quest for self-fulfillment. Instead of volunteering simply for the sake of giving, women had begun to ask what they could get in return for their services.

Leaders of the nation's major volunteer organizations speak of sharpened individual priorities as one of the most important characteristics of the new volunteerism. Joan Rich, chair of management and training service for the National League of Women Voters and a National League Board member, says that women are probably no less altruistic today than before, but that today they are simply more candid about their motives for volunteering. "Years ago we talked more in terms of what we would do for others, rather than what we were getting out of it for ourselves. In those days it would have been an embarrassment to say we were volunteering for ourselves. But people are more up front about that now. They're quite honest about saying they're interested in working on a particular issue for a particular reason."

Jane Freeman, president of the Girl Scouts of the U.S.A.,

says, "I think in scouting and in all volunteer organizations, when you're recruiting leaders, when you're asking for a commitment of time and energy, people need to understand what's in it for them. Now part of what is in it for them is the rendering of service and that brings a certain satisfaction. But today, women in particular are asking that question more openly and more specifically."

Dr. Ronald Smith, executive director of the National PTA, notes: "Over the years, there has been a marked change in the way PTAs have operated because more women have left their homes for work than ever before. Some of that slack in the membership has been picked up by the men. But while the women may have greater constraints on their time, they are both demanding more training and bringing more leadership skills which they have gained in the workplace into the organization."

Recent figures reflecting contemporary patterns of volunteerism suggest the direction of those new interests. According to studies conducted by the National Opinion Research Center on well-educated affluent Americans in 1978, the number of parent-school association members fell from 38 percent of the population in 1967 to 24 percent. Participation in political organizations declined from 17 percent to 8 percent. In the same years, however, membership in sports groups rose from 23 percent to 34 percent, in literary societies from 13 percent to 21 percent, and in professional societies from 26 percent to 39 percent. As Seth Reichlin writes, "The spirit of joining is not dead, but has been redirected away from civic organizations toward those that serve personal or professional objectives."

Volunteerism was once the mainstay of the suburbs. As long ago as 1925, Harlan Paul Douglass wrote that a heavy commitment to volunteerism seemed to be a particular characteristic of the suburban community. "Still another type of social agency which suburban peculiarities have thrown into importance beyond the usual place in the community is the local philanthropic institution. . . . The explanation is by no means that such communities have the most acute demands.

It is rather another symptom of suburban over-organization."

Later, in the 1950s and 1960s, during the golden age of suburbia, social critics were to make similar observations, that organizational activity was a hallmark of suburban sociability, and that volunteer participation among its women was practically a social mandate. As William H. Whyte wrote, "Only a minority of wives are really successful at handling both a large agenda of social or civic obligations and their home duties, but everyone puts up such a good front that many a wife begins to feel that something is wanting in her, that she is not the same. Determined to be as normal as anyone else, or a little more so, they take on a back-breaking load of duties—and a guilt feeling that they're not up to it."

Who among us in the over-25 category does not remember the PTA meetings, the Girl and Boy Scout troop meetings, the book clubs and League of Women Voters meetings that our mothers participated in so eagerly during our impressionable years? I still recall the dainty hand-decorated floral designs on the sugar cubes my mother used to set out along with the coffee, cakes and cookies for book club luncheons and PTA meetings. And how fondly I remember the Wednesdays of my eighth and ninth years, when I could wear my Brownie uniforms to school for our meetings! Those days were favorite times for me; they meant special afternoons of learning, a different kind of social experience from that which I received in school, a world of nature and crafts taught by the two scout leaders who were the mothers of my neighborhood friends. With what excitement the children in my neighborhood helped their parents collect newspapers for our biannual "paper drive" that was somehow supposed to contribute to the building of better playgrounds, libraries and hospitals! As children we never understood exactly how the money from such events would be used, but somehow it was the act of communal endeavor that made the event so pleasing and special.

What a contrast with a recent volunteer experience in my own life! It was a cold night in December 1980, and I arrived at the PTA meeting at my daughter's school in New Rochelle, where I was invited to speak on the subject of television. Although I had spoken in the schools before, I had been invited that particular night because of a story I had written on schools and television for the Education Survey of the *New York Times*. A representative from the New York Council on Children's Television had also been asked to speak, and that night she and I had arrived simultaneously. The auditorium was empty, except for the school PTA president, her husband, the school principal and two other women. Although it was already 8:00, we sat and waited for others to appear. The minutes ticked by and still nobody else arrived.

"Maybe it's the weather," one of the women finally suggested.

"Perhaps that has something to do with it," the PTA president said. "But last month our attendance was pretty poor, too. The parents in this school just don't seem to be interested in participating in the PTA. I don't really know why, although I understand there are a lot of single parents in the district and a lot of working mothers. In fact, that's really why I became president. Nobody else wanted the responsibility."

For the suburban women of earlier years, volunteer impulse went far beyond our nostalgia-tinted memories of our mothers' altruism. It was the duty of the affluent matron to participate in community events; it was simply what one did. Moreover, it was often the only acceptable outlet outside the house for women's energies. As a 53-year-old state vice-president of the League of Women Voters and mother of four sons explained, "It was the only thing we could do to get out of the house. For me, at least, it was a kind of saving grace. A chance to use my brains beyond the dishes and diapers of the daily routine."

The social protests against the "oughts" and "shoulds" of postwar America in the late 1960s and early 1970s dealt a death blow to the concept—if not the reality—of "woman's daily routine." Suddenly, for the first time in their history, there were no more hard and fast rules for young women. This was particularly true for middle- and upper-middle-class females—the children of the suburbs—who had the luxury of choice. Some followed the flower children to communes, or went to university towns like Berkeley, Ann Arbor, Madison and Cambridge, or began careers. Others, influenced by the sixties but still bound to convention, chose marriage and children, but with more tolerance for the nontraditionalists. Increasingly, by the early 1970s, the newly changed women of the suburbs began to find other outlets for their energies—especially work and higher education. Mounting government support of social service programs; a declining birth rate; crumbling national trust in institutions such as school, church and family; double-digit inflation, and the two-paycheck family also depleted the volunteer rolls.

Kerry Kenn Allen, executive vice-president of VOLUN-TEER, says that individuals are not discarding altruism at all, but are instead embracing it in a new, more individualistic manner. Mr. Allen points to the growth of the grass-roots political movement of the late 1970s and the more than 500,000 self-help groups that had sprung up in local communities by 1980. "I think you have to look beyond the fact that women are going back to work to account for the changes in volunteerism. A whole lot of changes are happening in our society about the way people look at themselves and their relationships to others that explain those trends. People are seeking power and control over their lives and participation and growth opportunities in the jobs they do. And if they want all of those things in their jobs, why shouldn't they want them in their volunteer work too?" Mr. Allen says that while some volunteer jobs may no longer be popular—for example, tending the gift shop at the local hospital—organization jobs involving volunteers in a direct, responsible way seldom have trouble attracting workers. "You'd be hard pressed to find a sexual abuse center, drug prevention clinic or suicide prevention hot line that's really having a hard time getting volunteers," observes Mr. Allen. "Why? Because those activities involve them in highly meaningful contact with other individuals in crisis."

"Meaningful" is a highly charged word and its very subjectivity has given the volunteer organizations difficulty as they

have tried to devise new programs to fit their memberships'
changing needs. For an attorney in Greenwich, Connecticut,
volunteer work serves an important personal need quite
different from what it might be for the full-time homemaker.
"For me, volunteer work means a chance to socialize with
other women in the community. Between my work and the
children I have little chance to meet other women here in any
other way. My husband can't quite understand why I continue
to volunteer when I'm already so pressed for time, but for me
it's a vital connection."

In contrast is a 33-ycar-old cx-schooltcachcr from Hollywood, Florida, who holds two master's degrees, is a full-time
wife and mother and describes herself as a "high-priced
chauffeur," but who hopes one day to go back for her
doctorate. For this woman, participation in her community's
PTA represents a way to stay intellectually active. "It's
important to me to continue to learn, to be able to voice my
views and to help make positive changes in the community.
And selfishly, it means I can have direct input into the quality
of our children's education."

Part of the difficulty with the traditional types of volunteer
assignments during the 1970s, volunteer leaders now say, was
that they still represented the female volunteer as an expend-
able commodity. "Our whole society has been geared on the
principle that the mother can wait. Volunteers received the
same treatment that mothers got because everyone assumed
that the professional volunteer had all day," observes Dr.
Elizabeth Metcalf, a child psychologist and president of the
Girl Scout Council of Tropical Florida. "But I think that's
changing. Women are becoming more assertive today. Because volunteers are harder to get now, they're becoming
more prized."

One measure of their improved status has been the new
attention to time limitations and task preferences of volunteers. Virtually every major voluntary agency now has night
meetings for those members who work during the day. Most
traditional volunteer organizations have also broken their tasks
and groups down into smaller components, or restructured

them into smaller short-term obligations. A Girl Scout troop that once contained twenty or twenty-five members is now often organized to contain ten or fifteen girls. A community fund-raising project for a hospital auxiliary may draw upon the public relations skills of one woman, the graphic skills of another, the secretarial acumen of a third and the mailing lists of a fourth.

The most important indication of a changing volunteer ethic is that organization leaders are now making concerted efforts to match volunteers' skills and interests with the tasks that need to be done. For with the new scarcity of the traditional female volunteer has come a somber realization—volunteerism is a two-way street, and a mutually satisfying arrangement must first be hammered out between the volunteer and the agency if tasks are to be accomplished.

At the Volunteer Bureau of San Mateo, Loyce Haran maintains that the coordination of the volunteer's interests with an agency's needs is the primary function of the clearinghouse. When a volunteer arrives at the center in search of placement, he or she is first carefully interviewed to determine job preferences. If there are no jobs currently available, the center helps the volunteer candidate create such a job. "What we do here is job develop. We go to where an agency needs a certain type of help and where the volunteer will also have something to offer. Then we try to make a match."

In Orlando, Julie Washburn, executive director of the Volunteer Service Bureau and president of the Association of Voluntary Bureaus, speaks of a "quiet courtship" that now exists between the volunteer candidate and the agency before any tasks are assigned. "What has happened is that a lot of women who volunteer are doing so to get jobs. They're volunteering to develop their own skills and when they get something out of it, they will stay on. It's not hard to get volunteers, but it's hard to keep them. The problem in the past has been the sieve-type of volunteer development and that's something we are working hard to avoid today."

In an effort to achieve a better fit between the agency and

the volunteer, the Volunteer Service Bureau of Orlando recently began to participate in a computerized "skill bank," which lists volunteers throughout the state of Florida and their specific skills, and matches them with agencies in need of services. Such banks will undoubtedly become a permanent fixture among volunteer organizations within the next decade. "The idea is not only to look at the pool of available volunteers, but to share them with other agencies," explains Mrs. Washburn. "If the voluntary agencies would join hands, everybody would be a lot happier, including the volunteer with specialized skills."

Of course matching volunteer talents with community needs has occurred throughout history. But until quite recently, it was men who were matched to positions calling upon their individual talents and abilities; women have traditionally served in a hodgepodge of volunteer capacities, reflecting their malleable, unfocused identities. In the past, the local male artist was expected to head the community art show or act as judge for a school district art project. The comptroller of the town's department store chain doubled in the evenings as the treasurer of the Kiwanis Club. And the senior business executive of a major corporation had a long tradition of serving on his local community service boards. The realization that a woman may volunteer in accordance with her talents is a healthy new trend. In the words of psychologist Dr. Bobbie McKay, she is "a woman who is not limited by the stereotypes of the past and who is free to discover her own uniqueness as she adds breadth and possibility to the world in which she moves."

A 46-year-old woman from Redwood City, who developed managerial skills as a volunteer that she was later able to use to obtain a paid staff position in a senior citizen center, echoes that feeling: "We found something for ourselves through specific volunteer service, something we had lost behind an apron and a vacuum cleaner."

Obviously some of the impetus for that recognition has come from the volunteer sector itself, which contains a high number of female directors, agency heads and staff assistants, many of whom have worked their way up through the ranks after serving as volunteers themselves. But increasingly, as today's young women have embraced careers in business, law, medicine and other nontraditional jobs, they have also become more confident and outspoken. Perceived as professionals in the workaday world, they see no reason to discard their roles while offering their services to a nonprofit organization. "I'll serve as a marketing expert or as communications chairman for our home-school association because there's where I can make a meaningful contribution," says a woman from Rockland County, New York, "but I'd never think to volunteer for that organization in another capacity."

A financial officer for a major oil company who now lives in Fairfield County, Connecticut, and who serves on the investment committee for her local YWCA, claims she volunteers primarily because she was called upon to exercise specific expertise. "I feel the things I'm doing are worthwhile and really keep my skills fresh," said the woman, who had taken a year off from her job to be with her infant son. With a polite smile she added, "But I wouldn't want to work on just anything for the sake of volunteering. It would be a waste of my time."

A 43-year-old airline pilot from Scarsdale, who offered a two-week career internship program to a teenage Girl Scout at the Westchester County airport, said: "It was a thrilling experience for me. But I have to say that it had as much to do with my interests in the idea of changing female roles in aviation as it did in helping the Girl Scouts. The gratification for me was that I enjoyed the challenge of working with a young girl on a one-to-one basis. I wouldn't take on a troop. But by taking on that internship, I could help assert the fact that women have a place in our country as pilots."

The concept of professionalism permeated the volunteer organizations of the late 1970s, revitalizing the faded programs and traditions of an earlier era and giving rise to a vibrant new volunteerism. Suddenly the middle-class suburban woman was a force to be reckoned with, one to be wooed, groomed and trained by volunteer organizations. As her numbers decreased, she became an increasingly valuable entity, and the burst of new programs and volunteer training courses testified to her formerly unrecognized power.

Organizations like the Girl Scouts developed more precise courses in management and leadership skills for their adult leaders. As an additional incentive, continuing education credits were offered to leaders participating in training sponsored by the national organization. Women with specific talents and skills who were unable or unwilling to head troops were invited to serve as council consultants or to make professional presentations. New scout leaders were provided with personal guidance, written guidelines and printed materials to help them organize troop meetings.

Study activities and research projects in organizations like the League of Women Voters and the PTA have proliferated. At the same time, leadership skills and management training have increasingly been stressed in virtually every aspect of these organizations. Members in both organizations have become more involved in legislative reform and advocacy work. And while both the League of Women Voters and the PTA have long drawn from their ranks to fill leadership positions, women were achieving those roles earlier. "While League women always had the opportunity to exercise and develop political skills, today's volunteers spend less time on typing and other routine tasks and more time representing the League in the public arena," says Joan Rich, a long-term local volunteer with the League of Women Voters of San Luis Obispo, California, before assuming a position on the National League Board.

And at the YWCAs, women who have participated in counseling programs for widowhood, divorce, spouse abuse and other kinds of life crises were encouraged to return as volunteers and volunteer trainers. Two programs that have been particularly successful have been "Encore," the Y's postmastectomy counseling program, and the abused spouse centers. The YWCA has just initiated a new "Career Volunteer

Development Program" designed to help volunteers develop skills and competencies that can be used in professional careers as well as volunteer work.

Concerned with the swelling tide of women to the workplace, the Association of Junior Leagues developed a Volunteer Career Development program as early as 1974 to help members evaluate and improve their personal and professional skills. The program, presented to members in five two-hour sessions, was so well received as a pilot project that by 1981 it had been brought to the League's 239 local chapters. The Association of Junior Leagues has also developed many new short-term community service tasks. Recently, the Association was asked to help develop "Leadership for Change," a course created by the National Association of Bank Women to help women achieve senior management positions in the business world and the volunteer sector.

In a similar manner, the 190,000-member American Association of University Women has intensified its training programs and urged women to assume increasingly active roles in their communities. Its two major projects in the years 1981 to 1983, "Money Talks" and "Taking Hold of Technology," are geared to help the volunteer translate her knowledge of financial and technological issues into applicable skills that will help her evaluate community service organizations, school boards, businesses, personal finances and her employment situation more realistically.

Some nonprofit agencies have initiated job development programs. One particularly successful program was created by the staff at the Valley Volunteer Board of Pleasanton, California, a suburb about twenty-five miles northeast of San Francisco. Faced with homemakers at the agency who requested volunteer work that could be used on a job resume, the Volunteer Board realized that there was a growing need for such a program. "We had become a kind of informal women's center. We were seeing the middle-class housewife who hadn't worked in ten to twenty-five years, who was feeling pretty incompetent and out of touch, but wanted to return to work," explained Betty Stallings, executive director of the

Board. "Most of them needed not only to have a job internship but emotional support for themselves as well." In order to help these women, the Board created a job internship program, and classroom instruction was offered at a nearby community college, including discussion of personal development, goal setting and time management. Those classes provided the women with immediate peer support as well. The Women's Re-Entry Program, as it came to be called, included placement for volunteers in jobs related to their interests. Two and a half years later, the results for the 200 women who have passed through the program have been remarkably successful. "Anybody who wants to get a job is usually able to do so," says staff member Barbara Tuck. "The internship seems to give them a lot of confidence."

One woman who participated in the program was Ruth Reilly, a 59-year-old widow from Livermore, California, who had remained home for many years raising her children. Although she had previously participated in a number of volunteer activities and fund-raising projects in her community, she had never thought to use her volunteer efforts to brush up on the skills that would make her job-marketable. But through the Women's Re-Entry Program, Mrs. Reilly was placed in a congressman's office where she worked as an aide. "It was the Valley Volunteer Board internship experience that fortified me. I had to get used to the reference books again and learn who to talk to to get the answers. I don't think I could have found anything closer to what I needed, or what any woman would need. It was all there in front of you. But it's that first step that comes the hardest. You don't know what you'd like to do, but that you'd like to do something." Today, Mrs. Reilly is employed by a major department store chain where she works in a variety of administrative capacities.

In a more comprehensive effort to attract and professionalize today's volunteer, a collaboration organized by the American Red Cross developed a new program to help volunteers evaluate and build on their skills. Called the "I CAN Interagency Collaboration for Volunteer Development," the program was created by eight national voluntary organizations—

the American Red Cross, the Association of Junior Leagues, the Association for Volunteer Administration, the Girl Scouts, the National Board of the Young Women's Christian Association, the National Center for Citizen Involvement, the National Council of Jewish Women and the National Council of Young Men's Christian Associations—and tested in twelve American cities.

According to Dr. Mark Cheren, assistant director of personnel training and development for the American Red Cross: "The assumption behind the program is that more and more volunteers are asking to be treated like professionals. It's a way to help those who volunteer to plan their lives, including their volunteer and paid work and their nonformal and formal learning in a process that is itself empowering." The "I CAN Volunteer Development Workbook" and accompanying administrative guides were published by the Red Cross in late 1981 and are now being disseminated through the country's major volunteer organizations.

Nonprofit agencies are starting to look to major corporations as a source of volunteer manpower. While business has traditionally contributed large sums of money to charities and even lent some of its top executives to altruistic causes, the widespread use of personnel is a relatively new trend. Corporations, voluntary agencies realize, have both the money and skilled personnel to contribute to the community at a time when public funds and free womanpower are disappearing. From the corporate viewpoint, the provision of people and services to the community has a multitude of benefits—not the least of which is a better public image. "Just the fact of giving money and walking away from the social problems in the community is not enough. In fact, it may sometimes even be the wrong thing to do," says Stanley Karson, director of the Clearinghouse on Corporate Social Responsibility, an organization created to promote public service efforts by the life and health insurance companies. "A hands-on approach to the problems in the community is often more valuable. Getting employees and the company itself involved is something that money can't really buy, but something from which the community can often benefit tremendously."

One result of increased attention to volunteerism by corporations has been the growing acceptance of release time for employees, of company-approved absences for civic work and study. Companies like Atlantic Richfield, American Airlines, Tenneco, Prudential Life Insurance, Fisher-Price and Xerox, to name a few, now have such programs in place. A sizable proportion of those volunteer employees, naturally enough, are women. The circle that began with the disappearance of the suburban homemaker into the workplace has thus been completed, as she once again steps back into the community— in the role of an employee-volunteer.

Even for the "liberated" woman who has put her energies into a career and postponed or bypassed marriage and children, the lure of bettering her community and helping the young, the poor and unfortunate still seems to hold her. A 31-year-old woman working for Xerox in Atlanta explained what she had already gained working with foster children through the Children and Family Services Department of suburban Rockdale County, Georgia. "I really enjoy the individual nitty-gritty contact with individuals I've had in this position," said Deborah Duchon, who has taken a year's "Social Service Leave" from Xerox to serve as a coordinator for the Rockdale County office. "Most people don't have that meaningful kind of human contact in daily life. And much as I love them, you certainly don't get it from selling Xerox machines!"

Another young woman who works as a television producer in San Francisco, but who devotes time to the Suicide Prevention and Crisis Center of San Mateo County answering calls on the hot line, said: "It's just something that's important to me, that's all. A feeling that you want to reach out to help others who may not have been as lucky as you have been. And you come away from those experiences richer, because by giving back to others, somehow you get recharged yourself."

Even in this age of tightened belts, it seems unlikely that volunteerism, that noble human impulse, will disappear. Like the changing image of the suburban woman herself, who once had 2.3 children, a breadwinning husband and membership in half a dozen community organizations, the form, not the substance, of her altruism has changed.

8

Skin Deep: The Minority Suburban Woman

∞∞∞∞∞∞∞∞∞∞∞∞∞∞∞∞∞∞∞∞∞∞∞∞∞∞∞∞∞∞∞∞∞∞∞∞∞

I have almost always had white people to do my housekeeping. That might make some people kind of chuckle, but those are the people available in my community. You know, there are a lot of people in Marin County who are artists, who have alternative life-styles and are looking for some unskilled work to do, who want to do housekeeping. I lose them from time to time like everybody else, because it's hard to get good help today. But with one exception, all my help has been white.

A 37-year-old black female attorney
in Mill Valley, California

"ONE MONTH AFTER I MOVED into that apartment in North Bergen where I had won the fair housing case, I was robbed. It was an inside job for sure. At least, that's what the police detective concluded. There I was, the only black in a forty-eight-unit building and a single parent. When I arrived home from work that night, someone had knocked out the dead-bolt lock and you could see the hole in the door from the outside. My neighbors must have seen it too, because they had to walk by my apartment to get to their own. But nobody said a word.

"When I saw what had happened, I wanted to call the police, but I was afraid to go into my apartment because somebody might still have been in there. I began knocking on my neighbors' doors for help. I could hear the people inside, but nobody would answer. I didn't want to come in, just have them call the police, I explained, but nobody paid attention to me.

"Later, what bothered me most was a feeling of having been intruded upon, of someone invading what is supposed to be yours. My daughter never did find anybody to play with in that neighborhood, except the superintendent's daughter. A year later I moved back home, right back with my parents to Englewood and the black community."

Although three years had passed, the willowy 28-year-old black woman sitting across from me at the Urban League for Bergen County was still stinging from the memory of the undisguised hostility she had encountered when she had moved into an all-white suburban community. Just a month before our interview, the woman had married, and now she and her husband were involved in a determined housing search that brought back the memories of her earlier experience. She and her husband were hoping to buy, rather than rent, a home in northern New Jersey. But in spite of recently litigated changes in real estate practices, and the increased appearance of blacks in the affluent communities of Bergen County, housing for middle-class black families still remained extraordinarily difficult to find.

"The communities where we would like to live we can't afford and the communities where we could buy just don't seem right for us," lamented the poised young professional. "I certainly don't want more of the kind of trouble I had before. At the same time, I also do not want to invest in an all-black community, where the real estate values may be on the decline. We would like to live in a mixed community, one that is more representative of the real world. But that is not easy. Discrimination may not be as open as it was years ago in the suburbs, but it's still there. It's a barrier that will probably always be there too, even if it becomes more discreet."

It was a dazzling white Sunday morning on the hilltops of. northern San Mateo County, the kind of morning that makes you forget the chilling fog that often steals through San Francisco and its innerlying suburbs. The air above the hills was crystal clear, and the traffic hushed, an atmosphere befitting the solemnity of a Sunday morning. Below, an endless vista of beige brick houses lined the hilltops like steps, the monotony of their design broken only here and there by bright bursts of flowers and the splashes of color from late-model cars neatly parked at street curbs.

Inside one of those well-kept homes, a 34-year-old black housewife serenely prepares Sunday brunch for her family amid the din of the color television set and her three children at play. Sharon Daws is proud to be a suburban housewife, as she first tells me when she meets me at the door. She is proud to be able to stay home all day, proud too that unlike most of the other black women on her block, she does not have to work to help her husband maintain their life. Her husband makes enough money for her and the children to live on. She is perplexed by the fact that white women seem anxious to hold jobs. From her point of view, she has attained the essence of the good life—a suburban home, a car of her own and a breadwinning husband. It hardly seems important to her that South San Francisco is largely composed of minorities and is therefore regarded by many outsiders as undesirable. It is, after all, a pleasant community, a well-kept suburb, the kind she always dreamed of living in as a young girl.

Sharon Daws and her husband have lived in South San Francisco for the last six years, far from the poverty of the black community in the inner city they once knew and fled, hoping to erase its memory forever. The Dawses feel they have a right to a better life than their poorer, inner-city contemporaries; they have contempt for those who live with the help of public assistance. "My husband and I worked hard to get where we are today, and we're proud of what we've accomplished," Sharon says as she pours coffee for me. "We moved here from the city to get better schools and to have a good environment for the children. We wanted a better opportunity for the family, one far from the drugs and hustling that we were constantly exposed to in the city. Out here, there is less of a chance for those problems to occur. We wouldn't ever consider going back."

"I'm glad we chose the suburbs over the city, glad to be able to go home to a quiet place with trees and a private yard after working in Chicago all day. The city places a stress on me that I wouldn't like to have all the time. The town I live in is another world altogether—a protective cocoon, a place where the kids can go around on their bikes without me worrying about what is happening to them. Still, I think we've paid a tremendous price for living in a place where there just aren't that many other black families.

"We know our kids are getting a good education and having the freedom to move around in a small community, but they are definitely missing something as far as their blackness is concerned. It's important for our kids to have black friends, especially as they approach puberty. It's important for them to have black adults as role models and to learn about black culture, because that's where their self-identity gets fostered. But we don't get a lot of selection for these things in a community like ours. To be honest, I wish there were more black people in my neighborhood."

The speaker, a 41-year-old woman from Chicago's North Shore, talked without any hint of bitterness or anger, but she sighed as she finished speaking, revealing the depth of the conflict that has raged in her for the decade that she and her family have lived in a predominantly white suburban community. As an administrative assistant in a fair housing program, she knew that even if her wish were granted—that more blacks did move into her neighborhood—the dream of racial balance would still probably not be fulfilled. For what is defined as a comfortable percentage of minorities by the white community is often thought too slight by the blacks; and vice versa. The result of an increasing black minority, the woman explained, is panic selling among whites. "The problem for those of us living in white middle-class suburbs today is in determining just how many blacks are considered a threat. For me, as for all black women in white middle-class suburbs, that means you have to be very sensitive to what is happening to your kids in school and in the neighborhood. It's a kind of special burden we have."

Foremost among the dreams of the middle-class minority woman is the image of the suburban home on the tree-shaded plot, the image which has inspired countless generations of Americans to leave the city for the middle landscape. With the civil rights movement of the 1960s and the rash of fair housing programs that followed, that goal seemed suddenly attainable, as the new minority groups moved to the suburbs in an unprecedented burst. But the integration of black and Hispanic families among the mainstream population has been remarkably slow and uneven.

Once having moved to the suburbs, the minority woman often finds her dreams abruptly shattered. Too often, beneath the promise of that bright new life, she collides with discrimination once again, relegating her to second-class status. Even worse, she and her children are often confused by questions of race and self-identity.

How black—or Hispanic—*is* my identity, the minority woman often asks herself, and how much of my identity should I expect my children to share? How much should I strive to become assimilated into the mainstream culture and how much should I identify with my racial or national roots? These questions have plagued minorities for decades. Once asked by the waves of first and second generation immigrants who moved en masse from the central city ghettos into the freshly constructed homes of the post-World War II era, they continue to haunt the new minority groups living in the suburbs. But with a difference. Color is a particularly powerful visual reminder of the differences among people. And it is that, far more than education and occupation, which continues to separate the suburban minority woman from her white contemporary.

Some minority women, like the one from Bergen County, have experienced overt racial discrimination when they have tried to settle in formerly all-white areas. Other minority people, like Sharon Daws and her family, fled purposefully to the suburbs in search of a better life—but once there, they found themselves living in predominantly segregated neighborhoods, as ghettoized as they once were in the inner city. Others, like the woman from the North Shore, have chosen predominantly white communities only to discover that they have separated themselves from the mainstream black culture.

Somewhere in that snarled mass of social contradictions, the minority woman has found a new order. Education and employment situations—two conditions that separated the traditional suburban woman from her minority sister—have begun to change dramatically in the last decade. Paid employment has become important for most modern suburban women, whatever their color or ethnicity. And with the improvement of education levels and job training for all women has come a blurring of formerly rigid social roles. After years of livng in the back bedroom of the suburban home as a maid, the minority woman has begun to emerge as a full-fledged citizen in the suburban community, persistent in her decision to forge a new identity for herself and her family. The appearance of the middle-class racial minority, and especially of its women, has created profound changes in the suburbs. Yesterday's suburban life-style—based on sharp divisions of income, education and color—has all but disappeared.

The black woman who a decade or two ago might have sought a job as a domestic in a neighboring "white" suburb, is more likely to be competing with the Caucasian suburban housewife for a secretarial job in a nearby corporate park. The upper-middle-class child, whose parents moved from the city to a high-income community, may attend school with the children of black professionals. And the newly divorced white woman of the suburbs may find herself looking to the black woman who is head of her own household as a model of strength, stability and perseverance.

Just as employment and divorce have fragmented social homogeneity among white suburban women, so has the appearance of the minority family. The arrival of the black or Hispanic woman in her new role as equal citizen is an unpredictable new factor portending the end of suburban elitism, forcing the traditional suburban female to confront contemporary social problems in surprisingly personal terms.

How does the white suburban woman react to the appearance of a new black or Hispanic neighbor? Some accept minorities quite easily. A sizable number, however, shy away from them altogether, and in time, if they are threatened enough by their appearance, may even move away from the community.

Sociological and demographic studies have established without a doubt that "white flight" is the rule rather than the exception. Once minorities appear, the tendency is for communities to become increasingly populated with minorities, while the more affluent white families move to newer, more distant, and more costly homes.

It was an unseasonably hot April in 1980 and I was visiting an old friend in Hollywood, Florida. She is a highly intelligent woman who had moved to that community three years before, and she openly admitted to me that one of the advantages of living in Broward County rather than closer to Miami was that Broward County was still nearly all white.

One afternoon, while trying to find my way back to her home, I passed through a neighborhood that seemed less maintained than the others, the houses noticeably shabby, with peeling paint and missing screens, the lawns filled with crabgrass and weeds. The neighborhood, I soon realized, was almost exclusively occupied by black families. Unlike other suburban communities I had observed in southern Florida that week, children were playing on the front lawns and the sidewalks rather than in their back yards. Men and women chatted on the street curbs and at their front walks, interrupting their conversation to stare curiously at me as I rode through the streets.

Suddenly, someone threw a stone at the back windshield of my rented compact car. There was loud laughter as I stepped on my brakes in reaction. Before long, two children began to follow me on their bikes, calling names I couldn't understand through the closed windows of my air-conditioned automobile. I began to feel distinctly uncomfortable, even though I had been lost many times before in suburban communities in my travels. There was an unmistakable sense of tension in the air of this particular suburban neighborhood, a feeling I couldn't quite fathom. Perhaps I was projecting my own fears about being in an all-black neighborhood, I thought, even though I frequently drove through Harlem on my way into New York City and live in an integrated neighborhood myself. Finally, I chalked up my rising paranoia to the fact that a white person must have been a rare sight on the streets of this southern black community.

Later that night I questioned my friend about the location of the neighborhood and what its past history had been. "Oh yes, there is a small black community around here somewhere," she replied vaguely, "but I really don't know exactly where it is. It's kind of an invisible population here—one we really don't pay much attention to."

The next morning, the *Fort Lauderdale News* carried a front-page story announcing the possibility that the high school gymnasium might be opened as a refugee center for the Cubans just then entering the United States through Miami in record numbers. "Oh no, that's just what we don't need in this community," my friend muttered over morning coffee as she read the newspaper. "It's going to make all of us very, very nervous to have such riffraff here."

Within the next month community pressure in Broward

County ran so high that the proposal was dropped. And within the same month, the black population of Liberty City of nearby Miami began a series of angry violent riots.

Usually the antipathy between the races in the middle landscape is expressed far more subtly, in keeping with the rules of suburban propriety. I recall a trip I made to a fashionable street in northwest Dallas, where I interviewed a black woman, the mother of four children, a professional volunteer married to a doctor. The street, as I later learned, was completely occupied by other black professional families and surrounded on both sides by a middle-class white community. Years before, when Dallas was smaller, the land where northwest Dallas now stood had been pasture, and a portion of that land had belonged to a black farmer. After World War II, when suburban sprawl transformed the Dallas countryside into suburban cul-de-sacs, the land owned by the black farmer was sold to a group of black families.

"No, we've never had any trouble in this neighborhood because of race," the woman, a long-term resident of the neighborhood, assured me as we sat on soft leather couches in her cathedral-ceilinged living room. "Nor have my kids had any difficulty. But we keep strong ties with the church and the black community, both of which are located in downtown Dallas. I guess if you have to characterize us, you would say that we are still tied to the black inner-city community—much more than we are to the white population around us."

Consider the experience of a black college professor from Peekskill, New York, who had moved with her husband and children to an all-white residential neighborhood in 1975. She witnessed little overt hostility from her neighbors when she moved in, but looking back, she realized that her family had had a powerful—if unstated—impact upon the community. "We were the first black family to integrate our neighborhood in this part of town, but today we are no longer alone. There are many more black families that have moved in here within the last six years. After we arrived, several white neighbors sold their homes to black families and moved away."

Within the last decade, this geographical game of hide and seek between the races has accelerated to a fine pitch. According to the 1980 census, over two million blacks migrated to the suburbs between 1970 and 1980, an increase of almost 40 percent, growing from 4.5 percent of the total suburban population in 1970 to 6.1 percent today. In the suburbs of the country's largest metropolitan areas (those with over a million people), blacks increased in number by more than 60 percent.

Although individuals of Spanish origin were notoriously underrepresented in the 1970 census, and are still thought by some to be undercounted, demographers believe that they are now the nation's fastest growing minority group. A major complication in defining that population is that Hispanics do not represent a single racial group, but instead derive their identity from places as diverse as Mexico, Cuba, Puerto Rico, Costa Rica and South America. The 1980 census reports that about 3.5 million people of Spanish origin live in America's suburbs, comprising about 5.4 percent of its suburban population. In some metropolitan areas, the proportion of Hispanics is considerably larger: in Los Angeles and Long Beach, 58 percent of the Hispanic population lives outside the central cities; in Miami, 67 percent of all Hispanics are suburbanites; in Chicago, 27 percent of the Hispanic community now resides in traditionally Anglo suburban communities.

Between 1970 and 1979, the number of families headed by women rose by 71 percent in the suburbs, compared to 51 percent in the rest of the nation. White female-headed households increased by 63 percent, but the rise among minority female-headed families was even larger. Black female-headed households have grown in number by 110 percent; by 1979, 25 percent of all suburban Spanish households were maintained by women.

With these changes in socio-economic composition has come a transformation in the status hierarchies of the suburban communities. What was once a fashionable suburban community may now have fallen into disrepute among elitists because it now contains a large number of minorities; what was once regarded as an insignificant village far from the city center may have become increasingly fashionable because of its lily-white composition.

The appearance in the suburbs of blacks and Hispanics has not necessarily meant an improved life for them. A comparison of income levels of the various racial and ethnic populations of the suburbs reveals that there is still a glaring disparity between white incomes and those of other populations. In 1979, the white suburban family had an average income of $23,093; in the same year, the black suburban family earned $13,852 and the Hispanic household $16,315.

More telling is the spatial distribution of the minority populations. Most of the suburban population growth of blacks and Hispanics has occurred in traditionally segregated communities, in well-defined minority corridors or in communities that have become newly segregated. New suburban ghettos, as blighted as those in the central cities, have proliferated, often with an accompanying deterioration of public services and educational standards in the schools.

Penetration by the middle-class minority into historically white mainstream communities has proceeded at a snail's pace, fraught with innumerable public and personal tensions. Often, the minority woman feels terribly isolated. Even the simple matter of where to get her hair dressed, her nails manicured or her clothes purchased becomes a major issue for many minority women living in the white suburban communities.

Although her social and educational status may be the same as her neighbors', the minority individual who moves into a predominantly white community is almost inevitably subjected to a negative first appraisal. As the black social psychologist Dr. Kenneth Clark observes, the physical distinctions between the Negro and Caucasian continue to act as powerful reminders of the long-standing low status historically assigned to American blacks. "The Negro's inferior status, unlike that of other American citizens, was historically fixed by law and reinforced by the cult of racism. The Negro was highly visible as the white immigrant was not . . . The Negro could not become indistinguishable from other Americans merely by changing his name, his speech, his style. Color was his continuing badge of inferiority."

Tom Gale, housing director for the National Urban League, reminds us that the unstable economy of the 1970s and the subsequent decline in the housing industry have had their most serious impact upon the low-income populations of America. "As the housing situation in the central cities has become more critical for the poor, there has been a kind of spillover effect into the suburbs. It shows up not only in the housing problems in the low-income populations of the cities, but in the increase of service calls [complaints] from the suburban ghettos. The same kind of rollover of deteriorating real estate that has occurred in the nation's central cities has begun to appear in the first band of near-in suburbs."

A July 1979 report by the Regional Plan Association, which monitors economic and residential patterns for the New York metropolitan area, confirms those observations. The Association found that less than 10 percent of all census tracts within the states of New York, New Jersey and Connecticut were racially balanced. Using figures based on 1979 census data, the Association discovered that almost two-thirds of the region's black families were confined to only about 1.35 percent of its residential land. There is ample evidence that other suburbs of large metropolitan areas have continued the same segregating trend.

In Dade County, Florida, 73 percent of all blacks lived in eighteen of the county's poverty census tracts. And in Columbus, Ohio, a 1977-78 study by the Housing Opportunity Center found that 70 percent of all prospective black home-owners were steered into segregated communities. Another report issued by the Mid-Ohio Regional Planning Commission disclosed that while the Columbus inner city had a black population approaching 20 percent, less than 2 percent of blacks lived in the surrounding suburbs.

Even in the West, where racial segregation is purportedly less noticeable than in other parts of the United States, the

migration of blacks out to the suburbs has been guarded. In
the San Francisco Bay area, which has an inner-city black
population of nearly 13 percent, suburban blacks rose in
number from 5.4 percent in 1970 to 6.5 percent in 1980, but
were still largely concentrated in communities like Oakland,
Berkeley, Richmond, Emeryville, Marin City and East Palo
Alto.

In Dallas, where the black population is heavily confined to
the southern part of the inner city, black suburban out-
migration increased a mere .3 percent, from 3.6 percent in
1970 to 3.9 percent in 1980.

It seems clear that the movement of minority groups to the
suburbs is a brave new trend, but one that still hovers on the
brink of a dangerous pattern of resegregation.

How do these housing patterns affect the minority woman?
If a minority woman can afford to purchase a high-priced
home, she may, thanks to civil rights and fair housing
legislation, legally be able to do so. Yet the very real obstacles
of discriminatory real estate practices, along with the natural
reluctance of most minority women to move into areas where
they might feel uncomfortable, often prevent them from doing
so. As a young law student, looking with her husband for a
house in Westchester County, said: "We keep looking at
houses in communities where people don't make as much
money as my husband, because those are the only communities where we seem to be accepted. It makes me angry that
we aren't able to share in the good quality of life found in
higher status suburban communities. On the other hand, we
wouldn't want to end up in a neighborhood where we weren't
wanted, or where there might even be a bomb threat against
our lives."

The woman, who rented an apartment in a quiet section of
Yonkers, was referring to an incident that had occurred to
Tom Porter, a black IBM executive, and his family. They had
purchased a new home in an affluent section of Yonkers in
August 1979, only to wake the night after they had moved in
to find their house in flames from a firebomb. Other incidents
of overt racism, such as the appearances of the Ku Klux Klan

in Hamden, Connecticut, and Tara Hills, California, have left indelible scars on the middle-class minorities.

There is also the long-standing belief among other blacks that separatism may be the best solution to social and economic inequities. While that separatist impulse, rooted in the Black Power movement of the 1960s, has been criticized by some black leaders today, it has resulted in a new sense of pride among young blacks. "Black is beautiful," they say. So why should blacks strive to be integrated into a community that refuses to consider their self-worth? The implication is that blacks should be wary—especially if they are members of the middle class who may be economically capable of buying into a predominantly white community.

A 37-year-old black professional from Mill Valley, California, expressed her own pride in separation from the white affluent suburbs of Marin County: "I have some white girl friends of my own here in Marin County, but all of our good black friends—the ones my husband and I do our weekend socializing with—live scattered in other counties throughout the San Francisco Bay area. It means we are always traveling long distances to see our friends, but we believe it's worth it."

Many minority women, like one 30-year-old black attorney from Wheaton, Illinois, prefer to live in a community with other middle-class blacks. "If I had a choice, I'd live in a predominantly black middle-class community. The trouble is, there just aren't any towns like that here. I live in a mixed community, work for a large corporation and spend most of my time in a white world, but my closest friends are still black. I guess I seek them out. I feel more comfortable with blacks. I've had too many experiences in my life where whites turned their backs on us to feel completely at ease with them."

I've heard the same attitude expressed by Hispanic women, who are often faced with a language barrier rather than distinctive physical features. More often than not, these women have told me they prefer to remain within their own culture when they move to the suburbs. A 38-year-old Puerto Rican woman, who has lived in the United States for twenty years and whose English is readily understandable, offered me some insights into the kind of self-consciousness language differences often present. The woman, who runs a luncheonette with her husband on a busy street in Brentwood, Long Island, told about her early efforts to become active in her daughter's school: "At first I thought it was my duty to visit the school and meet the teachers, and finally after months of putting it off, I attended a school meeting. But I never went back after that one time. I was scared to death to speak English, and I never got involved with the school for that reason. To this day, all of my friends are Spanish. Why? Because I know they won't make fun of my speech."

Even if she isn't handicapped by language, the Hispanic woman may feel that the difference in her appearance or in her name may make it difficult for her to be fully accepted in an Anglo suburb. As one dark-hued Hispanic woman living in Whitney Heights, New York, put it: "In the city you blend in with everybody else. You don't stand out like a sore thumb. But in the suburbs, it's different. Even though they are polite and nice here, they make a big point of the fact that you are different. If you're Spanish, they want to know just where you are from and what your customs are like. The fear is that you are going to bring in lots of others like yourself—that you are going to fill up your house with ten or twelve of your relatives, and wreck the neighborhood and property values. Even after they understand you aren't like that, there's always a line between you, a feeling that they are not going to let you forget that you are different."

A 47-year-old Hispanic widow living in Commack, New York, who could easily "pass" for Anglo-American, says, "People often talk about the Puerto Ricans and how bad they are without having the faintest idea who I am. When I tell them, they become terribly embarrassed. Once, when I was staying at a friend's house for the weekend, her husband said, 'You're awfully pretty, but just make sure you don't end up marrying a Puerto Rican or a black.' I was so upset I thought I might have to leave. That's the kind of prejudice I have come up against all my life on Long Island. But I've decided that I have to tell people who I am, because maybe if they do like and accept me, they will eventually learn to accept other Latins."

Some minority women, faced with what they perceive as inevitable hostility and mistrust between the racial and ethnic groups, simply resign themselves to living in segregated communities. A number of economically sophisticated minority women have come to believe that there may be little sense investing money in a house in a white middle-class community. For them, the American dream of the single-dwelling home in an affluent, tranquil setting has taken on a nightmarish quality, a loathsome reminder of the deep-rooted differences among the races. Some minority women may decide, as did one 45-year-old utility company executive living in a Columbus suburb, that there is little sense "moving up" to a better, less heavily integrated neighborhood, even when they can afford to do so. "Owning a home for a middle-class black may be part of the American dream, as it once was for me and my husband when we married, but we've come to realize that it may not be the best kind of investment a black could make. Having all your personal equity in your home can be a tricky venture if you're black. You might be better off investing your money in bonds, insurance or some other kind of security."

But most middle-class minority couples still invest the bulk of their personal equity in housing, even when they are aware that racial discrimination can erode the value of their home. A study published in 1979 by the Regional Plan Association on housing in the New York metropolitan area found that only about 6 percent of the discrepancy between black and white housing could be explained by income differences. The Bureau of the Census discovered that 47 percent of all whites with incomes below $3,000 lived in suburban areas; in contrast, only 28 percent of blacks with incomes above $10,000 lived in the suburbs—a clear indication that income has less to do with where individuals live than other, less obvious social factors.

Robert Lake, assistant research professor at the Rutgers University Center for Urban Policy Research, studied 1,004 recent homebuyers in suburban New Jersey and found that blacks spend 50 percent more time looking for homes in interracial neighborhoods than did whites, even though they looked at fewer units in a smaller number of communities. Blacks also looked at 10 percent fewer homes in interracial neighborhoods than whites looking at homes in all-white neighborhoods. Dr. Lake's conclusion was that blacks—even after adjusting for income and previous housing equity—not only had more difficulty finding homes in suburban communities, but also had fewer units to choose from.

One of the current forms of segregation is widespread "steering" by real estate brokers when they show homes to blacks in suburban communities. A study produced by the U.S. Department of Housing and Urban Development in 1979, which examined housing sales and rental market practices for blacks in forty metropolitan areas throughout the United States, showed that 27 percent of all rental agents and 12 percent of all housing sales agents were found to discriminate openly against blacks seeking to move. When the study compared real estate practices in metropolitan areas of over 100,000 population to those in smaller urban areas, blacks living in the larger communities were found subject to the most flagrant discriminatory behavior.

Racial steering, as Tom Gale points out, has unfortunate and direct economic consequences for the black homeowner, even perpetuating the financial hardship so common to the black experience. If a black family is steered into a community where property values are low and increase at a slower rate than those in white communities, the family will be put at an immediate economic disadvantage. "One of the consequences of black middle-class ghettoization in the suburbs is lower home values which, in turn, have many implications for the middle-class black's ability to move around the country. When blacks sell a house in Westchester and move to a Cleveland suburb, they don't have the same chip to play with in the real estate market as did their white counterpart when he sold his house."

Although little research has been conducted on Hispanic housing problems, one has only to look at the clustering of Hispanic groups in the communities surrounding any large

American city to see the pervasiveness of discrimination against them as well. In Los Angeles County, Hispanics tend to live in only a handful of communities—Montebello, Monterey Park, Van Nuys, North Hollywood, Alhambra, and San Fernandino. In Westchester County, Hispanics are found in greatest numbers in Mt. Vernon, New Rochelle, Port Chester, White Plains, Ossining, Peekskill and Tarrytown. In Connecticut, Hispanics frequent cities like Bridgeport, Norwalk, New Haven and New London and are seldom found in the tranquil bedroom towns of the surrounding countryside.

For those in the suburbs who are both members of minority groups and single, the obstacles are even greater. Housing, especially apartment rental, is a most critical issue. The Census Bureau reports that the single female is twice as likely to rent as the single male. In 1979, nearly 40 percent of all white female-headed households were likely to rent; those numbers rose even higher for minorities—47 percent for all black female-headed households and 64 percent for all Hispanics. Since apartments are in shorter supply than single-dwelling homes in the suburbs, the single minority woman almost inevitably finds herself competing for housing with limited opportunities. Faced with a lower income than her white sisters, handicapped by racial and ethnic differences and vying for jobs that are increasingly sought by white suburban women, the single minority woman is outbid at almost every step when she presents herself to a potential landlord. Housing experts maintain that the single minority woman has the most difficulty of any population group finding a place to live in the suburbs. As Celia Zager, director of the housing program for the Fair Employment and Fair Housing Department of the state of California says, "The trouble seems to stem from the fact that the old stereotypes and myths of the past remain meaningful to many landlords. They seem to be based on the male chauvinistic attitude that the single woman's job is tenuous and that she won't be able to keep up that property. Even while this may be changing for many women in real life today, all too often the old attitudes still hold sway."

The single minority woman who has children has even more difficulty finding a place to live. She may, like one Hispanic woman from Daly City, California, end up lying about her married status. "I just tell all my landlords that my husband is on the road all the time, that he is a trucker, and isn't home much. Usually it seems to work out okay, unless they ask to see check stubs from his paychecks." Other such women have resorted to more drastic stratagems. One woman, having looked for an apartment for months and about to be evicted from a building in Oak Park, Illinois, resorted to living with her children in the basement of a condemned building without heat and running water through the summer, before finally appearing at a local social service agency. "As soon as landlords learned I had young children, I'd find the door slammed in my face," said the woman, who was barely out of her teens. "There's something about being black, poor and female that doesn't give you an even chance."

At a recent conference on housing discrimination, Eli Kimels, fair housing administrator of the Westchester Residential Opportunities program, equated landlords' intolerance for families with children with racial discrimination. "What we are finding in Westchester is that minority families with children suffer overwhelming discrimination when it comes to renting apartments. When we've questioned the landlords, we can't get a satisfactory answer from them about why they don't allow children. Our conclusion is that the intent of the policy is a way of keeping racial minorities out of certain neighborhoods in Westchester County."

The single minority woman with a low income is almost certainly doomed to live in a suburban ghetto. Once there, it becomes even more difficult for her to achieve upward mobility than it is for her contemporaries in the central cities. If, as a single head of household, she is already seriously restricted in where she lives, she is even more likely to be frustrated in her ability to find or travel to a job. The very advantages she aspired to in the suburbs—decreased population density and geographical separation between homes and businesses—work against her. Most suburban businesses are dispersed over a large geographical area, in outlying shopping centers, in corporate and industrial parks, or in specially zoned residential areas. More often than not, the low-income minority woman does not have access to a car. She must depend upon public transportation—which is extremely poor compared to that in the central cities—to get to and from work. If she is applying for an entry-level position, she must compete with white housewives who are recently returning to work. And there are the limitations of suburban child care. Given these circumstances, it is little wonder that the single minority woman of suburbia often finds herself trapped in a pernicious cycle of poverty.

If she is fortunate, like the young single parent at the beginning of the chapter, she may be able to return to her parental home, where shelter and child care can be provided for her by other family members. If not, she may become another hopeless member of the welfare rolls. She may become, as one single mother of six children in Mt. Vernon, New York, described herself, "stuck in a puddle of regrets." "I've given up the idea of being anything ever but poor," she told me one day as I sat in the shabby living room of her cramped apartment. "I think of myself as the tar baby in that Uncle Remus story. I'm stuck here forever and so are my kids. I know that they don't get a fair shake in the schools and the kids on the streets are a bad influence. The question is, what kind of real chance do my children have to make good in a community like this anyway?" The grimness of her own situation is augmented by the affluence she sees around her in the neighboring suburban communities. For the minority woman who heads her own household, living in a suburban ghetto is a bit like living in a glass house with a sealed front door.

Happily, a growing number of young minority women have found the key to economic autonomy and learned to turn it to their advantage. With the increasing number of young blacks and Hispanics ascending the educational and economic ladder has come a burgeoning middle class which has moved to the suburbs. Sociologists and urban planners maintain that the current wave of black suburbanization is primarily a middle-class migration, one that is expected to accelerate in the 1980s as the baby-boom generation enters the homebuying and childrearing stages of life.

A 1979 study issued by the Census Bureau indicated that young black couples—husband-and-wife families under the age of 35—had recently achieved near economic parity with their white counterparts: young black families earned $15,116 in 1976, compared to $15,483 for white families. But such parity was achieved, it should be pointed out, because more black women worked to help their husbands than did white women: 45 percent of all young black wives held jobs compared to 33 percent of all white married women.

Until recently, few white suburban women anticipated that they might be forced to work in order to help their families survive. But as one black woman from Arlington, Texas, reminded me, minority women seldom have had the opportunity to enjoy their leisure time. "Black women almost always expect to work. If you're married to a black man, there's always the fear that he might lose his job—even in this age of affirmative action. He makes less money than the white man anyway. So when a black family finally does accomplish that move to the suburbs, the black woman rarely thinks about remaining home to play golf or tennis. Usually she's more concerned about finding a good job."

Labor Department figures indicate that, in 1980, 60 percent of all black suburban women were employed, compared to 53 percent of all white suburban women. If the minority female is to become part of the suburban community, if she is determined to successfully integrate her loved ones, she is forced to assume the role of social mediator—in much the same way as the traditional suburban woman was expected to be the mediator between her family and the community. But the highly formalized social structure of the suburbs may seem terribly awkward to the black or Hispanic woman. The suburban traditions of carpool, play date and dinner party—originally predicated on the existence of a female dependent class—may be impractical for her in view of her demanding work schedule, lower family income, commitment to an inner-city church, childrearing and other household obligations.

She may come to feel, as did one young black schoolteacher from Tarrytown who was seriously contemplating a return to New York City, that the suburban environment makes excessive demands on its women, that it necessitates the presence of the woman at home for the transportation and social life of its youngsters. "The suburban environment is highly artificial; it seems to demand a formal relationship between the mothers even before the children can get together and play. Somehow that doesn't seem a natural way for kids to grow up. Children should learn how to get along with their peers on their own terms, as a normal part of their personal development. At least where I grew up in Brooklyn, I could hop on my bike and go out on the streets and play. Here everything is structured, programmed, packaged and delivered."

Some experts, like Dr. Thomas Clarke at Rutgers, one of the nation's foremost specialists in black studies, predict that the difficulties experienced by today's generation of minority suburban women will likely diminish as more middle-class blacks move to the suburbs and achieve economic parity with the white mainstream. Dr. Clarke says: "Today, a far larger fraction of the black suburban population is on equal footing with the white. For these, the coarser forms of discrimination have been outlawed or lost their effect. . . . In the seventies and soon the eighties . . . a new superstructure of residential patterns is emerging which will set the tone of race relations for years to come."

Wilford Julius Wilson maintains that as more blacks adopt white middle-class values, they will become accepted into the American mainstream communities with unprecedented ease. Arguing that socio-economic class rather than race is the great divider today, Dr. Wilson traces a sharp new division between the poor minorities and the ascendant middle class—just as there was, I might point out, between the elite white suburbanites and their poorer inner-city contemporaries decades ago. Dr. Wilson writes: "The recent mobility patterns of the blacks lend strong support to the view that economic class is clearly more important than race in predetermining job placement and occupation mobility. . . . And as we begin the last quarter of the twentieth century, a deepening schism seems to be developing in the black community with the black poor falling further and further behind middle and upper income levels."

Hugh Wilson, director of the Institute of Suburban Studies at Adelphi University and co-author of *Moving Beyond the Myth: Women in the Suburbs,* observes: "The higher the level of education and the more accustomed the individual is to the concept of cosmopolitanism, the more tolerant he seems to be. The highly educated person is much more likely to feel comfortable around blacks than, say, the construction worker might be. Income and education are really the key levelers when we talk about discrimination."

I have noticed that another factor contributing to the easy transition some minority groups make in highly educated or affluent communities is the space and privacy often found in such enclaves. "If a black can afford to live in an affluent community like Old Westbury, Long Island, nobody will probably give him much trouble," Professor Wilson says. "With zoning restrictions that may require large amounts of acreage, as for instance, four-acre zoning between homes, privacy is assured. The differences between people are more easily tolerated with affluence."

A middle-aged Puerto Rican woman married to an Anglo physician told of her easy reception into Larchmont, an affluent community in Westchester County. The woman, who became involved in a variety of civic and community groups which, prior to her appearance, had no minority members, claimed she never encountered difficulty when she moved to Larchmont because her neighborhood was so private. "We live in such a large house here and we have so many grounds between us that we never see our neighbors anyway. Many people here have two homes and travel between the two of them a good part of the year. It's gotten to the point where we don't even know who are the old neighbors and who are the new ones. If you want to meet other people in this town, you do it through your church, your schools and your civic organizations."

I certainly hope that there will be more pleasant relations between the races in the years ahead; the contemporary experience for most middle-class blacks in the suburbs today has most certainly been uneasy. Some minority women, like one department store executive I interviewed in Miami, have ventured into upper-middle income communities only after enduring unpleasant social conditions in working-class communities. The woman, who rented a house in Carol City, described her experiences: "At first I thought it would be good for the kids to live in a real house. But the neighborhood we rented in was a blue-collar community and while there were some blacks, there were also lots of rednecks and hillbillies. They used to toss stones against our front door constantly. At night I would lie in bed and hear rocks come banging against our house. In the mornings, there was broken glass on the front walk and beer cans dumped in a heap. Our neighbors sat out back every afternoon, drinking and yelling nasty things to my kids while I was at work. I began to hear the word 'nigger' a lot. After a while, things got real hot in the neighborhood. You could feel the racial tensions in the air. That's when I decided it was time to move. Today, we live in a nice community west of Miami, where I have rented a condominium. We may not have many material possessions, but we haven't had any problems in this community on account of race. I think that's because our values are the same as those of the other people in town."

A Hispanic woman in Wyandanch, New York, had a similarly unpleasant experience. After living in that integrated community for a decade with her family, she found that the neighborhood was beginning to attract larger numbers of low-income families. With the changing population, the woman claimed that antagonism between the various population groups worsened. "Every day we'd find the word 'spic' written across the sidewalk of our home. Our oldest daughter was mugged right outside our door. Finally, some of the neighborhood rowdies threw our lawn mower into the swimming pool.

'We've got to get out of here and get away from these people,' I kept telling my husband. Eventually we did. About a year ago, we moved to a lovely neighborhood. We are the only Spanish family on the block, but so far everyone has treated us with politeness and courtesy."

Why, even with attempted friendliness, does the awkward-ness between the races still exist in some form? I think of my own family's experiences in Westchester, and still the answers remain hidden somewhere behind our myths about minorities and theirs about us. One summer day in 1975, when my husband was home alone in our new home in a quiet neighborhood of New Rochelle, a young well-dressed black couple appeared at the front door, explaining that our real estate broker had given them our name. Apparently they had seen our house before we had moved in, and because of the extensive renovations we had undertaken, were curious to see it in its newly restored form. As it happened, the young couple had also recently moved into the neighborhood: he was a banker with a major New York firm and she an executive with a Westchester corporation. Our new neighbors walked curi-ously throughout the house, quietly admiring the improve-ments we had accomplished. After the tour, my husband invited them to stay on for a cold drink. But our new neighbors declined, explaining that they had other obligations that afternoon.

"Your house is lovely," the woman said to my husband at the front door.

"Yes, you've done wonders," agreed her husband. "I wish we could have bought this house. We wanted to, you know. But you put in your bid first."

My husband smiled uncomfortably. The couple, as he had learned that afternoon, lived just a few streets away from us in what seemed like an equally charming neighborhood. "But you know what a terrible condition the house was in when we bought it," my husband reminded them. "From what I've heard, your house was in much better shape when you first moved in. It's too bad my wife isn't here now. But let's get together soon, the four of us. Maybe we can go out to dinner— explore some of those Westchester restaurants I've been hearing about on the radio."

"Sure, that sounds like fun," agreed our new neighbors pleasantly.

Later, I called the woman and her husband to introduce myself, and to invite them over for cocktails. But for one reason or another, they were busy whenever I tried to make plans. Eager to make new friends, I persisted through the summer and even into the fall. Eventually, of course, I gave up calling them. Today, if I met them on the street, I still would not know who they are.

Some years later, the phone rang one unseasonably hot May morning. It was one of my neighborhood friends, a young woman in her early thirties who had put her house on the market just three days before. Already, despite the skyrocketing mortgage rates of 1981, she and her husband had been bombarded with bids that nearly matched the asking price for their home. The night before, she and her husband tentatively accepted the highest bid, which had come from another white professional couple.

"Hi. You'll *never* guess what happened this morning," my friend Lorraine said breathlessly. "I got a call yesterday from a woman and her husband who had just been transferred here from California and wanted to look at our house. I told them they could come see the house, even though we were close to accepting another bid. This morning when they arrived at the door, I was absolutely shocked. They were black!"

"So?" I replied uncertainly.

"Oh, they were lovely people. Too lovely. And they made a bid even higher than the one we had just accepted," Lorraine continued, her voice rising. "I didn't know what to say. I mean, we could sure use the money. That extra $5,000 would mean new carpets, paint and paper for our new house—things I know I couldn't afford to do the first year if we did go ahead and sell it to the first family. What do you think I should do?"

"Well, did you already promise the first family?" I asked her.

"Yes, we told them last night they could have the house."

"A deal's a deal, right?"

"Yes, I suppose so," my friend conceded reluctantly, "but that extra money is so tempting. Legally we haven't signed a thing yet, so we could still technically back out. But here is the kicker. After the black couple left, one of my neighbors came right over and asked me if I would actually sell to a black family, reminding me that they would be the first ones on the block. I was really shocked at her reaction. I told her I didn't know, that they hadn't even made a bid yet. But my neighbor still looked real upset when she left. Later, when I went out to pick up Lisa from school, two of the women from the other end of the street gave me these really dirty looks. It was clear they knew all about it and were angry."

"Oh, come on, you're exaggerating," I scoffed.

"No, I'm not," she insisted. "I only *wish* I were."

"But what do you care what your neighbors think, anyway?" I reasoned. "You don't see them socially anyway."

"That's true, but if we do sell to that black family, I'm certainly not going to give out my new address to anybody in our old neighborhood."

"I think you're overreacting," I suggested softly.

"I'm not, I'm not," Lorraine protested. "Of course, what difference does it matter what color these people are, anyway, if they can afford to buy this house? After all, the guy is a corporate executive. He probably has more education and class than most of the other people on this block. But on the other hand, I ask myself, would I like living next door to a black family? It sounds awful to say it, but I wouldn't. Maybe their kids would start dating mine. It's a very tricky issue."

"Well, I wish I could help you, but if it was me, I'd feel obliged to keep my word to the first couple," I finally said.

"I know," Lorraine sighed. "But there's all that money. Thanks for listening to me, anyway. It helps to talk it out. I think I'm going to call a few other people and get their opinions."

Three days later, Lorraine called again, this time sounding much calmer. "We sold to the white couple," she said, after we had dispensed with the initial small talk. "That means no new carpets or wallpaper. But you should have seen some of the reactions around here. People are still asking us who is going to move in, even though it's all settled. Imagine, just by the appearance of a black couple looking for a home, how much hostility was created. What gets me is that this is already an integrated neighborhood anyway. What *is* it that people are getting so upset about, anyway?"

Some minority women, sensitive to the likelihood of neighborhood resistance to their presence and cognizant of the fact that they, more than their husbands, are likely to have contact with their neighbors, take precautions to avoid social discomfort. A few have met with heartening success. One middle-aged black woman, who described her move into a predominantly white community northwest of Chicago as a somewhat uneasy transition, decided that she and her husband would introduce themselves to their neighbors rather than wait for an invitation from them to get acquainted. "What we did was throw a housewarming party for ourselves when we first moved in. It turned out to be a great idea. It enabled our neighbors to become acquainted with us right away as solid citizens, as people who were interested in keeping our property up and who espoused the same values. The result has been that we have had a lovely experience living in Elk Grove for the last five years."

A 34-year-old black woman, a warm person with an infectious sense of humor who worked in an electronics plant in Delaware, Ohio, described her acceptance into that town's white community as an unexpected benefit of trying to improve the extracurricular activities of her daughter. Realizing that her child's elementary school class lacked a Girl Scout leader and that there would be no troop in her daughter's fourth grade class, she volunteered for troop leadership. "I felt that I had to step forward, because none of the other mothers seemed willing to take on the responsibility, and we had some real good times that year. I even got some of the other mothers to come along on an overnight camping trip with me in the spring. Not for a minute since have I or my daughters ever felt a bit of prejudice. The experiences we all shared together in the Girl Scouts seem to have neutralized whatever bad feelings the others might have had."

Another minority woman, who moved into an all-white section of North Bergen, New Jersey, fifteen years ago, said that she always considered her appearance in such a community as a unique opportunity for personal growth—not only for herself but also for those white suburban women who had never known another minority woman before. The woman, who holds an executive position with a public agency, attributes the easy acceptance she and her family experienced to the discovery of similar values. "I think I've educated a lot of people to the fact that just because a person is black, doesn't necessarily mean that she is poor, lazy or uncaring. When I came to town many of the women I met hadn't even known a black individual personally except as a domestic or gardener. But because I was one of the few blacks around and was involved in the community, we all got to know each other pretty well. And what we discovered was that we weren't really so different after all."

The kind of extra effort required to establish lines of communication between different racial groups is admittedly rare. More often there is only silence. Even today, as I write these words and as my 5-year-old daughter plays with a black friend under the sprinkler in our back yard, there are barriers that separate her mother and myself from becoming fast friends and that we do not yet have the courage to confront.

And yet I am for cautious optimism. The similarities between the mother of my daughter's friend and me have become more obvious of late than ever before. We both struggle with similar problems—of career, child care, transportation, home maintenance, carpools, job flexibility and family. It is these issues that drew us together as acquaintances in the first place.

I am convinced that, as the composition of the modern suburban family continues to evolve, as divorce, the unstable economy and feminism drive more women back to work, as female-headed households become more numerous, the differences between the white suburban woman and her minority sister will continue to dissolve. In time, white, black, Hispanic and Oriental women will come to understand that the differences between them are only skin deep. The fragmentation engendered by the appearance of the new trends and minorities in the middle landscape during the 1970s and 1980s may be mended by a true sisterhood based on the recognition of mutual needs and interests.

9

Options:
New Directions for the
Suburban Woman

>◇◇

What we are facing now is not an absolute division between women, but an evolving continuum—an evolution from those age-old roots of female identity in the family, in the biological necessity of child-bearing, to the new necessities of selfhood, person-hood, economically rewarding work and the new possibilities of choice, personal control, personal growth.

Betty Friedan, *The Second Stage*

Today it takes an act of courage to suggest that our biggest factories and office towers may, within our lifetimes, stand half empty, reduced to use as ghostly warehouses or converted into living space. Yet this is precisely what the new mode of produc-tion makes possible; a return to cottage industry on a new, higher, electronic basis and with it, a new emphasis on the home as the center of society.

Alvin Toffler, *The Third Wave*

*   *   *

WHO IS THE NEW SUBURBAN WOMAN? As I have come to understand her, she is someone who feels free to live her life and speak her mind in a highly individual way beyond the bonds of matrimony and motherhood, who has thrown off the shackles of tradition, who has cast social conventions to the winds in an environment that always tried to stifle her voice. In David Riesman's terms, she is no longer other-directed.

Today's suburban woman is inner-powered and has come to regard herself as more than a reproductive mannequin: Bob's wife or Susan's mother. She is a unique human being, defiant of description; therein lies her strength as a mediator for the jarring ideologies of our age. But there is a danger in her autonomy too. Will this distinctive new woman be able to effect a constructive evolution or will she fall into a privatism that alienates her from the rest of the community?

I worry about the future of the new suburban woman as I contemplate my own life and the lives of my friends. We are women so involved with our own families and careers that we sometimes overlook the concerns of our immediate surroundings. Sometimes my fears take precise shapes, nightmare dimensions, a landscape that seems neither so distant nor so impossible.

It is nightfall and already tomorrow's suburban landscape has taken on a luminous glow, the trees animated by the passage of electric cars, the blaze of solar-powered streetlights and the phosphorescent glare of multidwelling homes, transforming the twilight into a shimmering golden frieze. Decades ago, the neighborhood stores disappeared, replaced by a single shopping mall, a looming windowless structure encased in wood-toned aluminum. Beneath the neighborhood baseball field, with its synthetic evergreen grass, is an underground parking garage for the shopping mall that has become the social center for all suburban life. Several hundred feet beyond the mall stands a neighborhood of century-old split-level homes remodeled into multidwelling units for singles, childless couples and the elderly. Few children's voices are ever heard on these streets, and those youngsters have been silenced by nightfall, collected back into their homes and tucked into their beds, rare but prized specimens of the suburban landscape.

Few women know their neighbors. The differences between women have become accentuated by the urban atmosphere of these densely populated communities and their highly specialized occupations. Few women remain home during the day. Most disappear from the neighborhood in early morning in electric-powered automobiles and do not appear again until dusk, pausing momentarily in their driveways, waiting for the automatic garage doors to open, only to be swallowed up again into their starkly furnished homes. Virtually all ablebodied women in this society work. Some have made a full-time profession of mothering and spend their days in the module day-care centers. Others are employed as telecommunications technicians, construction workers, oceanographic farmers or domestic architects, depending on their training and aptitude. Times are harder now for all women than they were in the golden age of the suburbs, the affluent mid-twentieth century when most middle-class women had no profession, were married, leisured and dependent, homogeneous in their demographic composition and understanding of their life roles.

Less than a third of tomorrow's women are married, and those who are contribute to the family's financial welfare. Taxes are extraordinarily high: there is a long-lived elderly population, a dwindling social security system and an ill-financed national health care plan, which must all be supported by young, vigorous Americans. Children have become a luxury for most suburbanites, indulged in by only a small, highly specialized portion of the population.

Men and women no longer travel far to work; most commute to nearby parts of the suburban counties they live in, a ten or fifteen minute drive from their homes. Long ago, people abandoned commuting to the central cities, as the urban centers dwindled in importance. Gradually, the suburbs became the preferred area for most Americans, the dominant

way of life for people of all classes in the postindustrial era.
That migration began long ago, back in the twentieth century
when people began to move from the large cities back to the
small towns of America. Once settled in those tiny communities, the newcomers inadvertently spawned new suburbs,
sprawling municipalities with single-dwelling homes that had
to be served by new shopping centers and highways and were
built close to the corporate parks and product-distribution
centers. Suburbs reminiscent of the Levittowns and split-level
developments of the 1950s.

Today, most of the older suburban neighborhoods built in
the final years of the Industrial Age have been invaded by low-
income populations. In the third millennium, they are the
blighted offshoots of the outgrown central cities.

Considering current social and economic trends, such a
prediction for the suburbs of the future is possible. But I
believe even then the bucolic dream of the free-standing
cottage in a verdant setting with its tender female guardian
will persist deep in our collective subconscious.

Home for Thanksgiving. Mother and child. The log cabin in
the woods. The village green with its flowers and bandstand.
The sun-kissed sanctuary far from the din of city skyscrapers
and the workaday world. These images linger in our memory,
powerful cultural icons branded deep in our minds and hearts,
long after the realities of an earlier age have disappeared,
preventing us from believing that the environment described
above might indeed become a reality. The power of the
classical suburban ideal assures us we will never have to make
such accommodations in modern technological America.

Which of these two scenarios will be realized for our
suburbs and its women? We are now teetering on the edge of
a new social reality, moved by the economic, political and
demographic changes of the late twentieth century, a reality
foreshadowed by the emerging profile of the suburbs and the
suburban woman, fragmented and shaped as she has been by
a waning industrialism.

Who is the new suburban woman who has come to frequent

the middle landscape and what does her appearance presage for the future? With surprise, and perhaps understandable regret, I have come to understand that she is increasingly difficult to categorize, that, as we enter the last decades of the twentieth century and try to ferret a meaning out of the age, the suburban woman has become the most obvious symbol of social change. She has been transformed more radically than any other group in the last decade—into the forefront of social innovation.

How did she achieve this curious position—she who traditionally has been a reactor to the actions of others, rather than an initiator of actions? She who was always categorized as the staid, conformist symbol of American womanhood? Who is the new suburban woman after all?

She lives on every residential street. She is divorced. Employed. Remarried. A hard-line traditionalist. Leisured. Childfree. A member of a minority. A working mother. Torn between pursuit of a career and her duties at home. Worried about meeting the bills at the end of the month. Competing for law school. Protesting against pornographic movies. Growing vegetables in her back yard. Having an abortion. Working to prevent passage of the ERA. Coming to think of housework as less important than spending time with her family. Living with an unmarried member of the opposite sex. Having her tubes tied. Heading a volunteer organization. Spending her days in a station wagon which she is thinking of trading in for a smaller, gas-efficient automobile. Thinking of giving up carpooling altogether. She is a born-again Christian. A feminist. A born-again human being. A born for the first time autonomous individual.

Who is the new suburban woman? Unlike earlier generations of women who inhabited the suburbs with singular devotion to home and hearth, the new suburban woman is many possibilities, many different voices: some contradictory, some conciliatory, each a distinct, variegated example of the vast potential of female life in the last years of the twentieth century. And beyond.

She has become a bellwether for all American womanhood.

The suburban woman has always been the absorption point for changing American values, the translator of bright new city ideas and old rural values into a practical humanistic whole, the stuff that real people and real lives are made of. A litmus test for the latest fads in our society. In contrast to the trendy crowds of the central cities and the isolated individualists of the country, the suburban woman has represented the realistic compromise of modern life, an era when environments, relationships and social norms are evolving much more rapidly than at any previous time in history. Given the speed of contemporary life, the suburban woman has of necessity become a deft, cautious arbitrator who has navigated herself and her family through the rocky reaches of one transition after another—recession, radical feminism, right-wing economics, energy crises, rampant inflation—to maintain a semblance of order out of the chaotic events of our age. The divisions between social privatism and altruism, feminism and traditional womanly roles have been drawn. She has weathered the consequences of those divisions in her own neighborhood. It is up to her to synthesize them.

Looking back over the history of the suburbs, it is easy to understand why the suburban woman was so long neglected by historians and social critics, disparaged in the public view as a frivolous nonentity. At the peak of the Industrial Age, it was she who suffered the worst abuses and was confined to the most powerless role of all—the economic and social parasite of men and machines. It is no wonder that by the 1950s, when sexism was supreme, the suburban woman began to fall from her exalted position as a "wondrous creature" into being "just a housewife" a decade later.

For the suburbs were a striking symbol of what had gone wrong in America, and the changes that followed were inevitable attempts to correct the corruptions of a machine-mad materialism. Born in the deafening clatter of the Industrial Revolution, as income-selective sanctuaries, those early bedroom communities could only mirror its grandeur, and ultimately, its excesses.

The abuses of the Industrial Age—and the suburban life-style it created—inevitably gave birth to a new order. Out of the suffocation of their own lives, the cloistered women of the 1950s produced a generation of children who railed against the opulence and conformity of the postwar era. Our gluttonous thirst for goods and services expanded the suburban myth to remarkable dimensions, creating a larger-than-life cinematic vision for these impressionable young people. It was an impossible vision of affluence and perfectability, one which many young adults are still coming to terms with today. It has become a central obsession for them to carve out a more authentic, individualized reality.

"But this isn't the way I remember the suburbs of my childhood," the young women say when they move back there as adults today, disappointed that the dream of the perfect home, happy housewife and close-knit community of like-minded individuals is illusory. At the same time, the expectations raised by this generation of women, the new identity they have found through feminism, sexual revolution and individualism, do not yet work smoothly in the suburban environment. A new balance must be found.

I believe that progress is being made. We of the contemporary generation are beginning to realize that the suburbs, long thought of as "feminine" because of their tranquility, lack of social innovation and traditionalism, are actually preferred by men—that women frequently find them restrictive. As Dr. Susan Saegert, a professor in the Department of Environmental Psychology at the City University of New York discovered when she analyzed the satisfaction of men and women with the suburbs, men were almost always more pleased. She writes: "Women frequently feel a great loss of options after the move. For men, the range of home-related satisfactions is broadened in the suburbs, without as great a loss of other opportunities."

Ironically, while the suburbs were always painted as sanctuaries for women and children, they were more beneficial for men, vital retreats from the chaos of the cities. Despite the rhetoric of the nineteenth century portraying women as fragile, spiritual creatures, they were placed in the middle landscape not merely as members of a protected class, but as specially designated curators. Women have historically been sold a bill of goods. It has taken them over a century of living there fully to appreciate the subtley and long-range implications of that seduction. Today, decades after female suffrage, widened educational opportunities and amended property laws, affirmative action, equal opportunity, new matrimonial legislation, improved birth control and a raised feminist consciousness, we are just beginning to forge a new multidimensional approach to the possibilities of suburban life. I believe that today's young suburban women are setting forth with bold expectations, with as much vigor and attention as women of an earlier era lavished upon their suburban homes and gardens.

Today we hear a great deal about the "androgynous" lifestyle of our young men and women, that role differences between them are disappearing, that intellectual and emotional distinctions are few, that those that do exist are rapidly disappearing as men and women begin to share household and childrearing responsibilities more than ever before. The "new breed American," as pollster Daniel Yankelovich has dubbed him, is less likely to move his family around the country at the whim of his employer, less willing to sacrifice his personal life to the corporation.

For corporate life is changing: in the improved communication between worker and employer, in the increased attention to what has been called "the quality of life" in the workplace and in work innovations such as flextime, job-sharing, flexplace and the four-day work week. There is a lot of talk about these promising accommodations, but let's take a hard look at the realities. Institutions, especially in the business world, evolve slowly, usually only when management can justify changes as a way of realizing greater profits or productivity. Flextime and job-sharing may promise and even demonstrate greater worker productivity, but they are still too new—and too closely connected with the concept of the "new breed American"—to have found wide acceptance. As Jane Newitt, a senior researcher at the Hudson Institute, a futuristic think tank, has observed, such innovations may be muted by the fact that America will soon be faced with a rapidly growing elderly population: "It is hard to imagine that a society drawing close to explosively rapid growth of its aged population will be able to tax its productivity very much in order to provide more leisure and pleasanter work conditions for the young."

Dr. Stanley Nollen, an economics professor at Georgetown University's School of Business Administration, sees flextime, job-sharing and other innovative work practices as positive signs of changing worker mores, but maintains that such practices may have difficulty gaining acceptance. One example of how other potentially worthwhile employment practices sometimes suffer because of deep-rooted attitudes is part-time work: "Permanent part-time employment offers the employer and employee many advantages, but the notion that it is associated with women's work has made it suffer and relegated it to low status. The same thing might happen with flextime and job-sharing, even though probably just as many men as women would benefit from those innovations. Why shouldn't a man have just as many options spending time at home with his kids or his family as a woman? It's an important question, but would require an entire restructuring in the corporate world about the way we think of work and the family to make those innovations work well."

Dr. Michael Wachter, an economist at the University of Pennsylvania, predicts that even higher percentages of women will work and that they will fill more high-status jobs within the next decade. One inevitable result of their appearance, says Dr. Wachter, is that more accommodations will be made for innovations such as flextime, flexplace and job-sharing. But when the baby-boom generation ages and is replaced by a smaller work force who will, in turn, command higher wages for their services, Dr. Wachter predicts that many educated married women may find it economically feasible to remain home once again.

Such innovations therefore seem unlikely to be wholly embraced by corporations as the solution to the division between home and workplace—unless the entire system of production and consumption in our civilization is overhauled. Some believe that an entire reordering of our economic system is imminent, pointing out the new technologies, the declining commercial importance of the central cities, the service-oriented direction of our economy and the long-range potential of telecommunications and computers. But whatever direction our economy ultimately follows, I believe that work in relation to our personal lives has become the central controversial issue for a generation of young men and women. It is being seen in the suburbs—in the ways women have begun to manage their own lives, in the choices many have made about their own occupational potential and in some of the new ways, beyond flextime and job-sharing, that they have begun to develop new careers.

We are now entering an age of social and political conservatism; some say that the 1980s have already begun to resemble in many ways the reactionary period of the 1950s. In some ways I suppose that is true. But it would be foolhardy to suspect that the children of the fifties who rioted on the college campuses and in cities in the 1960s, who strove for self-expression and individuality in the 1970s and are now settling down into marriages, parenthood and careers in the 1980s, would consciously embrace the traditional life of their parents. We have simply come too far in our knowledge and technology, know too much as sons and daughters, as men and women and as parents, to fall back into a pattern so obviously fallacious. At the same time, many of us have become disenchanted with the extremes of feminism and individualism and are now striving to strike a balance between ourselves and our loved ones, between women and men, parents and children. As a result, some of those work conflicts are being reexamined by the new women of the suburbs, partially in the home.

The house may assume new significance as an economic unit in the way it did in preindustrial society, when the family often fed and clothed itself from products grown outside and manufactured under its thatched roof. As Alvin Toffler wrote in *The Third Wave,* tomorrow's homes may become "electronic cottages" acting as both producing and consuming units for individual families: "The home will assume a startling new importance in Third Wave civilization. The rise of the prosumer [one who both produces and consumes manufactured goods], the spread of the electronic cottage, the invention of new organizational structures in business, the automation and de-massification of production, all point to the home's reemergence as a central unit in the society of tomorrow—a unit with enhanced, rather than diminished, economic, medical, educational and social function."

The new suburban woman has already begun this process. The appearance of nontraditional women in the suburbs is an indication that the suburbs are becoming a dynamic place for all women to live and work—whatever their marital, ethnic or occupational status. Some have started businesses of their own. Others manage companies that hire women almost exclusively, or cater specifically to their needs. Others work in the helping professions, devoting themselves to the cares and concerns of troubled, divorced, aged or displaced women. Many others are vitally engaged in political activities to effect change in the community. However diverse their individual approach, these new women share a common characteristic: they have begun to turn the suburban environment from a crippling handicap into an advantageous proving ground, discovering new ways to work and bring the home and business community closer together.

I remember visiting a landscape artist in northeast Dallas. The mother of two children, Keith Lowry operates a thriving residential and commercial landscaping service from her home. For her, as for many other young women, the suburban community has been a solution to the highly individualized way she has chosen to organize her life—where she could at once raise children, maintain a comfortable home and pursue a career of her own. Interested in plants, designs and landscaping from an early age, Keith decided to start her business after years of remaining at home as a "bored housewife." She began simply, by knocking on the doors of

other suburbanites, interesting them in her ideas for landscape design and building up an enthusiastic clientele. Today
her business caters to major Dallas corporations as well as
residential clients. In the course of building her business,
Keith Lowry's perceptions of the suburbs changed. The
material accumulation of goods and the presentation of a
conformist image, once so important to Keith Lowry, and still
important to traditional suburban women, no longer have
much meaning. "A decade ago, my automatic response to any
neighborhood I was shown by a real estate broker that had a
pickup truck parked in the driveway was a resounding 'no.'
Here I am, ten years later, with the landscape truck I own and
drive now parked in front of my own house. What I've
discovered as I've grown stronger in my own identity is that
the superficial appearance of things has become less important than inner realities."

For years, Suzanne Thayer lived in a suburban community
near West Palm Beach, Florida, where she simultaneously
raised children, taught school part-time, gave piano lessons
and designed and sold clothes and pillows from her home. For
years, Mrs. Thayer's overworked, underpaid, frenzied way of
life continued, as she tried to juggle household responsibilities
and paid work. Finally her attempts to assume the "supermom" role rose to a mad crescendo, when meals were hastily
prepared, piano students were asked to stuff designer pillows
while they waited for their lessons and sewing equipment and
business invoices overran the house. Finally, the products Ms.
Thayer designed became so popular that she moved them out
of her home. Today, Suzanne Thayer heads her own company,
a multimillion dollar enterprise located in an industrial section
of West Palm Beach. Almost all the employees of Haphazard
Design, as the business is called, are women; most live in the
suburban communities surrounding West Palm Beach. Not
coincidentally, company hours coincide with the hours children attend the public schools—from 7:30 A.M. to 3:30 P.M.

Occasionally, of course, there are emergencies: a child gets
sick and has to be taken home from school. Sometimes there
are school vacations. And Ms. Thayer has hired a full-time

person just to answer the calls that come in on the company switchboard for her eighty employees from children, schools and spouses. But for Suzanne Thayer, the idea of running a business in which women are employed almost exclusively is an affirmation of her own belief, an expansion of her own earlier experiences as a suburban wife and mother who tried to supplement the family income. "So many of these suburban women are capable, intelligent and talented. The tragedy is that most of them have been so bogged down with houses, kids and families that they rarely get a chance to develop their own potential."

Laura Horowitz, a young suburban wife and mother in northern Virginia, found that her editorial skills were in demand even after she decided to quit work and remain home with her young children. That was in 1969. But the free-lance editorial work she agreed to do in her own house before she had children, and later, while they slept and played, grew so rapidly that she began to offer many of her assignments to other writers and editors. In 1972 she became so inspired by the number of other experienced, talented women she had encountered in the suburbs who were home with children but still wanted to work that she started her own business. Today her firm, Editorial Experts, Inc., has grown into a million dollar enterprise. Money has been one obvious reward, but Laura claims that her financial success has been dwarfed by a greater achievement—the fact that she is the source of employment for 200 writers, editors and typists who work from their homes. "At least half the women who work for me want to remain home because of their children. That pleases me very much, because one of my goals was to help the college-educated now-at-home housewife find a way to get decent professional work."

These dynamic new women of suburbia often emerge as economic entities to their own surprise. Typically, the metamorphosis of these women begins slowly: as a hobby or interest they have patiently nurtured, which blossoms, almost overnight, as in a fairy tale, into a viable money-making venture. I think of Babette Feibel, a married mother of four, a devoted community volunteer who lives in a pretty suburban subdivision of Columbus. Although Mrs. Feibel always thought of herself as a conventional nurturer with little interest in a career of her own, she had a high energy level and a penchant for bright ideas. One day she designed a series of hand-knit customized sweaters for teddy bears: it was a nice hobby, she thought, that she could have fun with and even earn a little pin money from. Quietly she began to sell her products to stores and boutiques in Columbus under the name of Abel Creations. Within a few months, requests for her product were pouring in so quickly that she had to hire several other women to work in their homes as knitters to help her keep up with the orders. A year later, her business has grown into a nationally distributed enterprise whose products appear in college stores, gift shops and department store chains.

Two suburban women from New Jersey, Marion Behr and Wendy Lazar, initiated a survey on female home-based businesses. After three years of research, they were startled to identify over 150 occupations conducted in the home—as diverse as importing firms, medical laboratories, data processing firms, dentistry and psychological counseling services. Public reaction to the survey of 500 women conducted by Ms. Behr and Ms. Lazar was so enthusiastic that they recently founded the National Alliance of Homebased Businesswomen.

Recent government studies indicate that there are at least a million women who run businesses from their homes, but the trend is expanding so rapidly today that even the Labor Department has no idea how many actually exist. Well over half the businesses identified by Marion Behr and Wendy Lazar are located in the suburbs, natural catalysts for the new, still largely unknown female American work force.

"What could make better sense?" says Marion Behr. "The problem most women face if they live in the suburbs is getting baby-sitters if they want to work. The best jobs are often in the city, but with young children at home, commuting is a problem. Home-based businesses are a natural solution."

There are other aspects of the coming renaissance for suburban women. I think of a whole other group of young women—attorneys, accountants, physicians, artists, designers and technicians—who have moved to the suburbs deliberately, feeling they have a better chance of building a career there than in the cities or the countryside. Most of these women have been pleased with their decision. For it is in the middle landscape, where homes have been increasingly surrounded by new business centers and corporate parks, that new services and talents are so badly needed. As the owner of a successful public relations company in Cedarhurst, Long Island, put it: "Out here, we're a prized commodity. Just the fact that the suburbs have for so long lacked services and that the brightest, most ambitious women in this field went to the cities makes this open territory for my company."

The trend is clear. Fewer women are moving to the suburbs as passive dependents, their sole motivation for relocating the acquisition of a high-status home. No longer do the home and the community modern women live in seem to be as important as they once were, when they were among the few means available to her for self-definition. "What do you do?" has become as important a question for middle-class women as "Where do you live?" Undoubtedly, there will always be value judgments made about particular communities because of their housing stock, their schools, the educational and income levels of their residents. But for today's women, their importance has dwindled.

The home of the future will be smaller. Dr. Floyd Lapp, assistant director of the Tri-State Regional Planning Commission, notes that the large, free-standing, single-dwelling suburban home has become anachronistic in an age of high energy costs, divorce, singlehood and prolonged life expectancy. "What we're into today is a kind of fossilized life-style in the suburbs. What way is there for us to go but back home again—back into the city, or into the conversion of the large old suburban homes into smaller apartment units which will reflect the decreased family size and greater number of individual households?"

I believe that the diminished physical size of our new homes reveals a larger conceptual change among our women as well—as women become increasingly self-actualized, they unconsciously begin to place less psychic value on their homes. It seems inevitable that as women devote more time to their occupations and less to the physical care of their residences, houses will continue to shrink in physical size.

Women will still continue to be drawn to the suburbs for traditional reasons—as respites from the congestion of the cities, as more living space, as good environments in which to raise children. The search for residential bliss in a semirustic setting is still a national obsession. According to the 1980 census, 44.8 percent of the American population, or 101 million people, now live in the suburbs, compared to 41 percent a decade ago. And while there has been a lot of publicity about the fact that rural parts of the country have recently gained population at the expense of the central cities, it is the suburbs that have grown the most. The trend shows little signs of changing.

A study by the Joint Center for Urban Studies of the Massachusetts Institute of Technology and Harvard University on attitudes of 900 Americans found that while many people expressed the desire to live in a more rural setting, most will probably continue to choose the suburbs for their homes. Richard Coleman, author of the report, maintains that the rural myth may be charming, but in this age of urban and suburban industrialization, not very practical. He wrote: "Most city people smitten with dreams of Ruralia admit they cannot get there soon. They are not ready to trade a job in hand for one in the bush. They have ties to aging parents, to brothers and sisters and other relatives which they cannot bring themselves to sever. . . . So the move is delayed, it remains a hope, a distant dream. Perhaps it will never be realized. Meanwhile there is a compromise possible, a move to the edge, or beyond the Houstons, Rochesters or Daytons they live in now."

A significant proportion of today's young women moving to the suburbs will continue to live their lives in a conventional mode, adhering to the old values of femininity and dependence in spite of the knowledge that they are anachronisms—

the only mothers home on the block during the day, the only ones left who still volunteer in the community service organizations. Some of these women will identify with conservative political and moral causes in an angry defense against what they correctly perceive as an erosion of traditional American values in an age of irremediable social change. For the foreseeable future, many politically apathetic young women will continue to arrive at the threshold of their first suburban homes with dewy-eyed excitement, even if later they find themselves trapped in a tedious household routine, or wondering at the futility of lives spent on the tennis courts, at the bridge tables or at the shopping centers.

There is another, more telling population of modern women who have come to live in today's suburbs, perhaps the most characteristic group of all, who have few worries about the relative advantages or disadvantages of suburban life and only some concern about the role of modern women. Most of these women live there because it is economically feasible, because they believe the schools are better and because they are closer to their jobs than they would be if they lived in the small towns. They are the pragmatists, readily accepting the suburban life as the best compromise between city and country. And they work, not because they are careerists or radical feminists, but because they have to, either because their husbands are not present or do not make enough money to insure a comfortable life for them or their children.

I think of a young mother I interviewed living in a new housing tract near Homestead, Florida, a fast-growing community southwest of Miami. "The hell with all this feminist rhetoric we've been listening to for the past ten years. If you really like men and know how to get along with them, you don't have trouble in marriage. You certainly don't worry about it. In our house, whoever gets home first at night makes dinner. We share the household chores on the weekends and take turns doing the laundry. I work, but not because I'm a feminist. My husband and I just want to have the good things in life for ourselves and our children and we know that we can't afford them on his salary alone."

Even for this ideologically uncommitted population, a crucial question remains: what *is* a comfortable life today? Does it mean a late model car, several color television sets, chic clothes, stereos, videotape machines, luxurious vacations, college and graduate school education for the kids? Have we deluded ourselves into thinking that the achievement of a material standard is the formula for personal happiness? Is materialism the ultimate betrayal of the suburban dream, in this day of runaway inflation and rapidly rising prices? Many men and women who have lived in the suburbs suspect that we may well be living out an erroneous pastiche of the Jeffersonian vision of having the best of both worlds. Such a prescription for happiness may have lost its potency, may be as phony as the fake brick wall and floor coverings that decorate our suburban kitchens.

Perhaps that is why some of us find ourselves skeptical when we think about the suburbs. We perceive its notions of the good life—prime ribs in every microwave, a luxury stereo system in every room, two cars in every garage—as symbols of a national dream turned nightmare. Perhaps that is why some of us desperately rush back to the small towns in an attempt to find purer values and escape the rat race of urbanized—and suburbanized—life. But before we return to rural America to make new cornfield suburbs from those communities, maybe we should take another step backward. Perhaps we should ask once again: what is it that women want?

Now, as before, the answer must be a simple dignified response: happiness. Whatever that means to each woman. And wherever she can find it. A 1979 *Redbook* survey on happiness conducted on 52,000 women by Gail Sheehy found that "inner harmony" was the most consistently stated definition for personal happiness. But curiously, among young women aged 18 to 29, material comfort took precedence over inner harmony as a life goal—an attitude uncomfortably reminiscent of the old suburban premise. That may offer us some insight into why so many young women have formed such a strong attachment to work today, why so many continue working throughout their lives whether they are married, have children or remain single.

I believe it is the issue of materialism more than any other that sparks the conflict between the various groups of women now struggling for power in America today. For it is the pursuit of material comforts that has sent many women back to work. The struggle has barely begun in earnest. We are just beginning to realize that we live in dangerously divided times, in an environment that seems to insure a new wariness among women. It is in the suburbs where we will be forced to pay the highest price for the abruptness of the transition among women, where we have already begun to witness the same type of social fragmentation characteristic of the cities.

Today the possibility exists that the woman on our block who shares a carpool might suddenly disappear, a casualty of the work force or the matrimonial courts. The working woman who lives next door may think of us as pampered, lazy housewives if we remain home all day. The neighbor who lives one street away and with whom we exchange recipes may be spending her days campaigning to cut funds from a day-care program our children attend. The political activist on our street who supports the ERA may sell her house to a minority family or a group of young single men and women. The mother who baby-sits for us so that we can pursue a full-time career may donate her salary to the Right-to-Life Committee. The divisive possibilities in the middle landscape are immense—much more so than the different views of childrearing separating traditional suburban women a generation ago. The conflict beneath the superficial suburban tranquility today is a potential volcano, which might suddenly erupt into political reaction that could change an entire way of life for young and old women alike.

One way to avoid the conflict is simply not to deal with our neighbors at all, to pretend that the possibilities for such an explosion don't exist. We say we don't have time for *those* women on our street; that because we don't have kids, we no longer know others in our neighborhood; that because we work we no longer have energy for community or political activities. In our private lives we remain silent about our conflicts regarding work, even as we pursue careers; we hesitate publicly to express our needs for quality child care, even as we struggle to find baby-sitters; we do little to insist upon better public transportation, as we juggle carpools, or wrangle with suburban taxicab companies. All too often we are closemouthed, even with our own friends and family, because these issues are painful ones which might touch upon soft spots in the lives of our loved ones or friends, inciting their anger or guilt.

As a result, we draw back. We close our doors. The divisions leave us in chilly isolation in our homes, apartments and condominiums. How shall we mold the remnants of our earlier community life into a new social order? Shall we continue to retreat into the "bell jar of amoral privatism," as Maxine Schnall has described the current social climate, or prolong what Christopher Lasch describes as the "culture of narcissism"?

I sometimes wonder if we are the unwitting victims in an era of rapid change, standing in the crosswinds between two completely different stages of civilization. Who among us is able to withstand the relentless torrents? Shall we end up, like the alienated suburban women pictured at the beginning of this chapter, segregated into strict occupational and nurturing roles, mistrustful of our nearest neighbors, blinded to our common needs, stripped of our womanly humanity? Are the emotional turbulence, the alienation, the special kind of loneliness so many women of the suburbs feel inevitable?

As Alvin Toffler explains, today's alienation has a special quality: "The loneliness we are witnessing is not necessarily caused by a function of individual aberration, eccentricity or anything the individual is doing wrong, but rather because the society is *manufacturing* loneliness—because we're going through a thirty or forty year period of inventing new forms of group living. The loneliness exists because we haven't yet learned to deal with social diversity. We want to be individuals, but part of that cost is finding other individuals with whom we can share things in common."

How do we find those individuals? And how can we work

together to resolve our differences? How shall we settle issues of home and family and career with our men, with other women and, most important, with ourselves?

I wonder if we are now confident enough to cast aside the extremes of feminism and enlist men in a cooperative effort to share the duties of home, hearth and childrearing. If women will be able to pursue careers on their own terms, not necessarily those based on the male model of success. If it will come to pass, as Betty Friedan predicts: "In the second stage, the woman will find and use her own strength and style at work, instead of trying so hard to do it man's way . . ." If, with our newly roused consciousness and heightened respect for all women, we will finally be able to put aside questions about the meaning of motherhood and femininity.

If so, if such an evolution is possible among women—and I believe we must make it possible—it will occur first in the suburbs. The very nature of the suburban community has always demanded compromise among women. Today, the potential for female unity depends upon flexibility of a special sort, the kind that capitalizes upon, that extols rather than denigrates, her strength as a woman. In the diversity of the new suburban woman, in the ingenious ways she is developing to link herself to the mainstream and work, even in the pain she feels in social fragmentation, such an evolution has already begun.

Notes

CHAPTER 1/*An Overview of the Modern Suburbs*

The opening quotation for this chapter by Antoinette Rehmann Perrett appeared in *Good Housekeeping* magazine in October 1909, Vol. XIIX, No. 4, on page 375.

The quotation from Elizabeth Janeway was taken from her book *Between Myth & Morning: Women Awakening*, William Morrow & Company, Inc., New York, 1975, pages 10 and 11.

The figures on suburban female employment were extracted from the U.S. Bureau of the Census report, *1979 Current Population Survey, Employment and Earnings Report*, Table 57, Annual Wages, published in January 1980.

League of Women Voter membership figures were provided in its *Membership Profile 1930–1979*.

The *Harper's* magazine article referring to thc 1950s was entitled, "The Big Change in Suburbia"; written by Frederick Lewis Allen, it appeared in June 1954.

The worrisome comments made about the women of the fities by the *New York Times Magazine* appeared in an article entitled, "Homogenized Children of New Suburbia," published on September 14, 1954.

Migration figures for people moving from the suburbs to the cities can be found in the U.S. Bureau of the Census report *Social and Economic Characteristics of the Metropolitan and Non-Metropolitan Population: 1977 and 1970,* Current Population Reports, Special Studies P-23, No. 75.

The *Chicago* magazine analysis of big-city gentrification was called, "About that Urban Renaissance"; written by Dan Rottenberg, it appeared in May 1980.

The *New York Times* analysis of national population patterns was called, "Study Says Old Cities Continue to Decline Despite Rejuvenation"; written by John Herbers, it appeared on July 7, 1980.

Information about the 5 percent population loss of the central cities was taken from a *Scientific American* magazine article entitled, "The Changing Demography of the Central City," published in August 1980.

The information about the increase in New England farmland acreage can be found in an August 16, 1980, *New York Times* article, "New England Farming Reawakens After 160 Years," by Michael Knight.

The quotation from Scott Donaldson's book, *The Suburban Myth,* published by Columbia University Press in New York, 1969, appeared on page 44.

Figures on the growth of female-headed families in the United States were provided by the U.S. Bureau of the Census from Current Population Reports *Population Characteristics,* Series P-20, No. 340, July 1979, and *Household and Family Characteristics: March 1978,* page 4. Additional information on this subject was documented in the U.S. Bureau of the Census reports *Household and Family Characteristics,* Series P-20, No. 352, March 1979, Table 4, and from *Families*

Maintained by Females Without Husbands Present: 1970–79,
Series P-23, No. 107, Table 9.

Figures concerning the number of divorced women who work
were provided by the Bureau of Labor Statistics, Division of
Labor Force Studies, from unpublished data for 1980, through
the courtesy of Beverly Johnson.

The statistics on childlessness in the United States as a new
national phenomenon can be found in the U.S. Bureau of the
Census report "Population Profile of the United States 1979,"
Series P-20, No. 350, published in May 1980.

The growth of single women as a normative social pattern was
documented in the U.S. Bureau of the Census report
*Population Characteristics: Marital Status and Living Ar-
rangements,* Series P-20, No. 349, published in February
1980. Information on the number of single women owning
homes was provided in a U.S. Bureau of the Census report,
Statistical Portrait of Women in the United States for 1978,
Series P-23, No. 100.

Information on the increase in the black and Hispanic
suburban population of America has been documented by the
U.S. Bureau of the Census in a report entitled, *Population
Characteristics: Population Profile of the United States, 1979,*
Series P-20, No. 350, May 1980.

The report produced by the Urban Institute *"The Graying of
Suburbia,* An Urban Institute Paper on Social Services,"
appeared in May 1979 and was written by Michael Gutowski
and Tracey Feild. The quotation was taken from pages 85–89.

CHAPTER 2/*From Rose-covered Cottage to Split-level Ranch: A History of the Suburban Woman*

The opening quotation was written by the feminist Harriet Martineau and appeared in *Society in America,* published by Saunders and Otley in London in 1837, Vol. 111, pp. 105–151.

The second quotation, by Thomas A. Edison, appeared in *Good Housekeeping* magazine in October 1912, Vol. LV, pages 436–444.

Ralph Waldo Emerson's quotation on the importance of nature was from his essay *Nature,* first published in 1834 and later reprinted in *Select Essays and Addresses* by Macmillan, New York, 1916.

Henry David Thoreau's quotation was taken from *Walden and Civil Disobedience,* edited by Sherman Paul, and published by Houghton Mifflin Company in Boston in 1960, page 138.

For a discussion of the power of the agrarian dream and its influence on American intellectual and political life, see Peter J. Schmitt's book *Back to Nature: The Arcadian Myth in Urban America,* published by Oxford University Press in New York in 1969, and Leo Marx's book *The Machine in the Garden: Technology and the Pastoral Ideal in America,* published by Oxford University Press in London, Oxford and New York in 1964.

Several books that proved helpful in tracking the social and architectural history of the early suburbs were *Carpenter Gothic: 19th Century Ornamental Houses of New England* by Alma C. McArdle and Deirdre Bartlett McArdle, published by Watson-Guptil in New York in 1978; *Mansions, Mills and Main Streets: Buildings and Places to Explore Within 50 Miles of New York City,* by Carol Rifkind and Carol Levine, published by Schocken Books in 1975, especially pages 9, 16 and 17; *Lost America: From the Atlantic to the Mississippi* by Constance M. Greiff, published by the Pyne Press in Princeton, New Jersey, in 1971; and Julia Treacy Wintje's *Along the Road to Bedford and Vermont: A Colonial Highway Through Mt. Vernon,* published by the Mt. Vernon Public Library in 1946.

The first quotation from Andrew Jackson Downing which appeared in *Horticulture* in July 1848 was from his essay "Hints to Rural Improvers," later reprinted in Downing's *Rural Essays.* The second quotation was from Downing's book of 1850, *The Architecture of Country Houses,* reprinted by D. Appleton & Company in New York in 1953.

The quotation from Elizabeth Cady Stanton and Lucretia Mott's famous 1848 *Declaration of Sentiments* was taken from Alice S. Rossi's reprint of that document in her book *The Feminist Papers: From Adams to de Beauvoir* published by Bantam Books in New York, 1973, pages 416–417. The original may be found in Elizabeth K. Stanton, Susan B. Anthony and Matilda J. Gage, editors, *History of Woman Suffrage,* Rochester, New York, Charles Mann, Volume 1, 1881.

My analysis of the diminished status of women in the nineteenth century compared to that of the eighteenth is based upon information found in several social histories of women. They include: Carl N. Degler's *At Odds: Women and the Family in America from the Revolution to the Present,* published by Oxford University Press in 1980, see chapters I–V; Alice S. Rossi's *The Feminist Papers: From Adams to de Beauvoir,* see pages 241–281; and Susan Torre's *Women in American Architecture: A Historic and Contemporary Perspective,* published by the Whitney Library of Design, in New York, 1977.

The quotations from Catherine Beecher's *A Treatise on Domestic Economy* can be found in Kathryn Kish Sklar's edition, published by Schocken Books, New York, 1977, pages 13, 20, and 26–27.

Harriet Martineau's treatise in *Harper's New Monthly Magazine* was called "How to Make Home Unhealthy," and was published in October 1850.

The city dweller's contempt for the new suburbanite of the late nineteenth century appeared in an article entitled, "Our Suburban Friends" by Richard Harding Davis in *Harper's New Monthly Magazine,* Vol. 89 in June 1894.

Concern with the female's role in the suburbs was first publicly expressed in Grace Duffield Goodwin's article "The Commuter's Wife: A Sisterly Talk by One Who Knows Her Problems," in the October 1909 *Good Housekeeping* magazine, Vol. 49.

The information about domestic science was gleaned from a variety of sources, including "Home Science to the Front," an editorial in *Good Housekeeping,* of November 1909, Vol. XLIX; "Home Science Education" from *The Encyclopedia of Education,* Crowell-Collier Educational Corporation, 1971, pages 447–479; and old magazine advertisements and covers courtesy of the New York Public Library Picture Collection.

Domestic science was cited by popular magazines as a mandate to the American housewife at the turn of the century. Two articles illustrating women's obsession with scientific management of the home were Mrs. Julian Heath's essay "The Housewife's Fight Is the Nation's," found in *Good Housekeeping* in October 1912, and "Suppose Our Servants Didn't Live with Us" by Mrs. Christine Frederick.

The Crisco ad appeared in the July 1913 *Ladies' Home Journal,* Vol. 30.

Census figures comparing city and suburban growth in the

early part of the twentieth century can be found in Harlan Paul Douglass's *The Suburban Trend,* published in 1925 by the Century Company in New York and London and reprinted by Arno Press and the *New York Times* in 1970.

Reference books on the 1920s were Constance McLaughlin Green's *The Rise of Urban America,* published by Harper & Row, New York, in 1965; Scott Donaldson's *The Suburban Myth,* published by Columbia University Press in 1969; John Gassner's *A Treasury of the Theatre: from Ibsen to Ionesco,* published by Simon and Schuster in 1966, especially the section "Modern American Drama," pages 770–1063; and Samuel Eliot Morison and Henry Steele Commager's *The Growth of the American Republic,* published by Oxford University Press in New York in 1942.

The questions raised by Ethel Puffer Howes about the significance of feminine political equality in an era when women were still tied to the home appeared in the September 1923 issue of *Woman's Home Companion* in an article called, "True and Substantial Happiness: A Talk About Cooperation for the Home, Past, Present and Future," Vol. 1, No. 9.

In June 1925, *Better Homes and Gardens* contained an article by Genevieve A. Callahan, "Bringing Color to Your Kitchen," which pointed out the intimate relationship between a woman and her kitchen.

The quotations from Harlan Paul Douglass's book *The Suburban Trend* can be found on pages 79 and 226 respectively.

The figures on female employment during and after World War II were drawn from the U.S. Bureau of the Census report *Labor Force and Employment and Unemployment in the United States, 1940–1960,* Current Population Reports, P-50. Statistics on the female labor force during the 1950s can be found in the Bureau of Labor Statistics' study *Women in the Labor Force, Selected Years 1900–1978,* as printed in *Women*

in the Labor Force: Some New Data Series by Janet L.
Norwood and Elizabeth Waldman, U.S. Department of Labor,
Bureau of Labor Statistics, 1979, Report 575, page 1, and in
*Labor Force Participation Rates of Married Women, Husband
Present, by presence and age of own children, selected years,
1950–1979,* as cited in Bureau of Labor Statistics, *Perspectives
on Working Women,* June 1980, Table 6, page 4.

The 1945 *Fortune* poll reflecting America's negative attitude
toward the employment of married women with breadwinner
husbands appeared in the August 1946 issue of *Fortune*
magazine.

Books that were particularly helpful in their discussions of the
1950s and their attitudes toward women are Landon Y.
Jones's *Great Expectations: America and the Baby Boom
Generation,* published by Coward, McCann & Geoghegan in
New York, 1980; Carl N. Degler's *At Odds: Women and the
Family in America from the Revolution to the Present,*
published by Oxford University Press in New York in 1980;
Constance McLaughlin Green's *The Rise of Urban America,*
published by Harper & Row in New York in 1965; and Donald
N. Rothblatt, Daniel J. Garr and Jo Sprague's *The Suburban
Environment and Women,* published by Praeger Publishers in
New York in 1979.

Figures documenting the suburban boom in housing were
found in Landon Jones's *Great Expectations: America and the
Baby Boom Generation;* in a *Time* magazine article entitled
"Flight to the Suburbs: Business Must Follow the Dollar" of
March 22, 1954, Vol. 63, No. 66; and in Frederick Gutheim's
story "What makes a good suburb?" from the July 25, 1955,
House and Garden magazine, Vol. 39, No. 4.

The quotation from sociologists George Masnick and Mary Jo
Bane can be found in their report *The Nation's Families:
1960–1990,* published by the Joint Center for Urban Studies
of MIT and Harvard University in 1980, on page 1.

For detailed information about the growth of the suburban population in America between 1950 and 1960, see the U.S. Bureau of the Census reports *Census of Population in Housing 1960* and *Census of Population in Housing 1970*.

The *New York Times* article referring to the urbanization of the Northeast appeared on January 14, 1957, on page 44. The *Reader's Digest* story about suburbia was called "Zoning Comes to Town"; written by Stuart Chase, it was published in February 1957.

Dr. Benjamin Spock's praise for the American housewife appeared in an article called, "What's She Got That I Haven't?" in the *Ladies' Home Journal* issue of October 1952.

Adlai Stevenson's commencement address to 1955 Smith College graduates was reprinted in the September 1955 *Woman's Home Companion* and entitled, "A Purpose for Modern Woman."

Two magazines that applauded the American housewife of the 1950s were *Look* with its article "A New Look at the American Modern Woman," which appeared on October 16, 1956, and the *Ladies' Home Journal,* whose story "Meet Mrs. $10,000 Executive in the House" appeared in September 1953.

The quotations from David Riesman's book *The Lonely Crowd: A Study of the Changing American Character,* published by Yale University Press in New Haven and London in 1950, were from pages 303 and 332 respectively.

Margaret Mead's analysis of mid-century American women can be found in *Life* magazine, December 24, 1956. The article she wrote was called "She Has Strength Based on a Pioneer Past."

Information about the new women workers of the 1950s was provided by the U.S. Bureau of Labor Statistics in their report

Labor Force Participation Rates of Men and Women 16 Years of Age and Over, 1950–76, Table 1, Annual Averages, as reprinted in *Labor Force Trends: A Synthesis and Analysis and a Bibliography,* Special Labor Force Report 208, page 4.

The *Fortune* magazine article about suburbia was called, "The Lush New Suburban Market," and appeared in November 1953. *Time* magazine also ran an article about the growth of the suburbs and the national economy in a story entitled, "Man, oh Man!" in its Modern Living section on February 1, 1954. A July 25, 1955, *Life* magazine story, "Pots, Pans and Prosperity," provided me with figures on the number of housewares and kitchen goods sold in 1954.

The 1955 *House and Garden* magazine article describing the ideal suburb was entitled, "What Makes a Good Suburb?"; written by Frank Gutheim, it appeared in January 1955.

The quotations from William H. Whyte, Jr.'s book *The Organization Man,* published by Anchor Books with arrangement through Simon and Schuster in 1956, appeared on page 401.

Information on the number of volunteer organizations found in the prototypical suburban community of Levittown, Pennsylvania, can be found in Herbert J. Gans's landmark sociology study, *The Levittowners: Ways of Life and Politics in a New Suburban Community,* published by Alfred A. Knopf and Random House in New York and Toronto in 1967.

The quotation from Vance Packard's book *The Status Seekers* can be found in the Pocket Books version of 1959 published in New York, page 4.

Eve Merriam's article was called, "Are Housewives Necessary?" and was published in *The Nation* on January 31, 1959.

Richard E. Gordon, M.D., Katherine K. Gordon and Max Gunther authored *The Split-Level Trap,* which was published by Bernard Geis & Associates in 1960. The quotation from the Gordons cited in this chapter can be found in that work on page 28.

The *New York Times* article on female alcoholism appeared on April 26, 1962, and was called "Alcoholism of Women Is Laid to Loneliness." The *Daily News* ran two sensational stories on "Lady Lushes" on April 25 and 26, 1962.

U.S. News & World Report's story about a potential exodus from the suburbs appeared on June 11, 1962, and was entitled "Is Flight from the Suburbs Starting?"

The quotations from Betty Friedan's *The Feminine Mystique,* published by W. W. Norton & Co., New York, in 1963, appeared on pages 25 and 235 respectively. Other articles reflecting concern about female suburban unhappiness included *Cosmopolitan*'s October 1960 article "Crackups in the Suburbs," *Good Housekeeping*'s September 1962 article "Loneliness," and *Redbook*'s story of September 1960, "Why Young Mothers Feel Trapped."

CHAPTER 3/*Nine to Five: The Working Suburban Woman*

The introductory quotation for this chapter is from Caroline Bird's *The Two-Paycheck Marriage,* published by Rawson, Wade Publishers, Inc., New York, in 1979, page 99. The second quotation in this chapter from *The Two-Paycheck Marriage* is from page 253.

Information on the labor force participation rates among women came from a variety of sources, including Bureau of Labor Statistics Press Release No. 80-767; a Bureau of Labor Statistics report *Perspectives on Working Women,* October 1980, Table 26, page 217; a Census Bureau publication,

Population Profile of the United States: 1979, Series P-20, No. 350, May 1980 (especially the section on Employment, pages 29-37); a Bureau of Labor Statistics report *Marital and Family Characteristics of Workers*, March 1980, to be in a forthcoming issue of the *Monthly Labor Review;* and unpublished 1980 employment data. Additional information on female employment in the United States was taken from *20 Facts on Women Workers* and the Bureau of Labor Statistics report *U.S. Working Women: A data book, 1977.*

Figures about the changing income level and work patterns in U.S. households were taken from the Bureau of Labor Statistics report *Women in the Labor Force: Some New Data Series*, Report 575, 1979, page 6; from the Census Bureau study *Money Income of Families and Persons in the United States: 1978*, Series P-60, No. 123, June 1980, pages 7-9, Table E; and from the Census Bureau report *Median Income, 1979*, Current Population Reports, page 40, No. 125.

The *New York Times* article "The Squeeze on the Middle Class," written by William Severini Kowinski, appeared on July 13, 1980.

The *Newsweek* cover story "Leading Two Lives/Women at Work and Home" appeared on May 19, 1980, and was also called "The Superwoman Squeeze."

Figures on the work patterns of suburban women were extracted from the Bureau of Labor Statistics, *1980 Annual Averages*, Current Population Survey.

Helena Z. Lopata's book *Occupation: Housewife*, published by the Oxford University Press in London in 1971, describes the role and relationship between the housewife and the larger society. In a comparison of Chicago suburban housewives and working women she found significant differences in marriage styles, friendship patterns and childrearing attitudes. Education was found to be a powerful factor in many behavioral patterns of these women.

In *The Nation's Families: 1960-1990,* written by George Masnick and Mary Jo Bane for The Joint Center for Urban Studies of MIT and Harvard University, the authors found that working wives contribute about a quarter of the family income, but that over one-third of all women who had worked as long as ten years often contributed more. Masnick and Bane conclude that because today's young women demonstrate a strong "attachment" to work, they are apt to contribute more to the family income than women have done in the past.

Lillian B. Rubin's book *Women of a Certain Age: The Midlife Search for Self* was published by Harper & Row, New York, in 1979. The quotations were taken from pages 164 and 167 respectively.

The quotation is from Elizabeth Janeway's book *Between Myth and Morning: Women Awakening,* published by William Morrow & Company, Inc., New York, in 1975, pages 70 and 71.

Information on education and its relationship to income and jobs was gathered from many different sources, including the Census Bureau report *Money Income of Families and Persons in the United States: 1978,* Current Population Reports, Series P-60, No. 123, June 1980; the Bureau of Labor Statistics report *Labor Force Trends: A Synthesis and Analysis and a Bibliography,* Special Labor Force Report 208, Chart 2, page 2; and the Census Bureau report *Educational Attainment of the United States,* March 1978 and 1979, Series 320, No. 356.

The data on part-time women workers was taken from the Bureau of Labor Statistics, *1980 Annual Averages,* Current Population Survey, and from an October 1978 *Monthly Labor*

Review article, "A profile of women on part-time schedules," by Carol Leon and Robert W. Bednarzik.

Dr. Janice Madden's study on the housing market and commuting behavior was published in *The American Economic Review*, Vol. 70, No. 2, May 1980, and entitled, "Urban Land Use and the Growth of Two-Earner Households." Using data collected by the Survey Research Center at the University of Michigan, Dr. Madden found that two-earner families are more suburbanized than one-earner families, and that unmarried individuals tend to live more centrally than all other household types.

Dianne Wescott's study "Employment and commuting patterns: a residential analysis," appeared in the *Monthly Labor Review*, July 1979.

The *Family Circle* study was conducted in 1978 and appeared on February 20, 1979. The study included 3,000 mothers who had worked full time and had children under 13 years of age. About 30 percent of these mothers said they allowed their children to stay home alone after school without a sitter, although fewer than 1 percent said they would have done so if they had other choices.

The National Survey of Working Women was sponsored by the National Commission on Working Women and was published in June 1979. Results were drawn from about 110,000 women who had participated in the survey. About 40 percent of these respondents were from suburban areas. About one-third of all women with dependent children listed child care as a major problem, but at the higher end of the occupational hierarchy more women found child care troublesome. About 36 percent of all professional, managerial and technical workers named child care as a major concern, but only about 29 percent of all blue-collar, sales and clerical workers thought of it as a problem.

According to Mary Petsche, executive director of the Coordinated Child Care Council of San Mateo County, Daly City, just south of San Francisco, has less than 10 percent of its childcare needs being met. Less than 25 percent of all children in Redwood City and less than 20 percent of those in the city of San Mateo in need of care currently receive services. Another study by the Coordinated Child Care Council of San Mateo County found that some 80 percent of all children aged 9 to 12 living in Pacifica, California, said they had no place to go after school because their parents work.

Judith Rosen, director of the Fairfax County Office for Children of Fairfax, Virginia, found that 50 percent of all children under the age of 2 had mothers who were employed and 62 percent of all children under the age of 5 had both adults in the family employed.

In 1978, Abt Associates conducted the National Day Care Study. A second study, published in 1981 by Abt Associates and called the National Day Care Home Study, found that 45 percent of all American families preferred family day care.

Figures on the declining number of domestic workers were found in a Department of Labor report, *Women in Domestic Work: Yesterday and Today,* Special Labor Force Report 242, January 1981. While official government figures reveal a shrinking domestic work force, Caroline Reed, executive director of the National Committee on Household Workers, believes there are about three unreported workers for each one who reports income.

CHAPTER 4/*The Circuit Breaker: The Divorced Suburban Woman*

The introductory quotation is from Jane O'Reilly's book *The Girl I Left Behind: The Housewife's Moment of Truth and*

Other Feminist Ravings, published by Macmillan Publishing Company, New York, in 1980, page 66.

The quotation is from Maxine Schnall's book *Limits: A Search for New Values,* published by Clarkson N. Potter, Inc., in New York in 1981, page 300.

Much of the information in this chapter on the rising divorce rate was drawn from Census Bureau reports *Population Profile of the United States: 1979,* Series P-20, No. 350, May 1980, and *Household and Family Characteristics,* March 1979, Series P-20, No. 352, July 1980.

A fair discussion on the divorce rate can be found in the Census Bureau reports *Families Maintained by Female Householders, 1970-79,* Current Population Reports, Special Studies, Series P-23, No. 107, and *Marital Status and Living Arrangements: March 1980,* Current Population Reports, Series P-20, No. 365; in the National Center for Health Statistics publications *Advance Report on Final Divorce Statistics, 1979,* Vol. 30, No. 2, Supplement to Monthly Vital Statistics Report, May 29, 1981, and *Annual Summary of Births, Deaths, Marriages and Divorces: United States, 1980,* No. 13, Monthly Vital Statistics Report.

Informal estimates of the number of divorced women now living in the suburbs are based on Census Bureau information found in *Household and Family Characteristics,* report of March 1979, Table 4, as well as in *Families Maintained by Female-Headed Households, 1970-79,* Table 9, P-23, No. 107. Information about the income level of female-headed households was found on page 33 of the latter.

A comparison of the earnings of those divorced with those separated, widowed and married is provided in the Census Bureau study *Money, Income and Poverty Status of Families and Persons in the United States, 1980,* Advance Data, Current Population Reports, P-60, No. 127.

The Census Bureau publication *Child Support and Alimony: 1978,* Current Population Reports, Special Studies, Series P-23, No. 106, provided much of the data for the discussion on child support and alimony. Additional information was gleaned from the Census Bureau *Statistical Abstract for 1976.*

A detailed discussion of the changing friendship patterns among the newly divorced was found in Robert S. Weiss's book *Marital Separation,* published by Basic Books in New York in 1975, especially Chapter 8. Other books that also examine the divorced woman's adjustment to single life include Robert S. Weiss's *The Family Life and Social Situation of the Single Parent,* published by Basic Books in New York in 1979, and Martha Yates's book *Coping: A Survival Manual for Women Alone,* published by Prentice-Hall in Englewood Cliffs, NJ, in 1976.

The study on single parents conducted by the National Committee for Citizens in Education during 1979-80 queried divorced parents on a variety of issues regarding school attitudes toward themselves and their children. One finding from special computer runs of that study indicated that fewer suburban parents believed the schools were aware of their divorced status than did parents from either the cities or rural areas. Suburban parents also tended to see school indifference to their status as a potentially more serious problem than did other parents.

Information about the growth and development of Parents Without Partners, Inc., came from the organization's membership files at their international headquarters in Bethesda, Maryland.

CHAPTER 5/*Liberation and Backlash: The Suburban Woman Who Stays at Home*

The first quotation is from Phyllis Schlafly's book *The Power of the Positive Woman,* Jove, HBJ, New York, 1977, page 63. The second quotation appeared on page 60. While Mrs. Schlafly concedes that there are women who do combine marriage successfully with a career, she maintains that it is always quite difficult, that these women have established a clear set of priorities ". . . under which business or professional demands must always give way to home and family whenever there is a conflict."

After years of expressing his public disapproval of day care, Harvard Professor of Human Development Jerome Kagan modified his stance. Writing in *Parents* magazine in April 1977 in "All About Day Care," Dr. Kagan explained that recent studies revealed that children raised in day-care situations fared just as well as those raised in the traditional home environment. In a 1978 study, *Infancy: Its Place in Human Development,* Harvard University Press, Cambridge, 1978, by Jerome Kagan, Richard Kearsley and Philip Zelazo, the researchers found that while social class and ethnicity were important determinants of a child's social and academic development, those raised in the day-care environment actually scored higher in their ability to replicate certain adult tasks.

Urie Bronfenbrenner, Cornell Professor of Human Development and Family Studies, maintains that every child needs the consistent attention of at least one parent "who is crazy about him" while he is growing up. While he supports the notion that day care is necessary and should be vastly expanded to meet the needs of working mothers, he still maintains that paid caretakers can in no way substitute for the care of a parent. As he said in a June 7, 1978, *U.S. News & World Report* article, "Liberated Women: How They're Changing

America," "I don't care whether it's the father who works and the mother who stays at home. Or the mother who works and the father who stays at home. Or both working part-time. But please, God, let there be somebody." Additional comments about the decline of the American family by Professor Bronfenbrenner can be found in "Nobody Home: The Erosion of the American Family," *Psychology Today*, Vol. 12, May 1977.

In a June 6, 1976, *New York Times Magazine* article, "Second Start," Dr. Joseph Glick, coordinator of the City University of New York's program in developmental psychology, has argued that day care might prove detrimental to young people, that it might provide a "narrowly structured environment that would emphasize the training of specific skills at the expense of flexible, adaptive open behavior." In the same article, Dr. Selma Chess, a child psychiatrist at New York University, expressed fears that day care might impede a child's development rather than improve it. She felt this might be especially true for poor and minority children who would be subject to still another cognitively graded atmosphere.

Other information of early childhood educational intervention programs suggests that they may be beneficial. A study conducted by Dr. Irving Lazar at Cornell University for the Consortium of Longitudinal Studies, on 820 children who participated in compensatory programs like Operation Head Start in the early and middle 1960s, found that early educational intervention had "significant long-term effects on school performance." Not only did the children demonstrate improved academic skills, but nearly 80 percent of them polled by the researchers had improved relationships with their families many years later. See January 6, 1980, *New York Times* article by Nancy Rubin, "Head Start Efforts Prove Their Value."

The comment by Gloria Steinem was extracted from "Feminist Notes: Now That It's Reagan," *Ms.*, January 1981, Vol. IX, No. 7.

Dr. Bobbie McKay's book *The Unabridged Woman* was published by the Pilgrim Press, New York, 1979, and was a direct outgrowth of her counseling experiences at the Glenview Community Church as a minister. Explaining the anger and depression that dependent women often experience, Dr. McKay writes, "Rather than take responsibility for our own lives, rather than make demands on those around us to make life better, we feel helpless and hopeless to change anything. Therefore, our only recourse in a depressed state is to tune out the world; to move inside ourselves; to feel bad about who we are; to feel angry and frustrated that we can't behave differently; perhaps to withdraw completely . . ."

Murray Straus, Richard Gelles and Suzanne Steinmetz wrote *Behind Closed Doors: Violence in the American Family*, published by Anchor Books/Doubleday, Garden City, New York, 1979, based on a 1976 survey of 2,200 American families.

The *New York Times Magazine* article by Colette Dowling was entitled "The Cinderella Syndrome" and appeared on March 22, 1981. Her book *The Cinderella Complex: Women's Hidden Fear of Independence* was published by Summit Books in New York in 1981.

The Eagle Forum brochure circulated to the public has as its subtitle, "the alternative to women's lib." The brochure also states that the Eagle Forum opposes ratification of the "so-called 'Equal Rights Amendment' because it is inconsistent with at least ten of the rights of women, families and individuals spelled out in this statement."

CHAPTER 6/*The New Pioneers: Single and Childless Suburban Women*

The first quotation in this chapter, written by Andrée Brooks, originally appeared in a *New York Times Magazine* article entitled, "Single at Midlife," on May 24, 1981.

Information on condominium construction in the United States was taken from *Housing Background,* a report prepared by the National Association of Home Builders, Public Affairs Division, July 1981.

The 1960, 1970 and 1979 data on childlessness, singles and unmarried couples was found in the U.S. Bureau of the Census report *Population of the United States, Population Characteristics,* Current Population Reports, Series P-20, No. 350, May 1980.

Additional information on single women living in the suburbs may be found in the U.S. Bureau of the Census reports *Special Studies,* P-23, No. 75, 1970, and *Social and Economic Characteristics of the Metropolitan and Non-Metropolitan Population,* 1977 and 1970, and in unpublished tabulations from the 1980 Current Population Survey, U.S. Bureau of the Census.

Information on childless women living in the suburbs was taken from the U.S. Bureau of the Census reports *Fertility of American Women,* Current Population Survey, Series P-20, No. 358, June 1979, Tables 7B and 9A, and *Birth Expectations and Fertility,* Current Population Reports, Series P-20, No. 248, June 1972, Table 12.

The singles study referred to at the University of Texas at Dallas in cooperation with *First Person Singular* was conducted upon 1,000 single men and women living in the Dallas-Fort Worth area during 1980. It was entitled, "Single Statistics," and was coordinated by Dr. Chuck Ingene of the University of Texas.

The quotation by Caryl Rivers, Rosalind Barnett and Grace Baruch was from their book *Beyond Sugar and Spice: How*

Women Grow, Learn and Thrive, published by G. P. Putnam's Sons, New York, 1979, page 200.

The decision rendered by United States Supreme Court Justice Douglas was called *Village of Belle Terre* v. *Boraas,* Supra, 94 Supreme Court Reporter, 416. U.S. 2.

The state supreme court case overruling the *Belle Terre* decision in the state of New Jersey was *New Jersey* v. *Baker,* 405A2d, 368, 371.

The citation for the California case which most recently overruled the *Belle Terre* decision was *City of Santa Barbara* v. *Adamson,* 610, p2d, 436, 441.

The Graying of Suburbia, by Michael Gutowski and Tracey Feild, was published in May 1979 through the Urban Institute in Washington, D.C. Although Gutowski and Feild do not directly address the problems of young single individuals unable to live in suburban communities, I have included their proposal for housing annuity programs, because I believe such proposals are just as relevant to young singles as to young married couples who could assume the burden of poorly maintained homes now occupied by the elderly suburban population.

The figures on the income levels for single, divorced and married women were taken from the U.S. Bureau of the Census reports *Money Income of Family and Persons in the United States, 1979,* Current Population Survey 1980, Series P-60, No. 129. According to the Census Bureau, married but childless couples had a median income in 1979 of $19,833 and a mean income of $23,150, compared to "all families," which had a median income of $19,661 and a mean income of $22,376.

CHAPTER 7/*Charity Begins at Home: The New Volunteer*

The Action Bureau report was entitled, *Americans Volunteer, 1974: A Statistical Study of Volunteers in the United States,* and was based on a survey by the U.S. Census Bureau.

The *New York Times* article on volunteerism, "Volunteers Now Are Getting Choosier," by Ethalia Walsh, was published on April 16, 1978.

The report referring to the December 1979 study on volunteer action centers was summarized in *Volunteering, 1979-80: A Status Report on America's Volunteer Community,* published by VOLUNTEER: The National Center for Citizen Involvement in April 1980.

The resolution adopted by NOW was reported by Enid Nemy in the story "NOW Attacks Volunteerism—But Others Rally to Its Defense," The *New York Times,* June 7, 1974. More recently, Betty Friedan refuted that resolution in a speech presented to the National Convocation on New Leadership sponsored by NOW Legal Defense and Education Fund. Calling for a "passionate voluntarism—we cannot rely on the federal government, Congress, or the courts," she said that women must begin to work together to effect social improvement. A report of that meeting can be found in an April 1, 1981, *New York Times* story, "NOW Convocation on 'New Leadership,'" also written by Enid Nemy.

For specific references to the writings of Tom Wolfe and Peter Marin on the age of individualism, see Tom Wolfe's "The 'Me' Decade" and Peter Marin's "The New Narcissism," in *Harper's,* October 1974. Jim Hougan's detailed analysis of the psychology of the 1970s may be found in *Radical Nostalgia, Narcissism and Decline in the 1970s,* published by William Morrow, New York, 1975.

The comments by Christopher Lasch were taken from his landmark book *The Culture of Narcissism: American Life in an Age of Diminishing Expectations,* published by W. W. Norton & Company, New York, 1979, pages 29-30.

Volunteerism was just one of many suburban issues examined by author Seth Reichlin in a December 15, 1980, *Fortune* magazine article, "The Aging of the Suburbs."

Harlan Paul Douglass's early references to suburban "over-organization" may be found in *The Suburban Trend,* published by the Century Company, New York and London, 1925, reprinted in 1970 by the Arno Press and the New York Times on page 196.

William H. Whyte's comments about civic overcommitment among suburban women can be found in his book *The Organization Man,* published by Doubleday/Anchor Books, Garden City, New York, 1956, page 401.

Daniel Yankelovich's article "New Rules in American Life: Searching for Self-Fulfillment in a World Turned Upside Down," published in an April 1981 *Psychology Today,* suggests that Americans are beginning to realize that to live fully they must become committed to deep personal and social values. In that article he wrote: "Though sparse, the survey data showing that Americans are growing less self-absorbed and better prepared to take a first step toward an ethic or commitment are fairly clear."

Dr. McKay's message—that women must learn to trust in their uniqueness if they are to lead full lives—can be found in *The Unabridged Woman: A Guide to Growing Up Female,* published by the Pilgrim Press, New York City, 1979, page 97.

CHAPTER 8/*Skin Deep: The Minority Suburban Women*

The figures on black and Hispanic suburbanization were taken from the U.S. Bureau of the Census, 1980 Current Population Survey, Provisional Totals for Racial and Spanish Origin Groups.

Information on the growth of female-headed households in the suburbs is found in the U.S. Bureau of the Census report *Families Maintained by Female Householders, 1970-79,* Special Studies, P-23, No. 107.

A comparison of the income levels of various racial and ethnic groups came from the U.S. Bureau of the Census report *Money, Income and Poverty Status of Families and Persons in the United States, 1979* (Advance Report), Consumer Income, *Number of Families and Median Income in 1979 and 1978, by Race and Spanish Origin of Households,* Current Population Report P-60, No. 125.

For the quotation from Kenneth B. Clark, see his book *Pathos of Power,* published by Harper & Row, New York, 1974, pages 108-109.

The 1979 Regional Plan Association report *Segregation and Opportunity in the Region's Housing* appeared in *Regional Plan News,* July 1979, No. 104.

The statistics on the segregation patterns of blacks in the Miami area were extracted from the report *Profile of Social and Economic Conditions in Low Income Areas in Dade County, Florida,* produced by the Metropolitan Dade County Department of Human Resources in 1980.

The information on black suburbanization patterns in Columbus, Ohio, was reported to me by Frank Lomax III, executive director of the Columbus Urban League. The study, sponsored by the Mid-Ohio Regional Planning Commission, was entitled, *The Franklin County Fair Housing Research Study: A Summary Report,* by David R. Larson and Gerald G. Newborg, Archival Systems, Inc.

Statistical information about patterns of suburban black migration in San Francisco and Dallas were obtained through the U.S. Bureau of the Census, 1980 Current Population Survey.

The suburban housing patterns and income discrepancies of blacks and whites reported by the U.S. Bureau of the Census was entitled, *Financial Characteristics of the Housing Inventory for the United States and Regions,* 1979 Current Housing Reports, Series H-150-77, Annual Housing Survey.

Dr. Lake's report was called, *Housing Search Experiences of Black and White Suburban Homebuyers,* and was found in *America's Housing: Prospects and Problems,* edited by George Sternlieb and James W. Hughes, and published by the Rutgers University Center for Urban Policy Research, New Brunswick, New Jersey, 1980.

The forty-city study by HUD on housing sales and rental practices was entitled, *Measuring Racial Discrimination in American Housing Markets: The Housing Market Survey,* by Ronald E. Wienk, Clifford E. Reid, John D. Simonson, Frederick J. Eggers, Division of Evaluation, U.S. Department of Housing and Urban Development, Office of Policy Development and Research, April 1979.

The *New York Times* article on the economic progress of young black families was entitled "Study Traces Progress of Blacks Since 1970." It was written by Robert Reinhold and appeared on June 19, 1979.

Figures on the employment of black and white suburban women were extracted from the Bureau of Labor Statistics,

Current Population Survey, *Employment Status of Black and Other Females in Metropolitan Areas*, 1980 Annual Averages.

Dr. Thomas A. Clarke's book *Blacks in Suburbs: A National Perspective* was published by the Rutgers University Center for Urban Policy Research, New Brunswick, New Jersey, 1979. The quotation cited in this chapter appeared on page 109.

The citation from William Julius Wilson's book *The Declining Significance of Race: Blacks and Changing American Institutions,* published by the University of Chicago Press, 1978, appeared on page 152.

CHAPTER 9/*Options: New Directions for the Suburban Woman*

The quotation from Alvin Toffler's book *The Third Wave,* published by Bantam Books, New York, in 1981, may be found on page 194. The second quotation from *The Third Wave* in this chapter appeared in Toffler's book on page 354.

The introductory quotation from Betty Friedan's *The Second Stage,* published by Summit Books, New York, in 1981, can be found on page 233.

The reference to Susan Saegert's analysis of the differences between male and female experiences in the suburbs came from her article, "Masculine Cities and Feminine Suburbs: Polarized Ideas, Contradictory Realities," published in *Signs: Journal of Women in Culture and Society*, Special Issue, Women and the American City, Supplement, Vol. 5, No. 3, page 106.

The quotation by Jane Newitt suggesting that the leisure values of the workers were apt to receive little attention in an age when the population is rapidly aging, came from *The*

Future of Westchester County: A Guide for Long-Range Social Needs Assessment, published by the Hudson Institute, Croton-on-Hudson, New York, 1979, page 148.

According to the U.S. Bureau of the Census, there were 702,000 female-owned businesses in the United States in 1977. These businesses accounted for 41.5 billion dollars in receipts. Source: U.S. Dept. of Commerce News, Bureau of the Census, May 23, 1980.

The U.S. Census Bureau 1980 Advance Reports as of August 1981 indicated that suburban growth increased from 41 percent of the nation's population, or 83,336,122 people, in 1970 to 101,474,674 by 1980, or 44.8 percent of the national population. At the same time, nonmetropolitan areas increased from 53,225,332 in 1970, or 26.1 percent of the population, to 57,099,807, or 25.2 percent of the population by 1980. Central cities meanwhile declined from 66,740,677, or 32.8 percent of the population, in 1970 to 67,930,344, or 30 percent of the nation's population, in 1980.

The report issued by The Joint Center for Urban Studies of the Massachusetts Institute of Technology and Harvard University by Richard P. Coleman was entitled, *Attitudes Toward Neighborhoods: How Americans Choose to Live.* The quotation was taken from page 47. In his final assessment of the study, Dr. Coleman concludes that while many Americans claim they would like to live in a rural setting, "not nearly so much out-of-the-metropolitan area movement will occur as is aspired to."

Gail Sheehy's study of happiness among women was published by *Redbook* magazine in July 1979 and entitled, "The Happiness Report." In that study Ms. Sheehy found that women cited "family security," mature love and inner harmony as the most important life goals.

An incisive interpretation of how American values regarding home, family life and interpersonal relationships have changed in the past generation is provided in Maxine Schnall's book *Limits: A Search for New Values,* published by Clarkson N. Potter, Publishers, New York, 1981.

Betty Friedan's article in the *New York Times Magazine* entitled, "Feminism's Next Step," appeared on July 5, 1981, and was based on her book *The Second Stage,* published by Summit in 1981.

Bibliography

Adams, Margaret. *Single Blessedness: Observations on the Single Status in Married Society.* New York: Basic Books, Inc., 1976.

Bailey, Liberty. *The Country-Life Movement in the United States.* New York: Macmillan, 1911.

Beecher, Catherine. *A Treatise on Domestic Economy.* Edited by Kathryn Kish Sklar. New York: Schocken Books, 1977.

Bernard, Jessie. *The Future of Motherhood.* New York: The Dial Press, 1974.

Bird, Caroline. *The Two-Paycheck Marriage: How Women at Work Are Changing Life in America.* New York: Rawson, Wade, 1979.

Birmingham, Stephen. *The Golden Dream: Suburbia in the 1970s.* New York: Harper & Row, 1978.

Bronstein, Don, and Weitzel, Tony. *Chicago: I Will.* Cleveland: World Publishing Company, 1967.

Brownmiller, Susan. *Against Our Will: Men, Women and Rape.* New York: Bantam Books, 1976.

Cheever, John. *The Wapshot Chronicle.* New York: Harper & Row, 1957.

Clark, Kenneth B. *Pathos of Power.* New York: Harper & Row, 1974.

Clark, Thomas A. *Blacks in Suburbs: A National Perspective.* New Brunswick, New Jersey: Rutgers University Center for Urban Policy Research, 1979.

Coleman, Richard P. *Attitudes Towards Neighborhoods: How Americans Choose to Live.* Cambridge, Mass.: The Joint Center for Urban Studies of MIT and Harvard University, 1978.

Degler, Carl N. *At Odds: Women and the Family in America from the Revolution to the Present.* New York and Oxford: Oxford University Press, 1980.

Didion, Joan. *The White Album.* New York: Pocket Books, 1979.

Dinnerstein, Dorothy. *The Mermaid and the Minotaur: Sexual Arrangements and Human Malaise.* New York: Harper & Row, 1976.

Donaldson, Scott. *The Suburban Myth.* New York: Columbia University Press, 1969.

Douglass, Harlan Paul. *The Suburban Trend.* New York and London: The Century Company, 1925, reprinted by The Arno Press in 1970.

Dowling, Colette. *The Cinderella Complex: Women's Hidden Fear of Independence.* New York: Summit Books, 1981.

Downing, Andrew Jackson. *The Architecture of Country Houses.* New York: D. Appleton & Company, 1953.

Firestone, Shulamith. *The Dialectic of Sex: The Case for Feminist Revolution*. New York: Bantam Books, 1971.

Fitzgerald, F. Scott. *The Great Gatsby*. New York: Charles Scribner's Sons, 1925.

French, Marilyn. *The Women's Room*. New York: Jove Publications, 1978.

Friday, Nancy. *My Mother/My Self: The Daughter's Search for Identity*. New York: Delacorte Press, 1977.

Friedan, Betty. *The Feminine Mystique*. New York: W. W. Norton & Company, 1963, 1974.

————. *The Second Stage*. New York: Summit Books, 1981.

Gans, Herbert, J. *The Levittowners: Ways of Life and Politics in a New Suburban Community*. New York: Pantheon Books, 1967.

Gassner, John. *Treasury of the Theatre: From Henrik Ibsen to Eugene Ionesco*. New York: Simon and Schuster, 1966.

Gordon, Richard E.; Gordon, Katherin K.; and Gunther, Max. *The Split-Level Trap*. New York: Bernard Geis & Associates, 1960.

Green, Constance McLaughlin. *The Rise of Urban America*. New York: Harper & Row, 1965.

Greer, Germaine. *The Female Eunuch*. New York: Bantam Books, 1972.

Greiff, Constance M. *Lost America: From the Atlantic to the Mississippi*. Princeton, New Jersey: The Pyne Press, 1971.

Gutowski, Michael, and Feild, Tracey. *The Graying of Subur-*

bia. Washington, D.C.: An Urban Institute Paper on Social Services, 1979.

Hansberry, Lorraine. "A Raisin in the Sun," from *Afro-American Literature Drama*. Edited by Adams, William; Conn, Peter; and Slepian, Barry. Boston: Houghton Mifflin Company, 1970.

Hope, Karol, and Young, Nancy. *Out of the Frying Pan: A Decade of Change in Women's Lives*. Garden City, New York: Anchor Press/Doubleday, 1979.

Hougan, Jim. *Radical Nostalgia, Narcissism and Decline in the 1970s*. New York: William Morrow & Company, 1975.

Howard, Jane. *Families*. New York: Simon and Schuster, 1978.

Janeway, Elizabeth. *Between Myth and Morning: Women Awakening*. New York: William Morrow & Company, 1975.

————. *Man's World, Woman's Place: A Study in Social Mythology*. New York: Dell Publishing Company, 1971.

Jones, Landon Y. *Great Expectations: America and the Baby Boom Generation*. New York: Coward, McCann & Geoghegan, 1980.

Kaplan, Samuel. *The Dream Deferred: People, Politics and Planning in Suburbia*. New York: Random House, Inc., 1976.

Keniston, Kenneth, and the Carnegie Council on Children. *All Our Children: The American Family Under Pressure*. New York and London: Harcourt, Brace Jovanovich, 1977.

Kerr, Clark, and Rosow, Jerome M., eds. *Work in America: The Decade Ahead*. New York: Van Nostrand Reinhold Company, 1979.

Kessler, Sheila. *The American Way of Divorce: Prescriptions for Change.* Chicago: Nelson-Hall, 1975.

Kleiman, Carol. *Women's Networks: The Complete Guide to Getting a Better Job, Advancing Your Career and Feeling Great as a Woman Through Networking.* New York: Lippincott & Crowell, Publishers, 1980.

Lasch, Christopher. *The Culture of Narcissism: American Life in an Age of Diminishing Expectations.* New York: Warner Books, 1979.

Leslie, Warren. *Dallas—Public and Private.* New York: Grossman Publishers, 1964.

Lopata, Helena Znaniecki. *Occupation: Housewife.* London, Oxford, and New York: Oxford University Press, 1971.

———. *Widowhood in an American City.* Cambridge, Mass.: Schenkman Publishing Company, 1973.

Lynch, James. *The Broken Heart: The Medical Consequences of Loneliness.* New York: Basic Books, Inc., 1979.

Manser, Gordon, and Cass, Rosemary Higgins. *Volunteerism at the Crossroads.* New York: Family Service Association of America, 1976.

Marx, Leo. *The Machine in the Garden: Technology and the Pastoral Ideal in America.* London, Oxford, and New York: Oxford University Press, 1964.

Masnick, George, and Bane, Mary Jo. *The Nation's Families: 1960-1990.* Cambridge, Mass.: The Joint Center for Urban Studies of MIT and Harvard University, 1980.

McArdle, Alma C., and McArdle, Deirdre Bartlett. *Carpenter*

Gothic: 19th Century Ornamental Houses of New England. New York: Watson-Guptil, 1978.

McFadden, Cyra. *The Serial: A Year in the Life of Marin County.* New York: Alfred A. Knopf, 1977.

McKay, Bobbie. *The Unabridged Woman. A Guide to Growing Up Female.* New York: The Pilgrim Press, 1977.

Millett, Kate. *Sexual Politics.* New York: Ballantine Books, 1978.

Morgan, Marabel. *Total Joy.* New York: Berkley Books, 1978.

Morison, Samuel Eliot, and Commager, Henry Steele. *The Growth of the American Republic.* Vol. 2. New York: Oxford University Press, 1942.

Muir, John. *Our National Parks.* Boston: Houghton Mifflin, 1901.

Mumford, Lewis. *The Golden Day: A Study in American Literature and Culture.* New York: Dover Publications, 1968.

Nathanson, Bernard N., with Ostling, Richard N. *Aborting America.* New York: Doubleday & Company, Inc., 1979.

Newitt, Jane. *The Future of Westchester County: A Guide for Long-Range Social Needs Assessment.* Croton-on-Hudson, New York: Hudson Institute, 1979.

O'Reilly, Jane. *The Girl I Left Behind: The Housewife's Moment of Truth and Other Feminist Ravings.* New York: Macmillan, 1980.

Packard, Vance. *A Nation of Strangers.* New York: David McKay Company, 1972.

———. *The Status Seekers.* New York: Pocket Books, 1959.

Peck, Ellen, and Senderowitz, Judith, eds. *Pronatalism: The Myth of Mom and Apple Pie.* New York: Thomas Y. Crowell Company, 1974.

Reich, Charles A. *The Greening of America.* New York: Random House, 1970.

Rich, Adrienne. *On Lies, Secrets and Silence: Selected Prose 1966-78.* New York and London: W. W. Norton & Company, 1979.

Riesman, David. *The Lonely Crowd: A Study of the Changing American Character.* New Haven and London: Yale University Press, 1950.

Rifkind, Carol, and Levine, Carol. *Mansions, Mills and Main Streets: Buildings and Places to Explore Within 50 Miles of New York City.* New York: Schocken Books, 1975.

Rivers, Caryl; Barnett, Rosalind; and Baruch, Grace. *Beyond Sugar and Spice: How Women Grow, Learn and Thrive.* New York: G. P. Putnam's Sons, 1979.

Rossi, Alice S. *The Feminist Papers: From Adams to de Beauvoir.* New York, Toronto, and London: Bantam Books, 1974.

Rothblatt, Donald N.; Garr, Daniel J.; and Sprague, Jo. *The Suburban Environment and Women.* New York: Praeger Publishers, 1979.

Rubin, Lillian B. *Women of a Certain Age: The Midlife Search for Self.* New York: Harper & Row, 1980.

Schlafly, Phyllis. *The Power of the Positive Woman.* New York: Jove Publications, Inc., 1977.

Schmitt, Peter J. *Back to Nature: The Arcadian Myth in Urban America.* New York: Oxford University Press, 1969.

Schnall, Maxine. *Limits: A Search for New Values.* New York: Clarkson N. Potter, Publishers, 1981.

Seeley, John R.; Sim, Alexander R.; and Loosley, Elizabeth W. *Crestwood Heights: A Study of the Culture of Suburban Life.* New York: Basic Books, Inc., 1956.

Sharp, Dallas Lore. *American Fields and Forests.* Boston and New York, Cambridge: The Riverside Press, 1909.

———. *The Lay of the Land.* Boston: Houghton Mifflin, 1908.

Staples, Robert. *The Black Woman in America.* Chicago: Nelson-Hall, 1973.

Straus, Murray A.; Gelles, Richard J.; and Steinmetz, Suzanne K. *Behind Closed Doors: Violence in the American Family.* Garden City, New York: Anchor Press/Doubleday, 1980.

Toffler, Alvin. *Future Shock.* New York: Bantam Books, 1970.

———. *The Third Wave.* New York: Bantam Books, 1981.

Torre, Susan. *Women in American Architecture: A Historic and Contemporary Perspective.* New York: Whitney Library of Design, 1977.

Trahey, Jane. *On Women and Power: Who's got it? How to get it?* New York: Rawson Associates Publishers, Inc., 1977.

Trecker, Harleigh B. *Citizen Boards at Work: New Challenges to Effective Action.* New York: Associated Press, 1970.

Vandervelde, Maryanne. *The Changing Life of the Corporate Wife.* New York: Warner Books, 1979.

Wallace, Michele. *Black Macho & the Myth of the Super-Woman.* New York: Warner Books, 1980.

Wallace, Samuel E. *The Urban Environment*. Homewood, Illinois: The Dorsey Press, 1980.

Weiss, Robert S. *The Family Life and Social Situation of the Single Parent*. New York: Basic Books, Inc., 1979.

————. *Marital Separation*. New York: Basic Books, Inc., 1975.

Whyte, William H., Jr. *The Organization Man*. Garden City, New York: Doubleday & Company, Inc., 1957.

Williams, James M. *Our Rural Heritage: The Social Psychology of Rural Development*. New York: Alfred A. Knopf, 1925.

Wilson, Hugh, and Ridgeway, Sally. *Moving Beyond the Myth: Women in the Suburbs, 1980*. Garden City, New York: Institute for Suburban Studies, Adelphi University, 1980.

Wilson, William Julius. *The Declining Significance of Race: Blacks and Changing American Institutions*. Chicago: University of Chicago Press, 1978.

Wintje, Julia Treacy. *Along the Road to Bedford and Vermont: A Colonial Highway Through Mt. Vernon*. Mt. Vernon Public Library, 1946.

Wood, Leonard A. *Changing Attitudes in the Family in the 1980s*. Atlanta, Georgia: 1979 Biennial Conference Family Service Association of America, The Gallup Organizations, 1979.

Wynne, Edward A. *Growing Up Suburban*. Austin, Texas: University of Texas Press, 1977.

Yates, Martha. *Coping: A Survival Manual for Women Alone*. Englewood Cliffs, New Jersey: Prentice-Hall, 1976.

Index

Abel Creations, 268
Abortion, 137–38, 157
ACTION, 205
Addams, Jane, 45
Alcott, Bronson, 41
Alexandria, Va., 79
Allen, Kerry Kenn, 214
American Airlines, 223
American Association of University
    Women, 20, 65, 220
American Cancer Society, 200
American Indians, 36
American Women's Opinion Poll, 80
Arlington, Texas, 28, 245
Association for Volunteer Administra-
    tion, 222
Atlanta, Ga., 223
Atlantic Richfield, 223

Baby boom, 55–64
Ball, Lucille, 66
Baltimore, Md., 31
Bane, May Joe, 58
Barnett, Rosalind, 188
Baruch, Grace, 188
Beare, Muriel "Nikki," 131
Beecher, Catherine, 45–46, 108
Behr, Marion, 268
Belle Terre, Long Island, 193, 194
Berkeley, Cal., 98
Berwyn, Ill., 116
Better Homes and Gardens, 53
Billingsley, Barbara, 66
Bird, Caroline, 72, 84
Blacks, see Minority women
Bolton, Roxcy, 136
Boston, Mass., 24, 48, 51, 150
Boy Scouts, 65
Boyce-Thompson Institute for Plant
    Research, 34
Brentwood, Long Island, 239
Brighton, N.Y., 62
Bronfenbrenner, Urie, 138
Brookline, Mass., 48, 126
Brooks, Andrée, 163
Bryant, William Cullen, 41

Buffalo Grove, Ill., 33
Bureau of Labor Statistics, 18, 101
Burlingame, Cal., 196, 200
Burroughs, John, 51

Campfire Girls, 65
Carol City, Fla., 248
Carter, Jimmy, 139
Catholic Church, 138
Catline, George, 41
Cedarhurst, Long Island, 170, 269
Census Bureau, U.S., 18, 34, 89, 112,
    169, 196, 242, 245
Census Occupational Classification
    System, 91
Chappaqua, N.Y., 202, 204
Cheren, Mark, 222
Chicago, Ill., 19, 31, 36, 48, 51, 58, 83,
    110, 113, 116, 119, 121, 137,
    144–45, 150, 228, 252
Chicago (magazine), 31
Child, Lydia Maria, 45
Child care, 95–102
    for divorced women, 125–26
Childless women, 35, 163–70, 187–92,
    195–99
Chinese, 36
Christian Fellowship, 156
Christian fundamentalists, 138
Cincinnati, Ohio, 36
Civil Rights Act (1964), 54
Clark, Kenneth, 235–36
Clarke, Thomas, 246
Clearinghouse on Corporate Social Re-
    sponsibility, 222
Cohler, Bertram, 30
Coiné, Stephen, 179
Cole, Thomas, 41
Columbia Presbyterian Hospital, 94
Columbia University Teacher's College,
    50
Columbus, Ohio, 19, 73, 81, 118, 120,
    123, 132, 200, 206, 236, 240,
    268
Commack, N.Y., 239
Commager, Henry Steele, 52

Condominiums, 36, 169
Consumer market, growth of, 62–64
Coral Gables, Fla., 101
Corgan, Anita, 21–23
Corporations
    changing employment practices of, 262–64
    suburban relocation of, 31, 32, 91
    volunteer work and, 222–23
Cosmopolitan, 69
Craig, Nancy, 208
Cross, Joan Robertson, 86, 155–56, 177
Cult of True Womanhood, 44
Currie, Arlyce, 98

Dallas, Texas, 19, 24, 31, 36, 76, 86, 116, 121, 155, 164, 170, 191, 233, 237, 265–66
Daly City, Cal., 143, 243
Daws, Sharon, 227–28, 230
Day care, see Child care
Day Care Council of Westchester, Inc., 98
Delaware, Ohio, 252
Des Plaines, Ill., 82
Displaced Homemakers, 134
Divorce, increasing rate of, 68, 107
Divorced women, 34–35, 104–30
    ambivalence of neighbors toward, 118–22
    children of, 125–26
    finances of, 112–17
    networks of, 127–30
    problems of, 108–12
    singles scene and, 122–24
Doctorow, Elly, 56, 57
Domestic science, 50–52
Donaldson, Scott, 34
Douglas, William O., 193
Douglass, Harlan Paul, 53, 211–12
Dowling, Colette, 155
Downing, Andrew Jackson, 41–42

Eagle Forum, 133, 135, 157
Economy, suburban, 18, 31–32, 90–92
Edison, Thomas A., 40
Editorial Experts, Inc., 267
Education, work and, 87–88
Eisner, Ann, 203
Elderly, 37
Elk Grove, Ill., 252
Emerson, Ralph Waldo, 40
Equal Rights Amendment (ERA), opposition to, 133–35, 139, 157
Evanston, Ill., 200

Exclusionary zoning, 194–95

Family Circle (magazine), 96
Family Protection Act, 126
Fassaden, Thomas Green, 45
Federal Housing Administration, 57
Federated Women's Clubs, 65
Feibel, Babette, 267–68
Female Society for the Promotion of Sabbath Schools, 45
Feminism, 54
    backlash against, 133–39, 156–58
    nineteenth-century, 44, 47
    volunteer work and, 209
    work and, 84
Field, Tracey, 195
Fisher-Price, 223
Fitzgerald, F. Scott, 51
Ford, Henry, 51
Fort Lauderdale, Fla., 118
Fort Worth, Texas, 36, 86
Fortune (magazine), 56, 62–63
Franklin Park, Long Island, 163, 172
Frederick, Christine, 50, 108
Freeman, Jane, 210
Friedan, Betty, 30, 69–70, 135–36, 255, 275
Fuller, Margaret, 41

Gale, Tom, 236, 241
Garden City, Long Island, 146
Garland, Texas, 171
Gelles, Richard, 150
Girl Scouts, 20, 29, 65, 200, 202, 204, 208–11, 215, 218, 219, 222, 252–53
Glencoe, Ill., 209
Glenview, Ill., 150
Goldsmith, Judy, 136
Good Housekeeping (magazine), 21, 40, 48–49, 69
Goodin, Joan, 91
Gordon, Katherine, 68
Gordon, Richard, 68
Graham, Phyllis, 157
Graller, Lois, 209
Great Books, 65
Great Neck, N.Y., 140, 142, 150
Green, Constance, 58
Greenwich, Conn., 88, 202, 204
Groveport, Ohio, 28, 133
Gutowski, Michael, 195

Hackensack, N.J., 183, 189
Hagstad, Gundhil, 116

Halpern, Gerald P., 194
Hamden, Conn., 238
Haphazard Design, 266
Haran, Loyce, 207, 216
Hargreave, Richard, 43
Harper's (magazine), 30
Harper's New Monthly Magazine, 47,
    48
Harwell, H. L., 45
Hawthorne, Nathaniel, 41
Hempstead, Long Island, 73, 117
Herman, Ceil, 157
Hicksville, Long Island, 155
Highland Park, Ill., 119, 197
Hispanics, *see* Minority women
Hollywood, Fla., 28, 83, 99, 114, 215,
    231
Homemakers, 131–62
    antifeminist backlash among,
        133–39, 156–58
    attitudes toward working women of,
        137, 140–44, 148–49, 151–52
    as consumers, 68
    domestic science view of, 50–52
    mother-support groups for, 144–49
    nineteenth-century concept of, 45–46
    Spock on, 59
    and value of motherhood, 152–58
Homemakers' Equal Rights Associa-
    tion, 134, 153
Homestead, Fla., 271
Horowitz, Laura, 267
Hougan, Jim, 210
House and Garden (magazine), 64
Housewives, *see* Homemakers
Housing Opportunity Center, 236
Housing and Urban Development, U.S.
    Department of, 241
Houston, Texas, 24, 36
Hull House, 45
Human Life Amendment, 127

Illinois, University of, 50
Indo-Chinese, 36
Industrial Revolution, 42, 260
Inflation, 77
Irvington, N.Y., 187

Jackson, Andrew, 41
Janeway, Elizabeth, 26, 87
Japanese, 36
John Birch Society, 138
Joint Center for Urban Studies, 270
Jones, Landon, 59

Journal of Home Economics, 50
Junior Leagues, 20, 65, 200, 202, 220,
    222

Kagan, Jerome, 138
Karson, Stanley, 222
Kessler, Sheila, 111
Kimels, Eli, 243
Ku Klux Klan, 237–38

Labor Department, U.S., 92, 245
Ladies' Home Journal, 50, 60, 71
Lafayette, Cal., 170
Lake, Robert, 240–41
Lake Forest, Ill., 168
Lapp, Floyd, 269
Larchmont, N.Y., 142, 247
Lasch, Christopher, 210, 274
Lawrenceville, N.J., 206
Lazar, Wendy, 268
League of Women Voters, 20, 29, 65,
    143, 146, 205, 207–8, 210, 213
Lesbians, 190–91
Levine, Jim, 126
Levittown, N.Y., 157
Levittown, Pa., 65
Lewis, Sinclair, 51
Libertyville, Ill., 105
Livermore, Cal., 221
Longfellow, Henry Wadsworth, 41
Look (magazine), 60
Lopata, Helena, 81
Los Angeles, Cal., 24, 58
Lowry, Keith, 265–66
Lyndhurst, N.J., 173
Lyons, Sharon, 178

McKay, Bobbie, 150, 152, 217
McKinney, Texas, 155
McKnight, Kathy, 202
Mamaroneck, N.Y., 127
Manhasset, Long Island, 154
Marin, Peter, 210
Martin, Virginia, 127
Martineau, Harriet, 39, 47
Masnick, George, 58
Mead, Margaret, 61
Menlo Park, Cal., 118
Merriam, Eve, 68
Metcalf, Elizabeth, 215
Miami, Fla., 19, 24, 30, 84, 232
Mid-Hio Regional Planning Commis-
    sion, 236
Mill Valley, Cal., 188, 225, 238

Minority women, 36, 225–54
  housing patterns for, 229–43
  middle-class values of, 246–48,
    252–53
  single, 242–44
  working, 244–46
Moral Majority, 133
Morison, Samuel Eliot, 52
Motherhood, value of, 152–58
Mothers' Centers, 134
Mother-support groups, 144–50, 154
Mott, Lucretia, 44
Mt. Vernon, N.Y., 48, 244
Muir, Jean, 51

Naperville, Ill., 189
Nation (magazine), 68
National Alliance of Homebased Busi-
  nesswomen, 268
National Alliance for Optional Parent-
  hood, 188
National Association for the
  Advancement of Colored
  People, 20
National Association of Bank Women,
  220
National Association of Commissions
  for Women, 20, 135
National Association of Home Builders,
  169
National Association of Women Busi-
  ness Owners, 131
National Center for Citizen
  Involvement, 222
National Commission on Working
  Women, 91, 96
National Committee of Household
  Workers, 101
National Congress of Mothers, 45
National Council of Jewish Women,
  222
National Day Care Study, 99
National Opinion Research Center, 29,
  211
National Organization for Women, 20,
  93, 136, 209
National Right to Life Committee, 133
New Rochelle, N.Y., 249
New York, 19, 24, 31, 48, 51, 58, 87,
  236, 240
New York Daily News, 69
New York Female Reform Society, 45
New York Times, 30, 31, 34, 58, 69,
  205
New York Times/CBS poll, 139

New York Times Magazine, 77
Nollen, Stanley, 263
North Bergen, N.J., 225, 253
North Palm Beach, Fla., 21, 100
Northvale, N.J., 140
Norwalk, Conn., 171

Oak Park, Ill., 208–9, 243
Ohio, University of, 73
Old Westbury, Long Island, 247
O'Reilly, Jane, 104
Orlando, Fla., 216–17
Owen, Henry, 145–47
Oyster Bay, Long Island, 194

Packard, Vance, 67, 68
Palo Alto, Cal., 28, 114
Parents Without Partners, 127–30
Park Ridge, Ill., 93, 119
Parton, Dolly, 75
Pasternack, Winifred, 194
Peekskill, N.Y., 233
Perrett, Antoinette Rehmann, 21
Petitipas, Rosemary, 202–3
Philadelphia, Pa., 24, 31, 58
Phoenix, Ariz., 24
Pittsburgh, Pa., 116
Plainfield, N.J., 193–94
Planned Parenthood, 138
Plano, Texas, 118, 124
Pleasanton, Cal., 220
Porter, Tom, 237
Potter, Jessie, 110
Pratt Institute, 50
Pro-Family Political Action Committee,
  133
Prudential Life Insurance, 223
Psychological stress, 68–69
PTA, National, 29, 65, 204, 211, 219

Rahway, N.J., 156
Reader's Digest, 59
Reagan, Ronald, 137, 139
Red Cross, 221–22
Redbook, 69, 272
Redwood City, Cal., 151, 190, 201, 204,
  217
Reed, Donna, 66
Rees, Kris, 204
Regional Plan Association, 236, 240
Reichlin, Seth, 211
Reilly, Ruth, 221
Reiss, Carol, 147
Return-to-the-land movement, 32
Rich, Joan, 210, 219

Richardson, Texas, 119, 143, 206
Ridgeway, Sally, 191–92, 197
Riesman, David, 60–61, 256
Rimberg, Felix, 206
Ripley, George, 41
Rivers, Caryl, 188
Riverside, Ill., 48
Roper Organization, 80
Rosenbaum, Maj-Britt, 86, 109, 113–14
Ross, Charlotte, 124
Rossi, Alice, 44
Rubin, Lillian, 84
Ruffins, Iris, 208–9
Rural areas, migration to, 32
Rutherford, N.J., 189

Saegert, Susan, 261
San Francisco, Cal., 19, 24, 51, 95,
    173, 177, 223, 227, 237
San Jose, Cal., 33, 95
San Luis Obispo, Cal., 219
San Rafael, Cal., 198
Santa Barbara, Cal., 194
Savvy (magazine), 75
Scarsdale, N.Y., 28, 218
Schlafly, Phyllis, 133–35
Schnall, Maxine, 105, 274
Selig, Marilyn, 98, 99
Seltzer, Michelle, 127
Sepulvedera, Cal., 187
Sevareid, Eric, 31
Sexuality
    divorced women and, 123
    in 1920s, 53
    in 1950s, 60–61
    nontraditional, 190–92
    single women and, 166–68, 185–87
    Victorian view of, 45, 46
Shackford, Jay, 169
Sharp, Dallas, 51
Sheehy, Gail, 272
Short Hills, N.J., 121
Siegle, Nancy, 153, 154
Sidney, William, 41
Simmons College, 50
Single parents, 125–30
Single women, 35–36, 163–87, 195–99
    bar scene and, 171–78, 182–85
    exclusionary zoning and, 193–95
    minority, 242–44
    sexuality and, 185–87
    social options for, 178–82
    See also Divorced women
Small towns, 33
Smith, Ronald, 211

Social Purity Movement, 45
Sosne, Ruth, 62
Spanier, Graham, 110
Spock, Benjamin, 59
Stallings, Betty, 220–21
Stamford, Conn., 198
Standard Metropolitan Statistical Area
    (SMSA), 18
Standefer, Paulette, 132
Stanton, Elizabeth Cady, 44
Steinem, Gloria, 139
Stop ERA, 133
Suburban, definition of, 18
Suicide, 124–25
Supreme Court, U.S., 138, 157, 193

Tara Hills, Cal., 238
Tarrytown, N.Y., 246
Teaneck, N.J., 102, 198
Tedrow, Mary, 132–33, 142
Television, image of women on, 66
Tenneco, 223
Texas, University of, 178
Texas Pro-Life Committee, 132
Thayer, Suzanne, 266–67
Thoreau, Henry David, 40
Time (magazine), 63
Tobin, Mary, 92
Toffler, Alvin, 255, 264–65, 274
Tooley, William, 155, 177
Tuck, Barbara, 221
Turrini, Patsy, 155
Tuttle, Lureen, 66

Ulmschneider, Ann, 188
Upper Arlington, Ohio, 97, 100, 115,
    186
Urban areas, return of middle-class to,
    30–31
Urban League, 20, 236
U.S. News and World Report, 69

Venture (magazine), 75
Victorian women, status of, 42–44
VOLUNTEER: The National Center
    for Citizen Involvement, 204,
    205, 214
Volunteer work, 28, 29, 64–65, 200–24
    corporations and, 222–23
    decline in, 205–9
    improved status of, 215–16
    professionalism in, 202–3, 216–22
Voorhees, N.J., 141

Wabrek, Lyn, 186, 189

Wachter, Michael, 263
Wallman, Lester, 109, 114
Walnut Creek, Cal., 74, 83, 99, 154
Washburn, Julie, 216–17
Wattleton, Faye, 138
Wedoff, Teri, 153
Weiss, Robert, 121
Wellesley College Center for Research
    on Women, 126
West Palm Beach, Fla., 141, 170, 266
Westport, Conn., 179
Wheaton, Ill., 238
White Plains, N.Y., 122, 174
Whitney Heights, N.Y., 239
Whyte, William H., 67, 212
Wilson, Hugh, 247
Wilson, Wilford Julius, 246–47
Winnetka, Ill., 118
Wolfe, Tom, 210
Wolkoff, Sandy, 154
Women's Christian Temperance Union,
    45, 138
Women's Home Companion, 52
Women's Re-Entry Program, 221
Woodside, Cal., 197
Working Mother (magazine), 75
Working Woman (magazine), 75
Working women, 21–23, 72–103
    child care and, 95–102
    childrearing and, 138
    divorced, 35, 114–16, 126

economic motivation of, 77–80
education of, 87–88
in future, 262–64
homemakers' attitudes toward, 137,
    140–44, 148–49, 151–52
job realities for, 89–95
middle-aged, 85–86
minority, 244–46
in 1950s, 56–57, 62
percentage of, 29
self-employed, 265–69
self-fulfillment as motive of, 80–83
social change and, 25–26
social power of, 83–84
during World War II, 56
World War II, 56, 57
Worthington, Ohio, 176
Wyandach, N.Y., 248

Xerox, 223

Yankelovich, Daniel, 262
Yonkers, N.Y., 237
Young Men's Christian Association,
    222
Young Women's Christian Association,
    20, 205, 219–20, 222

Zager, Celia, 242
Zoning, 58
    exclusionary, 193–95